"Wayne Grudem has assembled an impressive group of biblical and theological scholars to address one of the most important issues of our time. The book is especially valuable for its careful characterization of theistic evolution and the following case that theistic evolution is simply not consistent with the teachings of the Bible. I highly recommend this important book."

J. P. Moreland, Distinguished Professor of Philosophy, Talbot School of Theology, Biola University; author, *The God Question*

"In this new streamlined volume critiquing the concept of theistic evolution, Professor Grudem and several other distinguished theologians highlight the many theological problems that arise from trying to synthesize mainstream neo-Darwinian evolutionary theory with any theologically meaningful notion of design or creation. They show that facile claims about how 'God used the evolutionary process to create' conceal a host of incoherencies, ambiguities, and theological problems. This is a detailed, dispassionate and scholarly volume."

Stephen C. Meyer, Director, Center for Science and Culture, Discovery Institute; author, *Return of the God Hypothesis*

"An increasing number of evangelicals are advocating theistic evolution as the best explanation of human origins, thereby denying the special creation of a historical Adam. Without taking any specific view as to the age of the earth, this important book demonstrates that theistic evolution fails to take proper account of Genesis 1–3 as a historical narrative. Leading scholars argue that theistic evolution is exegetically ill-founded and theologically damaging. Written with an irenic tone toward those it critiques, this book will help guard against false teaching in the church that undermines the gospel."

John Stevens, National Director, Fellowship of Independent Evangelical Churches, United Kingdom

"The chapters are clear, detailed, and of a tone in keeping with 1 Peter 3:15: 'with gentleness and respect.' I consider this a valuable book for any Christian who wants to be able to give compelling answers to others who believe that theistic evolution is compatible with the Bible."

Richard A. Carhart, Professor Emeritus of Physics, University of Illinois at Chicago

"The theistic evolution solution to the creation-evolution controversy herein encounters a substantial critique from the teachings of Scripture. This is important reading for those who wrestle with the great questions surrounding the origins of life."

Peter A. Lillback, President, Westminster Theological Seminary

"As the debate over the origins of the universe, earth, and humans continues, and Christians grapple to understand the relationship between science and Scripture, evolution and creation, the voices in this book need to be heard. The big questions about life are simply beyond the reach of 'objective' analysis. This volume critiques theologically the flaws of positions that marginalize God from the process."

James Hoffmeier, Professor Emeritus of Old Testament and Ancient Near Eastern History and Archaeology, Trinity Evangelical Divinity School

"This book offers a much-needed critique of evolutionary creationism (theistic evolution), focusing on its biblical deficiencies."

Vern S. Poythress, Professor of New Testament Interpretation, Westminster Theological Seminary

A Biblical Case against Theistic Evolution

A Biblical Case against Theistic Evolution

Wayne Grudem, General Editor

Contributors

Wayne Grudem • John D. Currid • Guy Prentiss Waters
Gregg R. Allison • Fred G. Zaspel

:: CROSSWAY®

WHEATON, ILLINOIS

Library of Congress Cataloging-in-Publication Data

Names: Grudem, Wayne A., editor.
Title: A biblical case against theistic evolution / Wayne Grudem, editor ; contributors, Wayne Grudem, John D. Currid, Guy Prentiss Waters, Gregg R. Allison, Fred G. Zaspel.
Description: Wheaton, Illinois : Crossway, 2022. | Includes bibliographical references and index.
Identifiers: LCCN 2021012264 (print) | LCCN 2021012265 (ebook) | ISBN 9781433577031 (trade paperback) | ISBN 9781433577055 (epub) | ISBN 9781433577048 (pdf) | ISBN 9781433577062 (mobipocket)
Subjects: LCSH: Creationism—Biblical teaching. | Open theism. | Evolution—Religious aspects.
Classification: LCC BS651 .B475 2022 (print) | LCC BS651 (ebook) | DDC 231.7/652—dc23
LC record available at https://lccn.loc.gov/2021012264
LC ebook record available at https://lccn.loc.gov/2021012265

Contents

Contributors *9*

1 Introduction: What Is Theistic Evolution? *11*
   Wayne Grudem

2 Theistic Evolution Is Incompatible with the Teachings of the
   Old Testament *29*
   John D. Currid

3 Theistic Evolution Is Incompatible with the Teachings of the
   New Testament *73*
   Guy Prentiss Waters

4 Theistic Evolution Is Incompatible with Historical Christian
   Doctrine *125*
   Gregg R. Allison

5 Additional Note: B. B. Warfield Did Not Endorse Theistic
   Evolution as It Is Understood Today *155*
   Fred G. Zaspel

6. Theistic Evolution Undermines Twelve Creation Events and Several
   Crucial Christian Doctrines *177*
   Wayne Grudem

General Index *237*
Scripture Index *243*

Contributors

Gregg R. Allison (PhD, Trinity Evangelical Divinity School) is Professor of Christian Theology at The Southern Baptist Theological Seminary in Louisville, Kentucky. He is the author of several books, including *Historical Theology: An Introduction to Christian Doctrine*; *Sojourners and Strangers: The Doctrine of the Church*; *Roman Catholic Theology and Practice: An Evangelical Assessment*; *Embodied: Living as Whole People in a Fractured World*; and (with Andreas Köstenberger) *The Holy Spirit*.

John D. Currid (PhD, University of Chicago) is the Chancellor's Professor of Old Testament at Reformed Theological Seminary. He is the author of several books and Old Testament commentaries and has extensive archaeological field experience from projects throughout Israel and Tunisia. His latest book is *The Case for Biblical Archaeology: Uncovering the Historical Record of God's Old Testament People*.

Wayne Grudem (PhD, University of Cambridge) is Distinguished Research Professor of Theology and Biblical Studies at Phoenix Seminary. He has published more than twenty books, including *Systematic Theology*, was a translator for the English Standard Version of the Bible, and was the General Editor for the *ESV Study Bible*. He is a past president of the Evangelical Theological Society.

Guy Prentiss Waters (PhD, Duke University) is the James M. Baird Jr. Professor of New Testament at Reformed Theological Seminary in

Jackson, Mississippi. Books he has authored include *The Life and Theology of Paul*; *For the Mouth of the Lord Has Spoken: The Doctrine of Scripture*; and *The Lord's Supper as the Sign and Seal of the New Covenant*. He also served as senior editor for Crossway's *Covenant Theology: Biblical, Theological, and Historical Perspectives*.

Fred G. Zaspel (PhD, Free University of Amsterdam) is Pastor of Reformed Baptist Church of Franconia, Pennsylvania. He is also the Editor of Books at a Glance and Adjunct Professor of Christian Theology at The Southern Baptist Theological Seminary. His doctoral work was on the theology of Benjamin Breckinridge Warfield, and he has published two books and many articles on Warfield.

1

Introduction: What Is
Theistic Evolution?

Wayne Grudem

SEVERAL YEARS AGO, the contributors to this book were among the twenty-five authors of a much larger work offering a comprehensive scientific, philosophical, and theological critique of the idea known as theistic evolution.[1] Our contributions to that work focused on the Bible and theology. As we have observed the continued interest in theistic evolution among Christians, we determined that we should publish our chapters in a separate volume focusing on the incompatibility of theistic evolution with several of the most significant teachings of the Bible itself.

The ongoing debate about theistic evolution is not merely a debate about whether Adam and Eve really existed (though it is about that); nor is it merely a debate about some specific details such as whether Eve was formed from one of Adam's ribs; nor is it a debate about some minor doctrinal issues over which Christians have differed for centuries.

---

1   J. P. Moreland, Stephen C. Meyer, Christopher Shaw, Ann K. Gauger, and Wayne Grudem, eds., *Theistic Evolution: A Scientific, Philosophical, and Theological Critique* (Wheaton, IL: Crossway, 2017).

The debate is about much more than that. From the standpoint of theology, the debate is primarily about the proper interpretation of the first three chapters of the Bible, and particularly whether those chapters should be understood as truthful historical narrative, reporting events that actually happened. This is a question of much significance because those chapters provide the historical foundation for the rest of the Bible and for the entirety of the Christian faith.

That means the debate is also about the validity of several major Christian doctrines for which those three chapters are foundational. In Genesis 1–3, Scripture teaches essential truths about the activity of God in creation, the origin of the universe, the creation of plants and animals on the earth, the origin and unity of the human race, the creation of manhood and womanhood, the origin of marriage, the origin of human sin and human death, and man's need for redemption from sin.

Without the foundation laid down in those three chapters, the rest of the Bible would make no sense, and many of those doctrines would be undermined or lost. It is no exaggeration to say that those three chapters are essential to the rest of the Bible.

A. What This Book Is Not About

This book is not about the age of the earth. Many Christians hold a "young earth" position (the earth is no more than ten thousand years old), and many others hold an "old earth" position (the earth is about 4.5 billion years old). This book does not take a position on that issue, nor do we discuss it at any point in the book.

Furthermore, we did not think it wise to frame the discussion of this book in terms of whether the Bible's teachings about creation should be interpreted "literally." That is because, in biblical studies, the phrase "literal interpretation" is often a slippery expression that can mean a variety of different things.[2] For example, some interpreters take it to refer

---

2   See the discussion of various senses of "literal" interpretation in Vern Poythress, *Understanding Dispensationalists* (Grand Rapids, MI: Zondervan, 1987), 78–96. Poythress concludes, "What is literal interpretation? It is a confusing term, capable of being used to beg many of the questions at stake in the interpretation of the Bible. We had best not use the phrase" (96). See also his helpful discussion of the terms "literal" and "figurative" in "Correlations with Providence in Genesis 2,"

to a mistaken kind of wooden *literalism* that would rule out metaphors and other kinds of figurative speech, but that kind of literalism fails to allow for the wide diversity of literature found in the Bible.

In addition, any argument about a literal interpretation of Genesis 1 would run the risk of suggesting that we think each "day" in Genesis 1 must be a *literal* twenty-four-hour day. But we are aware of careful interpreters who argue that a "literal" interpretation of the Hebrew word for "day" still allows the "days" in Genesis 1 to be long periods of time, millions of years each. Yet other interpreters argue that the days could be normal (twenty-four-hour) days but with millions of years separating each creative day. Others understand the six creation days in Genesis to be a literary "framework" that portrays "days of forming" and "days of filling." Still others view the six days of creation in terms of an analogy with the work-week of a Hebrew laborer.[3] This book is not concerned with deciding which of these understandings of Genesis 1 is correct, or which ones are properly "literal."

Instead, the question is whether Genesis 1–3 should be understood as a *historical narrative* in the sense of *reporting events that the author wants readers to believe actually happened.*[4] In the following chapters, our argument will be that Genesis 1–3 should not be understood as

---

WTJ 78, no. 1 (Spring 2016): 44–48; also his insightful article, "Dealing with the Genre of Genesis and Its Opening Chapters," *WTJ* 78, no. 2 (Fall 2016): 217–30.

3 See John C. Lennox, *Seven Days That Divide the World: The Beginning according to Genesis and Science* (Grand Rapids, MI: Zondervan, 2011), 39–66, for a clear and perceptive explanation of these various understandings of the days of creation. Lennox favors the view (which I find quite plausible) that Genesis 1 speaks of "a sequence of six *creation* days; that is, days of normal length (with evenings and mornings as the text says) in which God acted to create something new, but days that might well have been separated by long periods of time" (54, emphasis original). He also favors the view that the original creation of the heavens and earth in Genesis 1:1–2 may have occurred long before the first "creation day" in Genesis 1:3–5, which would allow for a very old earth and universe (53).

4 In arguing for the historicity of the early chapters of Genesis, C. John Collins rightly says, "In ordinary English a story is 'historical' if the author wants his audience to believe the events really happened" (C. John Collins, "A Historical Adam: Old-Earth Creation View," in *Four Views on the Historical Adam*, ed. Matthew Barrett and Ardel B. Caneday [Grand Rapids, MI: Zondervan, 2013], 147). Collins has a helpful discussion of what is meant by "history" on pages 146–48.

Craig Blomberg says, "a historical narrative recounts that which actually happened; it is the opposite of fiction" (*The Historical Reliability of the Gospels* [Downers Grove, IL: InterVarsity Press, 1987], xviii, n2).

primarily figurative or allegorical literature, but should rather be understood as historical narrative, though it is historical narrative with certain unique characteristics.

Finally, this book is not about whether people who support theistic evolution are genuine Christians or are sincere in their beliefs. We do not claim in this book that anyone has carelessly or lightly questioned the truthfulness of Genesis 1–3. On the contrary, the supporters of theistic evolution with whom we interact give clear indications of being genuine, deeply committed Christians. Their writings show a sincere desire to understand the Bible in such a way that it does not contradict the findings of modern science regarding the origin of living creatures.

But we *are* concerned that they believe that the theory of evolution is so firmly established that they must accept it as true and must use it as their guiding framework for the interpretation of Genesis 1–3.

For example, Karl Giberson and Francis Collins write,

The evidence for macroevolution that has emerged in the past few years is now overwhelming. Virtually all geneticists consider that the evidence proves common ancestry with a level of certainty comparable to the evidence that the Earth goes around the sun.[5]

Our goal in this book is to say to our friends who support theistic evolution, and to many others who have not made up their minds about this issue, that the Bible repeatedly presents as actual historical events many specific aspects of the origin of human beings and other

---

See also the discussion by V. Phillips Long, *The Art of Biblical History* (Grand Rapids, MI: Zondervan, 1994), 58–87. Long prefers the term "historiography" (that is, the verbal report of events in the past) for what I am calling "historical narrative," but he recognizes that authors can define "history" and "historical narrative" in different ways. His conclusion is helpful: "We conclude then that historiography involves a creative, though constrained, attempt to depict and interpret significant events or sequences of events from the past" (87).

5 Karl Giberson and Francis Collins, *The Language of Science and Faith* (Downers Grove, IL: Inter-Varsity Press, 2011), 49.

living creatures that cannot be reconciled with theistic evolution, and that a denial of those historical specifics seriously undermines several crucial Christian doctrines.

B. A Definition of Theistic Evolution

In brief summary form, then, the theistic evolution that we are respect-fully taking issue with is this belief:

> God created matter and after that did not guide or intervene or act directly to cause any empirically detectable change in the natural behavior of matter until all living things had evolved by purely natural processes.[6]

This definition is consistent with the explanation of prominent theistic evolution advocates Karl Giberson and Francis Collins:

> The model for divinely guided evolution that we are proposing here thus requires no "intrusions from outside" for its account of God's creative process, except for the origins of the natural laws guiding the process.[7]

More detail is provided in an earlier book by Francis Collins, emi-nent geneticist and founder of the BioLogos Foundation.[8] He explains theistic evolution in this way:

1. The universe came into being out of nothingness, approximately 14 billion years ago.

---

6 This definition of theistic evolution was first published in *Theistic Evolution: A Scientific, Philo-sophical, and Theological Critique* (67), as a concise summary of the view we were opposing. In the paragraphs that follow, I have provided several quotations from authors who support theistic evolution in this sense, and these quotations give more detailed explanations of what the viewpoint involves.

7 Giberson and Collins, *Language of Science and Faith*, 115.

8 The website of the BioLogos Foundation (biologos.org) is the primary source for thoughtful material relating to theistic evolution.

2. Despite massive improbabilities, the properties of the universe appear to have been precisely tuned for life.

3. *While the precise mechanism of the origin of life on earth remains unknown, once life arose, the process of evolution and natural selection permitted the development of biological diversity and complexity over very long periods of time.*

4. *Once evolution got underway, no special supernatural intervention was required.*

5. Humans are part of this process, sharing a common ancestor with the great apes.

6. But humans are also unique in ways that defy evolutionary explanation and point to our spiritual nature. This includes the existence of the Moral Law (the knowledge of right and wrong) and the search for God that characterizes all human cultures throughout history.[9]

C. Objections to This Definition of Theistic Evolution

After *Theistic Evolution* was published with this definition in 2017, some reviews on the BioLogos website objected that our definition of theistic evolution misrepresented their position. The primary response was in a thoughtful and gracious review by Deborah Haarsma, president of BioLogos.[10] She proposes an alternative definition of theistic evolution (though she prefers to call it "evolutionary creation"[11]):

---

9   Francis S. Collins, *The Language of God: A Scientist Presents Evidence for Belief* (New York: Free Press, 2006), 200, emphasis added.

10   See Deborah Haarsma, "A Flawed Mirror: A Response to the Book 'Theistic Evolution,'" BioLogos, April 18, 2018, https://biologos.org/articles/a-flawed-mirror-a-response-to-the-book-theistic-evolution.

11   The authors of material on the BioLogos website usually prefer the term evolutionary creation to the term theistic evolution, but both terms are found in their literature. We have kept the term theistic evolution in this book because it has been the standard phrase used to describe this position for a century or more in theological discussion. See, e.g., Louis Berkhof, *Systematic Theology* (Grand Rapids, MI: Eerdmans, 1941), 162: "Theistic evolution is not tenable in the light of Scripture." Berkhof also refers to the earlier critique of theistic evolution in the book by Alfred Fairhurst, *Theistic Evolution* (Cincinnati: Standard Publishing, 1919).

In addition, the term evolutionary creation seems to us to be misleading, because people who support theistic evolution do not believe in "creation" in the ordinary sense that Christians use the term, to refer to God's direct activity in creating specific plants and animals and in creating

God creates all living things through Christ, including humans in his image, making use of intentionally designed, actively-sustained, natural processes that scientists today study as evolution.

Haarsma adds, "God guided evolution just as much as God guides the formation of a baby from an embryo" (in the previous sentence she had cited Psalm 139:13, which says, "You formed my inward parts; you knitted me together in my mother's womb"). She also says, "Although God in his sovereignty could have chosen to use supernatural action to create new species, evolutionary creationists are convinced by the evidence in the created order that God chose to use natural mechanisms."[12]

But it seems to me that Haarsma's objections only serve to confirm the accuracy of my definition given above.[13] We could modify the definition to add more things that Haarsma advocates, but the substance of the definition would remain, as in this example:

God created matter [with regular properties governed by "natural law"] and after that [God continued to sustain matter and preserve its natural properties but he] did not guide or intervene or act directly to cause any empirically detectable change in the natural behavior of matter until all living things had evolved by purely natural processes [which God actively sustained but did not change].

In this modified definition, I have explicitly added the BioLogos belief that God actively upholds and sustains the activity of the entire natural world (as affirmed in Col. 1:17 and Heb. 1:3). I agree with

---

human beings; they mean only the initial creation of matter with properties that would lead to the evolution of living things. Francis Collins himself had earlier argued against using the word "creation" in connection with theistic evolution "for fear of confusion" (Collins, *Language of God* [New York: Free Press, 2006], 203).

12 Haarsma, "Flawed Mirror."

13 The definition that I am using is also consistent with the previously noted explanation of prominent theistic evolution advocates Karl Giberson and Francis Collins: "The model for divinely guided evolution that we are proposing here thus requires no 'intrusions from outside' for its account of God's creative process, except for the origins of the natural laws guiding the process" (*Language of Science and Faith*, 115).

that belief (see chapter 6), so there is no disagreement at that point, and it is consistent with historical Christian doctrine. But the key point in our definition, and the point on which I strongly differ with supporters of theistic evolution, is their claim that God did not "cause any empirically detectable change in the natural behavior of matter" until all living things "had evolved by purely natural processes." (This wording is from my definition, to which they objected.)

Haarsma does not object to this part of our definition, and in fact her proposed definition affirms the same thing: "God creates all living things . . . making use of intentionally designed, actively-sustained natural processes."[14]

D. Theistic Evolution Confuses Creation with Providence

The problem with this understanding of creation is that it confuses the Bible's teaching about God's action in initially creating the world with the Bible's teaching about God's ongoing action of providentially sustaining the world. (Note the present tense verb in their definition of theistic evolution: not "God created" but "God creates.") In another BioLogos review, Jim Stump writes, "Yes, we believe that God guides evolution, the same as we believe God guides photosynthesis."[15]

But this is a misleading use of the word "guide." People ordinarily use the word guide to refer to an action that influences the course of an object so that it moves in a particular direction or toward a particular destination.[16] To influence the direction of something implies causing a change in the direction in which it was going. But the BioLogos explanation shows that they use the word guide to mean "does not influence the direction of an object but sustains it so that it continues in the direction in which it otherwise was going." So ordinary English speakers understand

---

14 See a similar viewpoint in Denis Alexander, *Creation or Evolution: Do We Have to Choose?*, 2nd ed., rev. and updated (Oxford and Grand Rapids, MI: Monarch, 2014), 436.

15 Jim Stump, "Does God Guide Evolution?," BioLogos, April 18, 2018, https://biologos.org/articles /does-god-guide-evolution.

16 Merriam-Webster's online dictionary defines "guide" as "direct in a way or course" or "direct, supervise, or influence usually to a particular end" (Merriam-Webster, s.v. "guide," https://www. merriam-webster.com/dictionary/guide).

guide to mean "influence the direction of something," but the BioLogos Foundation uses the word guide to mean "*not* influence the direction of something," which is just the opposite. They are using the word guide to mean the opposite of what people ordinarily mean by guide, and in this way their statement is misleading to ordinary readers.

Regarding the distinction between creation and providence, the narrative of God's creative activity in Genesis 1–2 gives overwhelming evidence that God's work of creation was fundamentally different from his providential work of preserving creation and maintaining its properties today. This is the reason that theistic evolution cannot be reconciled with any acceptable interpretation of Genesis 1–2, as we will attempt to demonstrate below. In Genesis, after God created man on day 6, "God saw everything that he had made, and behold, it was very good" (Gen. 1:31), and then God's initial work of creating things was done:

> Thus the heavens and the earth were finished, and all the host of them. And on the seventh day God finished his work that he had done, and he rested on the seventh day from all his work that he had done. (Gen. 2:1–2)

E. Theistic Evolution Understands Genesis 1–3 as Figurative or Allegorical Literature, Not Factual History

At the heart of theistic evolution is the claim that the first three chapters of the Bible should not be understood as a historical narrative in the sense of claiming that the events it records actually happened. That is, these chapters should rather be understood as primarily or entirely figurative, allegorical, or metaphorical literature.

As mentioned in note 8, above, the BioLogos Foundation hosts the primary website for thoughtful material relating to theistic evolution. Some of its writers are quite forthright in their claims, such as Denis Lamoureux, who says bluntly, "Adam never existed,"[17] and, "Holy Scripture makes statements about how God created living organisms that in

---

17 Denis Lamoureux, "No Historical Adam: Evolutionary Creation View," in Barrett and Caneday, *Four Views on the Historical Adam*, 58. The same statement by Lamoureux is found in his article

fact never happened," and, "Real history in the Bible begins roughly around Genesis 12 with Abraham."[18] Elsewhere on the Bio- Logos website, Peter Enns argues that the story about Adam in Genesis is not really a story about early human history but rather is a sort of parable about the history of the nation of Israel. He writes, "Maybe Israel's history happened first, and the Adam story was written to reflect that history. In other words, the Adam story is really an Israel story placed in primeval time. It is not a story of human origins but of Israel's origins."[19]

Others are less specific about these details but still claim that Genesis 1–3 is not historical narrative. Francis Collins says these chapters should be understood as "poetry and allegory,"[20] and Denis Alexander views Genesis 1–3 as "figurative and theological" literature.[21]

Yet another approach comes from John H. Walton. He says the accounts of the forming of Adam and Eve in Genesis 1–2 should not be understood as "accounts of how those two individuals were uniquely formed," but rather should be understood as stories about "archetypes," that is, stories that use an individual person as sort of an allegory for Everyman, someone who "embodies all others in the group" (in this case, the human race).[22] Therefore Walton says that the Bible makes "no claims" regarding "biological human origins," for Genesis 2 "talks about the *nature of all* people, not the unique *material origins* of Adam and Eve."[23] In fact, he says that "the Bible does not really offer any information about material human origins."[24]

In all of these approaches, the result is the same: Genesis 1–3 (or at least Genesis 1–2) should not be understood as claiming to be a report

---

on the BioLogos website at Denis Lamoureux, "Was Adam a Real Person? Part 2,"*BioLogos*, September 11, 2010, http://biologos.org/blogs/archive/was-adam-a-real-person-part-2.

18 Lamoureux, "No Historical Adam," 56, 44.

19 Peter Enns, "Adam Is Israel," *BioLogos*, March 2, 2010, http://biologos.org/blogs/archive/adam-is-israel. In the next paragraph, Enns says that he himself holds this view. Giberson and Collins mention Enns's view as another possible interpretation of the Adam and Eve story (*Language of Science and Faith*, 211).

20 Collins, *Language of God*, 206; see similar statements on 150, 151, 175, 207.

21 Alexander, *Creation or Evolution: Do We Have to Choose?*, 185; see also 189, 197, 230, 320.

22 John H. Walton, *The Lost World of Adam and Eve: Genesis 2–3 and the Human Origins Debate* (Downers Grove, IL: InterVarsity Press, 2015), 74.

23 Ibid., 181, emphasis original; see also 33–34, 35–45, 81.

24 Ibid., 192.

of actual historical events. John Currid responds at length to this claim in chapter 2 below.

F. Theistic Evolution Claims That God Was the Creator of Matter, But Not Directly of Living Creatures

What, then, do theistic evolutionists mean when they say that "God created all things, including human beings in his own image," as in this statement:

> "Evolutionary Creation (EC) is a Christian position on origins. It takes the Bible seriously as the inspired and authoritative word of God, and it takes science seriously as a way of understanding the world God has made. EC includes two basic ideas. First, that God created all things, including human beings in his own image. Second, that evolution is the best scientific explanation we currently have for the diversity and similarities of all life on Earth."[25]

They frequently mean that *God created matter* in the beginning with certain physical properties and then *the properties of matter* were enough to bring about all living things without any further direct activity by God.[26] This eliminates the problem of any conflict with science, because modern evolutionary theory also holds that *matter by itself* evolved over a long period of time into all living things.

---

25 https://biologos.org/common-questions/christianity-and-science/biologos-id-creationism), accessed 3-2-21.

26 See, e.g., Alexander, *Creation or Evolution*, 436. Since the question of the origin of life is different from the question of the evolution of simple living organisms into complex organisms, some proponents of theistic evolution seem to allow for the possibility of a direct intervention of God at the point of the first creation of life. E.g., note the unspecified possibilities suggested in the words of Francis Collins: "*While the precise mechanism of the origin of life on earth remains unknown*, once life arose, the process of evolution and natural selection permitted the development of biological diversity and complexity over very long periods of time. . . . Once evolution got underway, no special supernatural intervention was required" (Francis Collins, *Language of God*, 200, emphasis added).

   However, in a subsequent book Karl Giberson and Francis Collins seem to expect that eventually a materialistic hypothesis will explain how life could have originated from nonliving matter: see *Language of Science and Faith*, 169–75.

G. Theistic Evolution Claims That There Were Not Merely Two, but as Many as Ten Thousand Ancestors for the Human Race

Regarding the origin of the human race, Christians who support theistic evolution differ over whether Adam and Eve actually existed as historical persons. Some (such as Denis Lamoureux, cited above) do not believe that Adam and Eve ever existed, while others believe in a historical Adam and Eve. But even this "historical Adam and Eve" are still not the Adam and Eve of the Bible, because these theistic evolution proponents do not believe that their Adam and Eve were the first human beings or that the whole human race descended from them. They claim that current genetic studies indicate that the human race today is so diverse that we could not have descended from just two individuals such as an original Adam and Eve.

Francis Collins writes, "Population geneticists . . . conclude that . . . our species . . . descended from a common set of founders, approximately 10,000 in number, who lived about 100,000 to 150,000 years ago."[27] Similarly, Denis Alexander says, "The founder population that was the ancestor of all modern humans . . . was only 9,000-12,500 reproductively active individuals."[28]

Therefore, those Christians who support theistic evolution and also want to retain belief in a historical Adam and Eve propose that God chose one man and one woman from among the thousands of human beings who were living on the earth and designated the man as "Adam" and the woman as "Eve." He then began to relate to them personally, and made them to be representatives of the entire human race.

But on this view, where did this early population of 10,000 human beings come from? We should not think that they came from just one "first human being" in the process of evolution; there never was just one "first" human being from which everyone else descended. Rather, the evolutionary mutations in earlier life forms that led to the human race occurred bit by bit among thousands of different nearly human

27 Francis Collins, *Language of God*, 126; see also 207. Giberson and Collins claim that humans have descended from "several thousand people . . . not just two" (*Language of Science and Faith*, 209).
28 Alexander, *Creation or Evolution*, 265.

creatures. Some developed greater balance and the ability to walk upright. Others developed physical changes in their vocal organs that would enable complex human speech. Still others developed larger brains and the capacity for abstract human reasoning. And there were many other such changes. Over time, the creatures with *some* of these beneficial mutations had an adaptive advantage, and more of their offspring survived. Eventually they began to mate with other creatures who had *other* human-like mutations, and eventually many thousands of human beings emerged from this evolutionary process, all of them descended from earlier, more primitive organisms.[29]

H. Theistic Evolution Requires a Reinterpretation of the Identities of Adam and Eve

What happens, then, to the biblical narratives about Adam and Eve? Denis Alexander describes several possible models (which he labels A, B, C, D, E; see note 30) by which to understand both the biblical story of Adam and Eve and modern evolutionary theory.[30] He favors "model C,"[31] which he explains as follows:

> According to model C, God in his grace chose a couple of Neolithic farmers in the Near East, perhaps around 8,000 years ago (the precise date is of little importance for this model), or maybe a community of farmers, to whom he chose to reveal himself in a special way, calling

29 Alexander writes, "It should not be imagined that this [modern human] population somehow emerged 'all at once' with the distinctive features of anatomically modern humans. The . . . population . . . which eventually evolved into anatomically modern humans, must have done so over a period of tens of thousands of years. . . . Evolution, remember, is a gradual process" (*Creation or Evolution*, 298).

30 In model A, the narrative of Adam and Eve "is a myth" that teaches eternal truths without being constrained by historical particularity (*Creation or Evolution*, 288). In model B, Adam and Eve are either a mythical couple whose story represents something of the origin of the human race, or they are part of the earliest human population living in Africa perhaps 200,000 years ago (288–89). Model C is the one Alexander favors (see main text). Model D represents an old earth creationist view, with Adam and Eve created directly by God, and model E represents a young earth creationist view (294). Alexander thinks that models D and E are scientifically indefensible (282–304).

31 Alexander, *Creation or Evolution*, 303.

them into fellowship with himself—so that they might know him as a personal God. . . . This first couple, or community, have been termed Homo divinus, the divine humans, those who know the one true God, corresponding to the Adam and Eve of the Genesis account. . . . Certainly religious beliefs existed before this time, as people sought after God or gods in different parts of the world, offering their own explanations for the meaning of their lives, but Homo divinus marked the time at which God chose to reveal himself and his purposes for humankind for the first time. . . . [Adam] is . . . viewed as the federal head of the whole of humanity alive at that time. . . . The world population in Neolithic times is estimated to lie in the range of 1-10 million, genetically just like Adam and Eve, but in model C it was these two farmers out of all those millions to whom God chose to reveal himself.[32]

N. T. Wright proposes a similar explanation:

Perhaps what Genesis is telling us is that God chose one pair from the rest of the early hominids for a special, strange, demanding vocation. This pair (call them Adam and Eve if you like) were to be the representatives of the whole human race.[33]

Giberson and Collins propose a similar view:

A common synthetic view integrating the biblical and scientific accounts sees human-like creatures evolving as the scientific evidence indicates, steadily becoming more capable of relating to God. At a certain point in history, God entered into a special relationship with those who had developed the necessary characteristics, endowing

---

32 Ibid., 290–91.

33 N. T. Wright, "Excursus on Paul's Use of Adam," in Walton, *Lost World of Adam and Eve*, 177. John Walton himself proposes that Adam and Eve can be seen as "elect individuals drawn out of the human population and given a particular representative role in sacred space" (Walton, "A Historical Adam: Archetypal Creation View," in Barrett and Caneday, *Four Views on the Historical Adam*, 109).

them with the gift of his image. . . . this view can fit whether the humans in question constituted a group—symbolized by Adam and Eve—or a specific male-female pair.[34]

As the following chapters will argue, the difficulty with all of these theistic evolution explanations of "Adam and Eve" arises because they differ significantly from the biblical account in Genesis 1–3. They all propose that many thousands of human beings were on the earth prior to Adam and Eve, and so Adam and Eve were not the first human beings, nor has the entire human race descended from them. In addition, there was human death and human sin (such as violence, instinctive aggression, and worship of false gods)[35] long before Adam and Eve.

I. Twelve Differences between Events Recounted in the Bible and Theistic Evolution

We can now enumerate twelve points at which theistic evolution (as currently promoted by the prominent supporters cited) differs from the biblical creation account taken as a historical narrative. According to theistic evolution:

1. Adam and Eve were not the first human beings (and perhaps they never even existed).
2. Adam and Eve were born of human parents.
3. God did not act directly or specially to create Adam out of dust[36] from the ground.
4. God did not directly create Eve from a rib[37] taken from Adam's side.

---

34 Giberson and Collins, *Language of Science and Faith*, 212.

35 See, for example, the statement from Denis Alexander on page 23 above.

36 It is possible that "dust" in Genesis 2:7 refers to a collection of different kinds of nonliving materials from the earth. My argument in a later chapter does not depend on that interpretative detail. See the further discussion of the Hebrew word for "dust" by John Currid ("Theistic Evolution Is Incompatible with the Teachings of the Old Testament") on pages 61–62.

37 It is possible that the "rib" was accompanied by other material substances taken from Adam's body, for Adam himself says, "This at last is bone of my bones *and flesh of my flesh*" (Gen. 2:23). My overall argument in a later chapter is not affected by that difference. See the further discussion of the Hebrew word for "rib" on pages 51–52 and 198–199.

5. Adam and Eve were never sinless human beings.

6. Adam and Eve did not commit the first human sins, for human beings were doing morally evil things[38] long before Adam and Eve.

7. Human death did not begin as a result of Adam's sin, for human beings existed long before Adam and Eve and they were always subject to death.

8. Not all human beings have descended from Adam and Eve, for there were thousands of other human beings on Earth at the time that God chose two of them as Adam and Eve.

9. God did not directly act in the natural world to create different "kinds" of fish, birds, and land animals.

10. God did not "rest" from his work of creation or stop any special creative activity after plants, animals, and human beings appeared on the earth.

11. God never created an originally "very good" natural world in the sense of a safe environment that was free of thorns and thistles and similar harmful things.

12. After Adam and Eve sinned, God did not place any curse on the world that changed the workings of the natural world and made it more hostile to mankind.

Clearly, these statements denying what the Genesis text at least appears to teach about God's active role (or supernatural acts) in creation, about the existence of an original man and woman from whom the rest of the human race is descended, and about the moral fall of human beings as the result of the sin of Adam, presuppose the truth of contemporary evolutionary theory. They also presuppose the truth of the evolutionary narrative about the origin of man by way of undirected material processes from lower primates—as the proponents of theistic evolution openly acknowledge.

---

38 Some advocates of theistic evolution may claim that human beings prior to Adam and Eve did not have a human moral conscience, but they would still admit that these human beings were doing selfish and violent things, and worshiping various deities, things that from a biblical view of morality would be considered morally evil.

In fact, each of these twelve claims contradicts one or more parts of the text in Genesis 1–3, if it is understood as historical narrative (as we will argue that it must be understood).

The following chapters will attempt to demonstrate specific ways in which theistic evolution is incompatible with belief in the historical truthfulness of the Bible and with historical Christian doctrine.

In chapter 2, John Currid analyzes in further detail specific Old Testament passages that are incompatible with theistic evolution.

In chapter 3, Guy Waters similarly analyzes specific New Testament passages that are incompatible with theistic evolution.

In chapter 4, Gregg Allison argues that, throughout the history of the church, those who were recognized as leaders and teachers in the church were required to affirm the belief that God is the "Maker of heaven and earth, and of *all things visible* and invisible" (Nicene Creed), an affirmation incompatible with theistic evolution.

In chapter 5, Fred Zaspel concludes that the eminent nineteenth-century Princeton theologian B. B. Warfield, though often cited as a supporter of theistic evolution, would not have agreed with theistic evolution as it is understood today.

In chapter 6, I attempt to show that the aforementioned twelve details of the Genesis narrative that are denied by theistic evolution supporters are affirmed as historical fact by several New Testament writers. In addition, I will argue in chapter 6 that to deny all historical import to what the biblical text claims (as opposed to what an evolutionary reading of the text might impose on it) would undermine a number of core Christian doctrines.

2

Theistic Evolution Is Incompatible with the Teachings of the Old Testament

John D. Currid

"There is nothing new under the sun."

ECCLESIASTES 1:9

Summary

This chapter explores ways in which theistic evolution is incompatible with the teachings of the Old Testament. It closely examines Genesis 1–3 and responds to the five most common alternative explanations proposed by advocates of theistic evolution: (1) the "functional model" of Genesis 1–3; (2) the view that Genesis 1–3 is "myth"; (3) the view that Genesis 1–3 should be understood as "figurative and theological literature"; (4) the "sequential scheme" interpretation, which argues that the events of Genesis 2 occurred long after Genesis 1; and (5) the "etiology as methodology" interpretation, which claims that Genesis 1–3 was written not as factual history but as an explanation for certain features that we see in the world (though the explanation need not record actual historical events). Multiple features in the text of Genesis 1–3 show these alternative explanations to be unpersuasive.

———

In 1884, Dr. James Woodrow, who held the Perkins Professorship of Natural Science in Its Relation to Revealed Religion at Columbia Seminary in Columbia, South Carolina, was asked by the seminary trustees to deliver a lecture on the issue of evolution and the Bible.[1] He had been teaching at Columbia Seminary since 1861, and his views regarding the issues of creation had evolved over his twenty-plus years at the school. He had simply become more convinced of what he believed to be the scientific evidence in favor of evolutionary theory. Woodrow had made the following statement in 1883:

> The Bible teaches nothing as to God's method of creation, and therefore it is not teaching anything contradicting God's word to say that he may have formed the higher beings from the lower by successive differentiations; and . . . several series of facts, more or less independent of each other, seem to point this out as the method which he chose.[2]

In his lecture, Woodrow admitted that he had changed his position from one in which evolution was not true to one in which it likely was true. He concluded the following: "I am inclined to believe that it pleased God, the Almighty Creator, to create present and intermediate past organic forms not immediately but mediately."[3]

In regard to humanity, Woodrow alleged that only the soul of man was of immediate creation. His body, on the other hand, came from the "dust"

---

1 A summary of the lecture and the ensuing controversy is found in David B. Calhoun, *The Glory of the Lord Risen upon It: First Presbyterian Church, Columbia, South Carolina 1795–1995* (Columbia, SC: First Presbyterian Church, 1994), 147–49.

2 Quoted in Ernest Trice Thompson, *Presbyterians in the South*, vol. 2 (Richmond: John Knox Press, 1963, 1973), 461.

3 James Woodrow, *Evolution: An Address Delivered May 7th, 1884 before the Alumni Association of the Columbia Theological Seminary* (Columbia, SC: Presbyterian Publishing House, 1884), 28.

(Gen. 2:7). He argued that this creative act is open to varying interpretations, and perhaps "dust" refers merely to preexisting material. Therefore, mankind may have descended from some type of animal ancestor.

This lecture by Woodrow created a firestorm, and it produced a division in the Southern Presbyterian Church. The board of Columbia Seminary, who had called for Woodrow's lecture, met to consider his position on origins. Frank Smith comments that the board concluded

> that, while not agreeing with his belief regarding the probable way in which Adam's body was created, there was nothing with his carefully-delineated views on evolution that was incompatible with the faith.[4]

The courts of the Presbyterian Church were not quite as forgiving. After a complicated and detailed debate and controversy at the synod levels, the issue came to the General Assembly of 1886. The Assembly debated the question for five days. At the end it overwhelmingly voted, 137 to 13, that "Adam and Eve were created, body and soul, by immediate acts of God's power" and that Adam's body was made "without any human parentage of any kind."[5]

The General Assembly took further action by recommending to the four synods in charge of Columbia Seminary that Dr. Woodrow be dismissed from his teaching position (the vote was 65 to 25).[6] Eventually, he was dismissed from the seminary. However, he was allowed to remain an ordained Presbyterian minister in good standing because when he came under trial in 1886 by the Augusta (Georgia) Presbytery, he was acquitted of heresy by a vast majority of presbyters.

The evangelical church today is facing increasing controversies over the relationship of science and the Bible and, in particular, over the view of theistic evolution.[7] But as we can see from what happened with

---

4   F. J. Smith, "Presbyterians and Evolution in the 19th Century: The Case of James Woodrow," *Contra Mundum* 6 (1993): 7.

5   Calhoun, *Glory of the Lord Risen upon It*, 149.

6   Smith, "Presbyterians and Evolution," 17.

7   See, e.g., Denis Alexander, *Creation or Evolution: Do We Have to Choose?* 2nd ed., rev. and updated (Oxford: Monarch, 2014); Francis S. Collins, *The Language of God: A Scientist Presents Evidence for*

Dr. Woodrow more than 130 years ago, this debate at its core is nothing new. The relationship between the Bible and science, especially in regard to origins, has been at the forefront of discussion since the mid-nineteenth century. Perhaps the arguments today are more nuanced, but the basic issues are the same. The difference today, as I see it, is that there is an increasing acceptance of theistic evolution (or "evolutionary creation," as it is often called) in evangelicalism, and that acceptance is growing by the day.

Some evangelical scholars have joined the ranks that advocate theistic evolution. Bruce Waltke, currently distinguished professor emeritus of Old Testament at Knox Theological Seminary, made a video for BioLogos in which he argued that evolution is compatible with evangelical, orthodox Christianity. In the video, titled "Why Must the Church Come to Accept Evolution?," Waltke gives warning that if the church does not accept evolution then it risks becoming "a cult," "an odd group," "not credible," and "marginalized."[8] Peter Enns and John Walton, both highly respected Old Testament scholars, have made significant contributions in favor of evolutionary creation on the BioLogos website and in other writings. These men are accomplished Old Testament exegetes, and their work must be taken seriously and discussed. Tremper Longman, Robert H. Gundry Professor of Biblical Studies at Westmont College, fits squarely into this camp.[9] In a 2014 blog post, Longman concluded the following: "But it seems to me that there is a good case, especially on genetic evidence, that God used evolution. So I find myself affirming an evolutionary creation-

---

Belief (New York: Free Press, 2006); and H. J. Van Till, D. A. Young, and C. Menninga, *Science Held Hostage* (Downers Grove, IL: InterVarsity Press, 1988).

8   The video was originally posted on March 24, 2010, on the BioLogos website biologos.org, and it created a significant controversy. Waltke subsequently asked BioLogos to remove the video, which they did. But then on April 6, 2010, Reformed Theological Seminary accepted Waltke's resignation, an action that was widely understood as directly related to Waltke's endorsement of theistic evolution. See "OT Scholar Bruce Waltke Resigns following Evolution Comments," *Christianity Today*, April 9, 2010, http://www.christianitytoday.com/gleanings/2010/april/ot-scholar-bruce -waltke-resigns-following-evolution.html.

9   See, e.g., his most recent commentary: Tremper Longman, *Genesis* (Grand Rapids, MI: Zondervan, 2015).

ist perspective."[10] Longman also serves on the Advisory Council of BioLogos.

Others who are not Old Testament scholars but have great influence in evangelicalism have come out in favor of evolutionary creation. For example, Presbyterian Church in America pastor Tim Keller authored an article for BioLogos titled "Creation, Evolution, and Christian Lay People," in which, at the very least, he shows sympathy to the theistic evolution viewpoint.[11] New Testament scholar N. T. Wright is clear in his support of evolutionary creation.[12] My point here is not simply to name names but to show that the evolutionary creation movement is stronger than it has ever been and is making inroads into evangelical thought today.[13]

In this chapter, I would like to consider some of the more recent developments in the debate over the early chapters of Genesis, and especially human origins, in Old Testament studies. I will examine five models that advocates of theistic evolution have proposed to explain how Genesis 1–3 can be interpreted as consistent with theistic evolution:

I. The Functional Model

II. Genesis 1–3 as Myth

III. Genesis 1–3 as Figurative and Theological Literature

10 See Jonathan Watson, "Temper Longman Responds to Justin Taylor on the Historicity of Adam," *Academic*, March 24, 2014, accessed August 25, 2016, https://academic.logos.com/2014/03/25 /tremper-longman-responds-to-justin-taylor-on-the-historicity-of-adam/.

11 See Tim Keller, "Creation, Evolution, and Christian Laypeople," *BioLogos*, 2006, https://biologos .org/uploads/projects/Keller_white_paper.pdf.

12 See his "Excursus on Paul's Use of Adam," in John H. Walton, *The Lost World of Adam and Eve: Genesis 2–3 and the Human Origins Debate* (Downers Grove, IL: InterVarsity Press, 2015), 170–80.

13 Some would argue that this position has had long-standing acceptance in evangelicalism, and rarely is the name of the Princeton theologian B. B. Warfield not raised in support of that contention. See, e.g., B. B. Warfield, *Evolution, Scripture, and Science: Selected Writings*, ed. D. N. Livingstone and M. A. Noll (Grand Rapids, MI: Baker, 2000). However, see the response of Fred Zaspel elsewhere in this volume (pages 155–176); see also Fred G. Zaspel, "B. B. Warfield on Creation and Evolution," *Themelios* 35, no. 2 (2010): 198–211. Zaspel argues that, while Warfield entertained the *possibility* that God used an evolutionary process as part of his creative work, he never affirmed evolutionary theories as true, and he explicitly denied that someone could hold to the teachings of the Bible and affirm several of the key concepts of modern theistic evolution proponents, such as there being sinful humans prior to Adam and Eve, or human death before Adam and Eve, or that Adam and Eve were not created sinless.

IV. The Sequential Scheme

V. Etiology as Methodology

I. THE FUNCTIONAL MODEL:
GENESIS 1–3 IS NOT ABOUT ORIGINS

John Walton, professor of Old Testament at Wheaton College, is perhaps the most prominent evangelical Old Testament scholar presenting the case for the compatibility of the Bible and a divinely guided process of evolution. Walton has written extensively on the nature of the creation account in Genesis 1–3.[14] In general, he proposes that these chapters are about the assigning of *roles and functions* to the various elements of the universe and not about the historical origins of the universe.[15]

Walton does some excellent work in highlighting the presence of concern for functions in Genesis 1–3, and I am in agreement with him that such a concern is present in the text. However, where I take exception to his writings is the claim that Genesis 1–3 has nothing to do with *material origins*, and that it is merely about establishing *functions* alone. I want to focus on one critical, foundational aspect of his model.[16]

One linchpin of Walton's design is the proposition that Genesis 1–3 is an ancient Near Eastern text, and, as such, is similar to other creation accounts of antiquity. He believes that ancient Near Eastern creation documents are primarily interested in function and not material origins. Therefore, Genesis 1, like those texts, is merely about the function and role of the various elements of the cosmos. This understanding extends

---

14 Among his many works, I would point the reader to the following ones that get at the heart of his position on Genesis 1–3: John H. Walton, *Genesis*, NIV Application Commentary (Grand Rapids, MI: Zondervan, 2011); Walton, *Genesis 1 as Ancient Cosmology* (Winona Lake, IN: Eisenbrauns, 2011); Walton, *Lost World of Adam and Eve*; and Walton, *The Lost World of Genesis One: Ancient Cosmology and the Origins Debate* (Downers Grove, IL: InterVarsity Press, 2009).

15 Walton's position is making its way into recent literature in regard to the interpretation of Genesis 1–3. See, for example, Scot McKnight's acceptance of it—hook, line, and sinker—in Dennis R. Venema and Scot McKnight, *Adam and the Genome* (Grand Rapids, MI: Baker, 2017), 124–25. My critique in this section thus applies not only to Walton but to McKnight as well.

16 For an extensive and perceptive review of Walton's most recent work, see R. E. Averbeck, "The Lost World of Adam and Eve: A Review Essay," *Themelios* 40, no. 2 (2015): 226–39.

into Genesis 2, which, he claims, *does not teach the material creation of humankind* but deals with the nature of humanity's function and purpose in the world.

In relation to our discussion in this book, Walton's argument has an important consequence: if the opening chapters of Genesis have nothing to do with material beginnings of the universe, including the origin of humanity, then the historical clash between science and the Bible regarding the nature of physical origins is a moot point. In other words, the early chapters of Genesis are not really interested in material origins and, therefore, there is no conflict between them and science.

It is my intention to test Walton's view of the design and purpose of ancient Near Eastern creation documents, and to see if his position stands on firm ground or not. The question simply put is, do the creation accounts of the ancient Near East have a concern not only for functions but also for the *material origins* of the cosmos and, in particular, of mankind? Or, to put it another way, are the ancient Near Eastern creation documents *solely* interested in functions and roles of the various elements of the cosmos?

A. Egyptian Creation Texts

The first thing one must realize when dealing with ancient Egyptian creation accounts is that there are many of them, and some of them are antithetical to one another.[17] The Egyptologist John A. Wilson gives expression to this reality when he says, "It is significant that a plural should be necessary, that we cannot settle down to a single codified account of beginnings. The Egyptians accepted various myths and discarded none of them."[18] Henri Frankfort calls this the mythopoeic mind, which admits "the validity of several avenues of approach at one

---

17 I give a more extensive discussion of these Egyptian texts in my book *Ancient Egypt and the Old Testament* (Grand Rapids, MI: Baker, 1997). For other studies on Egyptian creation accounts, see, e.g., J. P. Allen, *Genesis in Egypt: The Philosophy of Ancient Egyptian Creation Accounts* (New Haven, CT: Yale Egyptological Seminar, 1988); and J. K. Hoffmeier, "Some Thoughts on Genesis 1 and 2 and Egyptian Cosmology," *Journal of Ancient Near Eastern Studies* 15 (1983): 39–49.

18 John A. Wilson, in Henri Frankfort et al., *Before Philosophy* (1951; repr., Baltimore: Penguin, 1973), 59.

and the same time."[19] In addition, one must be aware that many of the references in Egyptian literature to the origin of the universe appear sporadically in various contexts, such as in the Coffin Texts, the Pyramid Texts, and elsewhere. So, for example, there is no single documented account of the creation of mankind, but the subject of human origins is found in various places in a wide array of texts. Siegfried Morenz properly concludes that there is "an abundance of more or less scanty references in the most varied texts which give us some very disjointed information about Egyptian notions concerning God the creator and the evolution of the world (and life on it)."[20] It is important to keep these thoughts in mind as we consider the views of the ancient Egyptians regarding creation.

After an extensive investigation of these Egyptian texts, my conclusion is this: while it is true that Egyptian creation texts do, in fact, have a focus on how the universe operates and how mankind functions within it, this is not to the exclusion of concerns about the origins of the material creation. It is clear, at least to me, that material origins were of utmost importance to the ancient Egyptians in their literature. The beginning of physical objects in the universe is a distinct aspect of the various creation accounts.

1. Self-Creation of a Creator-God

A number of texts not only describe the creation of the universe but even picture the creator-god materializing in an act of self-creation. Utterance 587 of the Pyramid Texts states,

> Praise to you, Atum!
> Praise to you, Kheprer, *who created himself!*
> You became high in this your name High Ground.
> *You created yourself* in this your name Kheprer.[21]

---

19 Henri Frankfort, in *Before Philosophy*, 29.

20 Siegfried Morenz, *Egyptian Religion* (Ithaca, NY: Cornell University Press, 1973), 160.

21 My own translation, emphasis added. For various other renderings, see R. O. Faulkner, *The Ancient Egyptian Pyramid Texts* (New York: Oxford University Press, 1969), 238–41; and R. T.

That is an early text that dates to the end of the third millennium (c. 2400–2200) BC.

Later Egyptian creation texts echo this belief that the creator-god was a product of self-creation. Coffin Text 714 says,

> I [am] Nu the one with no equal.
> I came into being on the
> Great Occasion of the inundation, when I came into being.
> I am he who flew, who became Dbnn
> Who is in his egg.
> I am he who began there [in] Nu.
> See, the chaos-god came forth from me.
> See, I am prosperous.
> I created my body in my glory.
> *I am he who made myself,*
> I formed myself according to my will and according to my
>   heart.[22]

This idea that the creator-god brought himself into being is a common element of Egyptian creation texts, including The Sun Hymn of Haremhab, Spell 601 of the Coffin Texts, and Spell 85 of the Book of the Dead.[23] The ancient Egyptians were interested in where the creator-god came from and when he began his existence.

2. Creation of Other Gods

Numerous texts then describe the acts of the creator-god in bringing into existence the lesser gods of the cosmos that are personified in the various physical elements of the universe. These acts are pictured in a

---

Rundle Clark, *Myth and Symbol in Ancient Egypt* (London: Thames and Hudson, 1959), 37–38. For original texts, see K. Sethe, *Die Altaegyptischen Pyramidentexte* (Leipzig: J. C. Hinrichs, 1908–1922).

22 My own translation, emphasis added. For Coffin Texts, see *Oriental Institute Publications*, 8 vols. (Chicago: University of Chicago Press, 1935–2006).

23 For the Book of the Dead, see R. O. Faulkner and C. Andrews, *The Ancient Egyptian Book of the Dead* (Austin: University of Texas Press, 1972).

variety of ways. In some texts, the creator-god is portrayed as creating the elements of the cosmos by expectoration or spitting out of the lesser gods.[24] Other creation texts describe the creator-god exhaling or sneezing the lesser gods from his nostrils, such as in Coffin Texts 75, 80, and 81. A third method spelled out in the Pyramid Texts is creation by an act of onanism (masturbation) by the creator (see Utterance 527). Spell 245 of the Coffin Texts alludes to that earlier text when the god Shu says to the creator-god Atum, "This was the manner of your engendering: you conceived with your mouth and you gave birth from your hand in the pleasure of emission. I am the star that came forth from the two."[25] One further description of creation is the Memphite theology of the Old Kingdom found on the Shabaka Stone. It tells of the god Ptah, "who made all and brought the gods into being."[26] Ptah is glorified in this text because he formed the universe by speech, that is, by mere verbal fiat. He spoke, and the gods burst forth.

These stories are frankly and directly concerned with explaining the details of the history of the physical universe as it comes into being. Ancient Egyptian theogony[27] is cosmogonic (it explains the origin of the universe) because each of the gods fashioned by the creator-god is a personification of an element of nature. As I have written elsewhere,

> Thus in some of the myths the creator-god produces four children who correspond to the basic structure of the universe: Shu (= air), Tefnut (= atmosphere), Geb (= earth), and Nut (= heavens). They in turn breed another generation of gods who represent elements of nature (e.g., Seth = storm). So we must in no way think that

24 See, e.g., Utterance 600 of the Pyramid Texts, trans. J. A. Wilson, in J. B. Pritchard, ed., *Ancient Near Eastern Texts Relating to the Old Testament* (*ANET*) (Princeton, NJ: Princeton University Press, 1955); and Spell 76 of the Coffin Texts, trans. J. Zandee, "Sargtexte Spruch 76," *Zeitschrift für ägyptische Sprache und Altertumskunde* 100 (1973): 60–71.

25 Translation in Clark, *Myth and Symbol*, 44.

26 *ANET*, 5.

27 "Theogony" refers to ancient attempts to explain the origins of gods.

the Egyptian creation myths describe merely a metaphysical or spiritual creation.[28]

3. Creation of Mankind

The same is true of the creation of mankind in Egyptian literature. Many texts refer to that event and to the fact that humanity was specially formed by a creator-god. Some texts portray the creator-god as a potter who creates mankind by molding it on a potter's wheel or table. For instance, the creator-god Khnum is pictured as "modeling people on his wheel. He has fashioned men."[29] The creator-god Ptah is similarly represented as a potter crafting mankind out of a lump of clay.[30] "Man is clay and straw, and God is his potter" is a pronouncement in the Instruction of Amenemope.[31]

Thus, in contrast to Walton's contention that Genesis 1–3, like other ancient Near Eastern texts, is primarily interested in function rather than origins, in Egyptian texts there is a substantial focus on the origins of the universe. The purpose and function of mankind in creation are not central ideas. The Egyptian texts have much more to do with humanity's origins than with humanity's utility and capacity.

B. A Significant Mesopotamian Creation Text

Among the cosmological texts of Mesopotamia, perhaps the most important is the Babylonian epic called *Enuma Elish*.[32] This document does spend a lot of time describing the order, function, and purpose of the various elements of creation. For instance, the purpose of mankind in the universe is stated directly:

---

28 Currid, *Ancient Egypt and the Old Testament*, 60.

29 From *The Great Hymn to Khnum*, in Miriam Lichtheim, *Ancient Egyptian Literature*, 3 vols. (Berkeley: University of California Press, 1975–1980), 3:114.

30 A. H. Sayce, *The Religions of Ancient Egypt and Babylonia* (Edinburgh: T&T Clark, 1903), 138.

31 W. K. Simpson, ed., *The Literature of Ancient Egypt* (New Haven, CT: Yale University Press, 1973), 262.

32 This title derives from the opening words of the account, which are "When on high" or "When . . . above." The literature on this text is vast; see, e.g., Alexander Heidel, *The Babylonian Genesis*, 2nd ed. (Chicago: University of Chicago Press, 1951); and W. G. Lambert, *Babylonian Creation Myths* (Winona Lake, IN: Eisenbrauns, 2013).

He shall be charged with the service of the gods,
That they might be at ease![33]

However, such descriptions are not to the exclusion of descriptions of material creation. Thus, the passage just quoted begins with the following words by the creator-god Marduk:

Blood I will mass and cause bones to be,
I will establish a savage, "man" shall be his name.
Verily, savage-man I will create.

A rift between origins (the act of creation of mankind) and function (man's place in the order of creation) is not evident here. Both are present.

The same holds true for the rest of the universe as described in the *Enuma Elish*. While Walton and others are certainly correct that a good part of the text deals with the creator-god's ordering of the universe and the assigning of functions to its various parts, this text certainly does not omit attention to material origins. For example, central to the story is a cosmic battle between the gods of order and the gods of chaos, and this supports Walton's claim that there is a concern for function. Yet, the beginning of the text describes a situation in which material things did not exist and then tells how they were brought into being through divine agency:

When the heavens above did not exist,
And earth beneath had not come into being—
There was Apsu, the first in order, their begetter,
And the demiurge Tiamat, who gave birth to them all;
They mingled their waters together
Before meadow-land had coalesced and reed-bed was to be
       found—

---

33 For a study of this idea, see W. R. Mayer, "Ein Mythos von der Erschaffung des Menschen und des Königs," *Orientalia* 56 (1987): 55–68.

When not one of the gods had been formed

Or had come into being, when no destinies had been decreed,

The gods were created in them.[34]

The watery chaos pictured in this text consists of two gods, Apsu and Tiamat, who create other deities through sexual procreation. The created gods each represent a vital element of the universe, such as sky, water, and earth. This second generation desires order rather than the chaotic status quo of Apsu and Tiamat. Order wins the day in a great cosmic battle. The point is, again, that the text is concerned about both the ordering of the universe and its material origins. Averbeck puts it well when he concludes, "Driving a wedge between material creation as over against giving order to the cosmos by assigning functions or roles is a false dichotomy that cannot bear the weight of the text."[35]

It is interesting that Walton comments, "Our first proposition is that Genesis 1 is ancient cosmology. . . . In these ways, and many others, [the ancient Israelites] thought about the cosmos in much the same way that anyone in the ancient world thought . . ."[36] I agree that Genesis 1 is similar to other ancient cosmology in several important ways. But since it is evident that ancient Near Eastern creation accounts had great concern for *both function and material origins*, we would expect the biblical creation account to have the same focus and interests. Consequently, the idea that the origins debate can be swept away because Genesis 1–3 is not paying attention to physical, material beginnings is simply mistaken.

C. Functions and Origins in Genesis 1–3

The Hebrew creation account begins with the words "In the beginning, God created . . ." In ancient Hebrew there are a variety of words meaning to make or to form something; and these words have various subjects, that is, either men or God. The verb used in Genesis 1:1 for "create" is only and always used for the work of God when it appears

---

34 Quoted in Lambert, *Babylonian Creation Myths*, 50–51.

35 Averbeck, "Lost World of Adam and Eve: A Review Essay," 235.

36 Walton, *Lost World of Genesis One*, 16.

in the qal (simple active tense) stem as it does here. In the qal stem, it is not used for the action of mankind. Simply put, it is God who is at work in Genesis 1; this is his creation. Verse 1 then describes the object of God's creative activity: it was "the heavens and the earth"; here we see a figure of speech called a "merism," which is a set of opposites that are all-inclusive (see, e.g., Ps. 139:8; Rev. 22:13). It is a designation for all that exists. God has simply created all things.

In verse 2 the universe and, in particular, the earth is pictured in the process of creation. It is described as *tohu*, that is, "without form." This is a Hebrew word that commonly reflects a state of wildness and wilderness; it indicates a circumstance of chaos and what is unordered. The earth is also described as *bohu*, which is often translated as "void" (ESV). It denotes "emptiness." So at this point in the account, the earth is wild and empty. It is *tohu* and *bohu*. These two words are important because they serve as headings for the remainder of the creation account in Genesis 1. In days 1–3, God brings order out of the *tohu* by putting things in their right places. That is followed by days 4–6, in which God takes care of the *bohu* by filling the universe with celestial bodies and filling the earth with plants, animals, and humans.

The account does report the various roles and functions of various elements of the creation. For example, he placed the lights in the heavens "to separate the day from the night" (v. 14) and "to give light upon the earth" (v. 15). Mankind, as well, was created for a purpose, and that was to "have dominion over the fish of the sea and over the birds of the heavens and over the livestock . . ." (v. 26) and to "be fruitful and multiply and fill the earth and subdue it . . ." (v. 28) We certainly do not want to underappreciate this aspect of the creation account. God made things for specific roles, functions, and purposes.

The problem with Walton's functional model is that it highlights the roles of the elements of the universe at the expense of their actual creation. The reality is that God was not only ordering the cosmos and assigning roles to the different parts of nature, but he was filling the universe as well. In other words, he created light (v. 3), oceans (v. 9), land (v. 9), plants (v. 11), celestial bodies (v. 14), animals (v. 24), and humans (v. 26). To interpret Genesis 1 as merely about functions and not about origins is a failure to account for some of the very prominent features of the narrative.

II. GENESIS 1–3 AS MYTH

Another way that supporters of theistic evolution attempt to resolve the conflict between the Bible and evolution is by claiming that Genesis 1–3 is not factual history but is an ancient Near Eastern "myth." They are using the word "myth" in the sense of a legendary story without determinable basis in fact or history. In regard to creation, they see myth as a symbolic tale of primordial times that deals principally with the realm of the gods. It is a "narrative only in the sense that the stories have a linear forward movement, but they are simply ahistorical. Their purpose is to explain the order and meaning of the universe as it stands."[37]

Eastern University professor Peter Enns argues for the "Genesis 1–3 as myth" position with his claim that ". . . the opening chapters of Genesis participate in a worldview that the earliest Israelites shared with their Mesopotamian neighbors. . . . the stories of Genesis had a context within which they were first understood. And that context was not a modern scientific one *but an ancient mythic one.*"[38]

The belief that the Hebrew creation account is based on the Babylonian creation myth, and is itself mythic, has been standard fare for a long time among liberal Old Testament scholars. A dominant early advocate of this position was the German professor Hermann Gunkel (1862–1932).[39] He states that the biblical creation narrative "is only the Jewish elaboration of far older material, which must have been originally

---

37   See J. D. Currid, *Against the Gods: The Polemical Theology of the Old Testament* (Wheaton, IL: Crossway, 2013), 43. Cf. P. Veyne, *Did the Greeks Believe in Their Myths? An Essay on Constitutive Imagination*, trans. P. Wissing (Chicago: University of Chicago Press, 1988).

38   Peter Enns, *Inspiration and Incarnation: Evangelicals and the Problem of the Old Testament* (Grand Rapids, MI: Baker, 2005), 55, emphasis added.

39   See, in particular, Hermann Gunkel, *Schöpfung und Chaos in Urzeit und Endzeit* (Gottingen: Vandenhoeck & Ruprecht, 1895); and Gunkel, *Die Sagen der Genesis* (Gottingen: Vandenhoeck & Ruprecht, 1901).

much more mythological."[40] More modern critical scholars continue to hold this core belief, but with a few more twists and turns.[41] Joseph Blenkinsopp, for example, comments on the nature of Genesis 1–11, saying, "For its basic structure and major themes it has drawn on a well established literary tradition best represented by the Mesopotamian *Atrahasis* text, and in this limited respect it is comparable with the work of early Greek mythographers."[42]

But this approach raises a question: Why does Genesis 1–3 contain so many elements that appear to be literal history if in fact it was borrowed from an ancient Near Eastern myth? Many liberal scholars answer that the writer of Genesis borrowed ancient Near Eastern myths of creation, and then stripped them of their mythological elements and made them look like historical records. The author thus employed a form of *demythologization* to rid the creation story of myth and then replaced it with a monotheistic, non-mythic orthodoxy.

But then how can they be so sure it originated with a myth? These same commentators believe that, through a close reading of Genesis 1–3, they can still see some of the original mythic character. And this is important for our study, for if Genesis 1–3 is merely a sanitized text that is really mythic at its core, then the question of origins, including human beginnings, is a moot one—myths are never intended to be taken as real history in the first place. Those who embrace a mythic interpretation simply have no trouble accepting evolution as a means of material and human origins; there is no tension between the Genesis myth and science in this regard.

No doubt there are many parallels between the Hebrew creation account and the myths of the ancient Near East.[43] The question is, is the

---

40 Quoted in J. Niehaus, *Ancient Near Eastern Themes in Biblical Theology* (Grand Rapids, MI: Kregel, 2008), 23–24.

41 See the recent contribution of K. L. Sparks, "Genesis 1–11 as Ancient Historiography," in C. Halton, ed., *Genesis: History, Fiction, or Neither? Three Views on the Bible's Earliest Chapters* (Grand Rapids, MI: Zondervan, 2015). He argues that the various parts of Genesis 1–11 are "myth, legend, and tale" (109).

42 Joseph Blenkinsopp, *The Pentateuch: An Introduction to the First Five Books of the Bible* (New York: Doubleday, 1992), 93–94.

43 See Heidel, *Babylonian Genesis*.

position of *demythologization* the best explanation for the relationship between the two literatures? This interpretation clearly highlights the close association of Genesis 1–3 and other ancient Near Eastern texts, while it undervalues the uniqueness and originality of the Hebrew account. But are the early chapters of Genesis in their original form merely another myth that is later partially cleansed, or are they unique and distinct in their own right?

There are compelling reasons for rejecting the "Genesis as myth" view. The mythic explanation underestimates the deep, fervent resistance of the Hebrews to anything that even smacks of the mythological. Again, many modern commentators view any reticence to myth as a very late aspect of the compositional process of the early chapters of Genesis. To the contrary, I would argue that Genesis 1–3 is at its very core anti-mythological, and this can be seen in its polemical quality and disposition.[44] Since I have dealt elsewhere with the polemical nature of the Hebrew creation account, I will not take time to restate my entire case in detail, but will give some specific examples of polemic at work in the general account of the creation and of human origins in particular.[45]

A. Anti-Mythic Polemic on the Creation of Humanity

In the Mesopotamian creation myth, the gods created mankind for the specific purpose of easing the workload of the deities. The *Atrahasis* text says,

> The gods' load was too great,
> The work too hard, the trouble too much . . .
> The gods dug out the Tigris river
> And then dug out the Euphrates . . .
> For 3,600 years they bore the excess,

---

44 Consider the groundbreaking work of G. F. Hasel, "The Polemic Nature of the Genesis Cosmology," *Evangelical Quarterly* 46 (1974): 81–102. The strength of this article is his sound argument that a primary purpose of the Genesis account is anti-mythological.

45 See Currid, *Against the Gods*, 33–46.

Hard work, night and day,
They groaned and blamed each other.[46]

Mankind's function was to be a slave to the gods so that "they might be at ease." After their creation, humans multiply quickly and they become a thorn in the sides of the gods. People are tumultuous, and they disturb the sleep of the gods, in particular Enlil, the head of the pantheon:

And the country was as noisy as a bellowing bull.
The god grew restless at their racket . . .
He addressed the great gods,
"The noise of mankind has become too much,
I am losing sleep over their racket.
Give the order that *suruppu*-disease shall break out."

Enlil's attempt to destroy humanity with a plague is a failure. He then tries to inflict them with a famine, but that fails as well. Finally, he orders a flood to consume them all. It is clear that the deluge in the *Atrahasis* epic contains several similarities and has parallels with the biblical account of the flood.[47]

But there are far greater differences. Israel's account of mankind's creation and the subsequent flood is opposed at its very heart to the worldview conceptions of the rest of the ancient Near East. Humanity's creation is not for the purpose of being slaves to the gods and to carry their workload, but rather mankind is created in the image of God (Gen. 1:27), as the "crown of creation," and as God's co-regent, ruling over the created order. Humanity's very purpose and dignity arise from this special, sovereign act of the Creator.

The flood in Scripture is not a consequence of mankind's not caring for the ease of the gods or of their awakening the gods from their slumber (these gods have all the foibles of human character); rather, it is due to mankind's

---

46 Trans. Stephanie Dalley, *Myths from Mesopotamia* (Oxford: Oxford University Press, 1997).
47 For a good study of the Mesopotamian flood account, see W. G. Lambert and A. R. Millard, *Atrahasis: The Babylonian Story of the Flood* (Winona Lake, IN: Eisenbrauns, 1999).

unholiness in contrast to a holy God (Gen. 6:5). Such major distinctions cannot be accounted for by a simple cleansing of myth from the text.

B. Anti-Mythic Polemic on the Creation of the Luminaries

In ancient Near Eastern creation texts, a dominant feature is theogony, which, as noted above, refers to the creation of the gods who are personified in the elements of the universe. The forming of astral bodies of the sun, moon, and stars is theogonic. So, in the Mesopotamian *Enuma Elish*, the creator-god Marduk made the gods and then "constructed stations for the great gods, fixing their astral likenesses as constellations."[48]

The biblical author, in contrast, presents God as creating the luminaries, but there is no interest in theogony. He is rigidly monotheistic and sanctions no deification of the heavenly bodies. Alexander Heidel comments, "The opening chapters of Genesis, as well as the Old Testament in general, refer to only one Creator and Maintainer of all things, one God who created and transcends all cosmic matter. In the entire Old Testament, there is not a trace of theogony, such as we find, for example, in *Enuma Elish* and Hesiod."[49]

It is significant that the luminaries are not given names in the Genesis 1 account. They are merely called "the two great lights," one being "the greater light" and the other being "the lesser light," and "the stars" (1:16). While some commentators believe this fact has no significance or that it is simply "the rhetorically high style of the narrative,"[50] it clearly distinguishes the Israelite worldview from the other ancient Near Eastern theogonic views. The creation texts from the ancient Near East present the luminaries as gods, and they bear deific names. To the contrary, Hebrew religion conceives of the luminaries as mere material objects that are not to be worshiped. G. F. Hasel correctly comments, "They share in the creatureliness of all creation and have no autonomous divine quality."[51]

---

48 *ANET*, 67.
49 Heidel, *Babylonian Genesis*, 97.
50 C. John Collins, *Genesis 1–4: A Linguistic, Literary, and Theological Commentary* (Phillipsburg, NJ: P&R, 2006), 82–83.
51 Hasel, "Polemic Nature," 89.

Other examples could easily be cited of Hebrew polemic in the Genesis creation account against common ancient Near Eastern creation documents.[52] The conclusion is obvious: ancient Near Eastern creation texts are myth, and they bear all the identifying marks of myth—things such as polytheism, theogony, magic, and fertility.[53] But Genesis 1–3 is zealously anti-mythological. It is monotheistic to its very core, and it in no way sanctions the existence of other gods or the creation of other gods. It also promotes a high view of mankind and their creation over against the man-as-a-slave morality of other religions. These are issues that are central to the Hebrew world and life view, and they are not attained by some sort of mythological cleansing. Contrary to some supporters of theistic evolution, Genesis 1–3 is not dark mythological polytheism but stands in stark contrast to it and is in fact a sustained polemic against it.

III. FIGURATIVE AND THEOLOGICAL LITERATURE

One of the most common and popular ways to deal with the issue of origins in Genesis 1–3 is to argue that the account is figurative. In other words, it is not the biblical author's intention to present his material in a historical or scientific manner. His aim is really theological; that is, the account exalts the Lord as the Creator of the universe, but the writer is not interested in the manner of creation. As Denis Alexander says, "The purpose of Genesis 2, like Genesis 1, is to teach theology."[54] Thus, a wedge is driven between what some call "theological history" (i.e., Genesis 1–3) and modern scientific inquiry (geology, geography, physics, etc.) and modern social sciences (history, anthropology, and other fields of research). The end-all, of course, is a sweeping dismissal of Genesis 1–3 having any concern about the methods and manners of creation. Modern scientific research provides the answers to the issue of the mechanics of origins, and the Bible does not.

---

52 See, again, Currid, *Against the Gods*, 33–46.

53 See my article "Cosmologies of Myth," in W. A. Hoffecker, ed., *Building a Christian World View*, vol. 2 (Phillipsburg, NJ: P&R, 1988), 9–20.

54 Alexander, *Creation or Evolution*, 196.

The approach of Francis Collins also falls into this general category. He classifies Genesis 1–3 as "poetry and allegory"[55] and therefore not intended to be understood as factually true historical narrative.

John Walton is a third author to adopt this "figurative literature" approach, although his descriptive label is "archetypal literature." By "archetype" he means a kind of Everyman allegorical story in which what happens to Adam and Eve is a kind of allegory (an archetype) to tell us what happens to every person. For example, after discussing Genesis 2:7, in which "the LORD God formed the man of dust from the ground and breathed into his nostrils the breath of life, and the man became a living creature," Walton writes,

> the next question to consider is whether this statement about Adam pertains to him uniquely or to all of us. The core proposal of this book is that the forming accounts of Adam and Eve should be understood archetypally rather than as accounts of how those two individuals were uniquely formed. When I use the word *archetype* . . . I am referring to the simple concept that an archetype embodies all others in the group.[56]

Another commentator, New Testament scholar Scot McKnight, calls Adam and Eve in Genesis 1–3 "literary," and certainly what he means is that in the text there is "no sign of a historical or biological or genetic Adam and Eve."[57]

The end result is the same from the approaches of Denis Alexander, Francis Collins, John Walton, and Scot McKnight: Genesis 1–3 should not be understood as historical narrative reporting actual events that

---

55 Francis Collins, *The Language of God: A Scientist Presents Evidence for Belief* (New York: Free Press, 2006), 206; see also 150–51, 175, 207.

56 Walton, *Lost World of Adam and Eve*, 74. Walton goes on to explain that an "archetype" will sometimes be a historical figure and sometimes not (74–75, 96). He decides that Adam and Eve were "real people who existed in a real past" (96) with regard to the account of Genesis 3 of their fall into sin (101–3), but the accounts of how they were initially created in Genesis 2 are not historical, and we do not need to consider them to be the first human beings (75–77, 101, 103).

57 Scot McKnight, in Venema and McKnight, *Adam and the Genome*, 136.

happened in the past, but instead we should understand these chapters as "figurative" or "allegorical" or "archetypal" or "literary" literature. My objections here will apply to all four of these approaches, because my contention is that Genesis 1–3 should be understood as historical narrative.

Alexander supplies a number of examples to demonstrate why Genesis 1–3 should be understood figuratively and theologically, but not historically or scientifically. For instance, he states the following:

> For myself I have never met a Christian who, upon reading Genesis 3:8—"the man and his wife heard the sound of the Lord God as he was walking in the garden in the cool of the day"—imagines that God was physically walking around in the garden with two legs. No Hebrew reading this would have imagined that the God of Israel, of whom no form was seen when he spoke out of the fire (Deuteronomy 4:15), was clattering round the garden in noisy footwear. In reality, this is a rather vivid and heart-aching picture of the results of sin . . .[58]

Actually, the Hebrew reader would have no trouble understanding that what is being described in this incident is a *theophany*, that is, a temporary appearance of God in physical form.[59] At times, the Lord even takes on a theophanic form as a human being. In Genesis 18:1–2, for example, the text tells us that "Yahweh appeared" before Abraham at the tent-door when three men stood before the patriarch. Two of the "men" are designated as angels later in the story (18:22; 19:1), and the third figure is the Lord himself (see 18:13, 17). Thus we see the Lord appearing in human form, accompanied by two of his angels. There is nothing figurative about this account of the Lord's appearance in physical form.

The warning that the proponents of the "figurative only" position give is that the primary purpose of the early chapters of Genesis is

58 Alexander, *Creation or Evolution*, 198.
59 See J. Niehaus, "In the Wind of the Storm: Another Look at Genesis III 8," *Vetus Testamentum* 44, no. 2 (1994): 263–67.

theological, and, therefore, one should not expect these chapters to be scientific in regard to how God made the universe or the biological intricacies of existence. Again, Alexander presents this position well when he says,

> These chapters represent the opening manifesto of the Bible, setting its parameters and its priorities, and the danger is that if we start interpreting the text as if it were scientific literature, or was intended to tell us how God created biological diversity, then we run the risk of missing the central theological messages.[60]

This argument, of course, is a non sequitur. The mere fact that one views the text as historical literature, and not as some type of figurative manifesto, certainly does not mean that one will miss the main theological points of the text. In reality, the reverse is true: the person who views the early chapters of Genesis as figurative will miss some of the principal teachings of the account. Let us turn to consider this point.

Walton's argument for taking Genesis 2 as "archetypal literature" is based on a simple test. Walton comments,

> In order to determine whether the treatment of Adam in the text focuses on him primarily as an archetype or as an individual, we can ask a simple question: is the text describing something that is uniquely true of Adam, or is it describing something that is true of all of us? If only Adam is formed from dust, then it is treating him as a discrete and unique individual. . . . If Eve's formation conveys a truth about her that is true of her alone, then it is the history of an individual.[61]

But then, in order to demonstrate that Genesis 2 is not describing the unique creation of Adam and Eve but is in fact "describing something that is true of all of us," Walton has to do violence to the actual words

60 Ibid., 196–97.
61 Walton, *Lost World of Adam and Eve*, 75.

of the text. In the midst of an entire chapter that speaks repeatedly of numerous specific actions that the Lord God carried out (Gen. 2:2, 3, 7, 8, 9, 15, 16, 19, 21, 22), Walton tells us that verse 7, "then the Lord God formed man of dust from the ground," does not mean that the Lord God formed man of dust from the ground. It means, rather, that all people are created mortal, subject to death.[62] He says that "the LORD God caused a deep sleep to fall upon the man, and while he slept took one of his ribs and closed up its place with flesh . . . the rib that the Lord God had taken from the man he made into a woman" (Gen. 2:21–22) does not mean that God created Eve from a rib that he took from Adam's side. It simply implies something that is true of all human beings generally, and that is that a man's wife "is his ally, his other half."[63]

However, several decisive considerations in Genesis 1–3 show that these chapters are rightly understood not as poetry or allegory or figurative literature, but as historical narrative.

A. Genre of Genesis 1–3

Genesis 1–3 bears all the markings of Hebrew historical narrative. One common grammatical device that reflects a historical genre is the Hebrew verbal construction of the vav-consecutive with an imperfective verb.[64] This construction appears frequently in the first three chapters of Genesis: for instance, this device of historical sequence occurs fifty-one times in Genesis 1 alone ("And God said," v. 3; "And God saw," v. 4; etc.). Another indicator of prose narrative is the use of the small Hebrew word *'eth* as the sign of the direct object.[65] The early chapters of Genesis actually contain little indication of figurative language. There are few tropes, symbols, or metaphors. The dearth of figurative language is quite striking. A question thus arises: if the text was not

---

62   Ibid., 72–74.

63   Ibid., 81.

64   B. T. Arnold and J. H. Choi, *A Guide to Biblical Hebrew Syntax* (Cambridge: Cambridge University Press, 2003), 84–87. This function is quite rare in Hebrew poetry.

65   R. J. Williams, *Hebrew Syntax: An Outline*, 2nd ed. (Toronto: University of Toronto Press, 1976), 78, comments that this accusative marker "is rare in poetry but normal in prose."

meant to be taken historically and sequentially, why did the biblical author employ narrative devices so freely?

Yes, Genesis 1, in particular, is highly structured. Elements like the repetition of "evening and morning" throughout the passage reflect its compositional grid. However, repetitive formulas do not necessarily signify nonhistorical, figurative accounts. For example, the entire book of Genesis is structured according to the repeated formula "This is the book of the generations of . . ." (2:4; 5:1; 6:9; 10:1; 11:10, 27; 25:12, 19; 36:1, 9; 37:2),[66] but that in no way indicates that the entire book is figurative in what it relays to its readers. Genesis 1 has an elevated style, yet it is still historical narrative. C. John Collins perhaps has the best genre definition of Genesis 1 when he calls it "exalted prose narrative."[67] As I conclude elsewhere, "This description properly reflects the sequence, chronology, and historicity of the account, while at the same time underscoring its exceptional quality."[68]

The historical nature of the Hebrew creation account underscores the reality that God invented time and history. And the history that God created in Genesis 1 is one that is moving and unfolding: it is a linear history that moves from inception to consummation. The universe had a beginning, and it is moving toward an end. This truth distinguishes the biblical creation account from the cosmogonical texts of the ancient Near East. The non-Israelite accounts are legendary stories that have no determinable basis in fact or history. They are symbolic sagas of primordial times that describe the realm and activities of deities. They are what can be called "mythic narrative"; that is, the stories have linear forward movement, but they are simply ahistorical. Models such as the figurative approach simply de-historicize the Hebrew creation account and, therefore, minimize this important "theological" aspect of the text.

The deeply historical nature of Genesis 1–3 is profoundly important to the entire Bible because these chapters stand at the beginning

---

66 See my discussion of this formula below, in the section "C. *Toledoth* Formula ("These Are the Generations of . . .")."

67 C. John Collins, *Genesis 1–4*, 44.

68 Currid, *Against the Gods*, 44.

of the Bible, whose overall structure is historical. The Bible shows the great scope of the work of God from the beginning of time to a final judgment and a new heavens and new earth. The first three chapters of Genesis do not stand alone in the Bible as isolated chapters but are structurally tied to the narrative in Genesis 4 about Adam and Eve and their children Cain, Abel, and Seth; and to the genealogies of human beings found in Genesis 5; and to the historical record in Genesis 6–9 of Noah's family and the flood; and to the historical narrative in Genesis 10 of the nations that descended from Noah's sons; and to the tower of Babel and to the descendants of Shem in Genesis 11; and to Abraham and the patriarchs in Genesis 12–50. Genesis 1–3 does not stand alone but is closely linked to the rest of this entire historical narrative.

The macro-structure of the Bible is a historical account of God's actions from beginning to end. If we remove the profoundly historical nature of Genesis 1–3, we will remove the historical foundation on which all the remainder of the Bible rests.

B. Context of Genesis 1–3

The most basic premise of hermeneutics from the time of the Reformation is that when one faces a difficult text, one must proceed on the assumption that Scripture interprets Scripture. The Westminster Confession of Faith (1646) puts it well: "The infallible rule of interpretation of Scripture is the Scripture itself: and therefore, when there is a question about the true and full sense of any Scripture (which is not manifold, but one), it must be searched and known by other places that speak more clearly."[69] I am certain that few would disagree that the early chapters of Genesis are difficult. The obvious question, then, is how does the remainder of Scripture handle the Genesis creation account? I know of no text in the Bible that suggests that Genesis 1–3 is a figurative passage or that would counter the basic chronological/ sequential structure of the account. In fact, whenever the creation texts are referred to in the rest of Scripture, chronology and history

---

69 Westminster Confession of Faith, 1.9.

predominate. So, for example, Exodus 20:8–11 reflects the reality that mankind's earthly seven-day week has a set and solid foundation in God's activity in the creation week. Psalm 104, which reviews the creative work of God at the beginning of time, confirms the sequence and history of the early chapters of Genesis. While it is true that not every jot and tittle of the creation account is dealt with in the rest of the Bible, yet when it is considered, it is not understood as figurative in any way but as a report of actual historical events.

Often those who promote a figurative view of Genesis 1, in particular, use Genesis 2:5 as evidence: the claim is that this verse cannot be harmonized with the progression of the week in Genesis 1.[70] This is an important issue, and I will deal with it in the next section of this essay.

More could be added regarding the sequential and historical nature of the early chapters of Genesis, but space and time do not allow us to go into much greater detail.[71] In any event, although some authors merely dismiss the Hebrew account as figurative and not historical, some by a mere flick of the wrist, the nature of the text is much more complicated and complex than they suppose. They do not do proper justice to the chronological reality of Genesis 1–3, and to the fact that God is the God of history. Surely the intention of the author cannot be merely to theologize and to divorce history from the account?

IV. THE SEQUENTIAL SCHEME

For many decades, the question of the relationship between the account of Genesis 1:1–2:3 and Genesis 2:4–3:24 has been a dominant issue in Old Testament studies. The liberal higher critics, with few exceptions, argue that the two accounts are from different sources, and they are therefore not complementary but competing narratives of creation.[72]

---

70 See, in particular, M. G. Kline, "Because It Had Not Rained," *Westminster Theological Journal* (*WTJ*) 20 (1958): 146–57; and M. Futato, "Because It Had Rained: A Study of Gen. 2:5–7 with Implications for Gen. 2:4–25 and Gen. 1:1–2:3," *WTJ* 60 (1998): 1–21.

71 For further study, see my response to the "Framework View of Gen. 1:1–2:3" in John Currid, *Genesis*, vol. 1, EP Study Commentary (Darlington, UK: Evangelical Press, 2003), 34–42.

72 See E. A. Speiser, *Genesis*, vol. 1 (Garden City, NY: Doubleday, 1964), 18–20.

They are "two excerpts from two separate compositions, which a later editor arranged consecutively by pure chance."[73]

Others dismiss that claim. Brandeis professor Nahum Sarna, for example, simply concludes that "Chapter 2 is not another creation story."[74] More traditional and conservative commentators take the position that the two texts harmonize, and the second narrative is a more detailed exposition focused especially on Adam and Eve and events of the sixth day of creation.

More recently, John Walton has proposed a third alternative.[75] He says that perhaps "the second account might be considered a sequel to the first. . . . the second account is not detailing the sixth day, but identifying a sequel scenario, that is, recounting events that potentially and arguably could have occurred long after the first account."[76]

But here are some of the key verses in Genesis 2 that have long been understood to give a more detailed explanation of the creation of Adam and Eve that is just mentioned briefly in Genesis 1:

> Then the LORD God formed the man of dust from the ground and breathed into his nostrils the breath of life, and the man became a living creature. (Gen. 2:7)

> So the LORD God caused a deep sleep to fall upon the man, and while he slept took one of his ribs and closed up its place with flesh. And the rib that the LORD God had taken from the man he made into a woman and brought her to the man. (Gen. 2:21–22)

Making these verses talk about something other than the creation of Adam and Eve as the first human beings would provide a convenient

---

73 Umberto Cassuto, *A Commentary on the Book of Genesis, Part One: From Adam to Noah* (Jerusalem: Magnes, 1989 ed.), 85.

74 N. M. Sarna, *The JPS Torah Commentary: Genesis* (Philadelphia: Jewish Publication Society, 1989), 16.

75 John H. Walton, "A Historical Adam: Archetypal Creation View," in *Four Views on the Historical Adam*, ed. Matthew Barrett and Ardel B. Caneday (Grand Rapids, MI: Zondervan, 2013), 89–118.

76 Ibid., 109.

solution for theistic evolutionists. This is because, if Genesis 2 is a more detailed explanation of the creation events of Genesis 1 (as Christians have historically held), then the statements "formed the man of dust from the ground" and "the rib that the LORD God had taken from the man he made into a woman" simply cannot be reconciled with the theistic evolution view that Adam and Eve were born from previously existing human beings.

So Walton's sequential scheme has weighty consequences for the issue of the origin of humanity in Scripture. Walton recognizes the significance of this when, after proposing his "sequel scenario," he goes on to say,

> In such a case, Adam and Eve would not necessarily be envisioned as the first human beings, but would be elect individuals drawn out of the human population and given a particular representative role in sacred space.[77]

If, as Walton suggests, Genesis 2–3 is not representing Adam and Eve as the first humans created, then the issue of human origins is thrown wide open. Walton himself recognizes this reality when he comments on the idea that Adam and Eve were not the first humans: "If the Bible makes no such claims, then the Bible will not stand opposed to any views that science might offer (e.g., evolutionary models or population genetics), as long as God is not eliminated from the picture."[78]

In other words, Walton is proposing that God created humanity as a species in Genesis 1, but at a later time or stage he chose Adam and Eve "out of the human population" to serve as an archetype of humankind. This allows Walton to affirm that he believes in Adam and Eve as historical personages. However, he also contends that perhaps they were not the first humans nor were they the parents of the entire human species. Those conclusions certainly make his position controversial.

But Walton's proposal faces several decisive objections.

77 Ibid.
78 Ibid., 112–13.

A. Clear Indicators of Historical Narrative in Genesis 2

On Walton's proposal, key portions of Genesis 2 must be understood not as straightforward narrative history but as some kind of poetic or figurative descriptions of God's activity. For example, there are explicit statements about God forming Adam and Eve from the dust of the ground and making Eve from a rib taken from Adam's side. But in Walton's view these become part of a description of the time, perhaps "tens of thousands of years" after human beings first appeared on the earth, when "individuals whom the Bible designates as Adam and Eve are chosen by God as representative priests in sacred space."[79]

This means that if we follow Walton's view, "the LORD God formed the man of dust from the ground" does not really mean that the Lord God formed man from the dust of the ground. Rather, it has something to do with God choosing a specific human being as a representative of the human race. And "the rib that the LORD God had taken from the man he made into a woman and brought her to the man" does not mean that the rib that the Lord God had taken from the man he made into a woman. Rather, it has something to do with God choosing a specific female human being as a representative priest with Adam.

Several factors in Genesis 1–2 stand in clear opposition to Walton's position. The two accounts of Genesis 1–2 are both of the genre of historical narrative, not poetic or allegorical literature, and they bear the markings of it (see discussion above, under "A. Genre of Genesis 1–3"). However, although both chapters are presented as historical prose narrative, they are stylistically different. As noted above, Genesis 1 is what C. John Collins appropriately calls "exalted prose narrative."[80] It is exceptional narrative that is highly structured, with much repetitive material. The text that begins in Genesis 2:4 is also unusual material, but it employs the common historical prose narrative normally used in Old Testament literature.

Corresponding to the stylistic differences, the nature of the content of the two accounts is distinct. Whereas Genesis 1:1–2:3 provides a

---

79 Ibid., 114–15.
80 C. John Collins, *Genesis 1–4*, 44.

broad sweep in its description of the creation of the universe, Genesis 2:4ff. is a pointed, localized record of events in the garden of Eden. In the opening narrative, God is the sole actor; in the second one, there are other participants working in the story besides God. This latter difference is reflected in the distinct names for God in the two narrations. In Genesis 1:1–2:3 the only name for God used in Hebrew is Elohim (translated as "God"); it appears thirty-six times in those thirty-four verses. The use of only this name perhaps carried a universal sense for the original audience, in which the transcendence of God is being emphasized. But in Genesis 2:4–24, the Hebrew name used for God is Yahweh Elohim (eleven times, translated "the Lord God"), and the addition of Yahweh to Elohim may be for the purpose of defining the universal Creator God as none other than the covenant God of Israel, Yahweh. The idea is to see the movement from the general to the particular: the transcendent God of Genesis 1 is the same as the immanent God of Genesis 2.[81]

The distinctiveness of the two narratives is also highlighted by the closing words of Genesis 2:4, which reads, "in the day Yahweh Elohim made *the earth and the heavens.*" This expression echoes the phrase "heavens and earth" of Genesis 1:1, but the order is reversed. This is probably because the heavens are at center stage in the opening account as God displays his mighty acts to produce the universe, while the second episode focuses on the earth and, in particular, the garden of Eden with mankind in it.

Therefore, both of the episodes are historical narrative and they are not diametrically opposed; rather, they highlight different aspects of God's creative activity. Again, this appears to be a stylistic move from the general to the particular: a change of focus from the larger universal picture to a telescopic view of one part of the universal picture. This means that Genesis 2 does not describe events perhaps "tens of thousands of years" after the creation account of Genesis 1 but gives a more particular description of the original creation of Adam and Eve.

---

81 The compounding of the two divine names occurs twenty times in Genesis 2–3, but on only one other occasion in the entire Pentateuch (Ex. 9:30).

Such a movement from the general to the particular in Hebrew narrative is a common rhetorical device. For example, we read in Joshua 14:6–14 about the episode of Caleb requesting an inheritance of land that had been promised to him. At the close of the passage the text says that Joshua "gave Hebron to Caleb. . . . [and] Hebron became the inheritance of Caleb the son of Jephunneh the Kenizzite to this day. . . . And the land had rest from war" (vv. 13–15). Later, in Joshua 15:13–17, we read the particulars of Caleb's capture of the Hebron region that helped to lead to peace in the land. Although this passage occurs later in the text, it is not sequential to 14:6–14 but is homing in on some specifics and particulars of the earlier passage.

B. Genesis 2:5

> When no bush of the field was yet in the land and no small plant of the field had yet sprung up—for the Lord God had not caused it to rain on the land, and there was no man to work the ground . . .

This verse is commonly used by commentators to deny that Genesis 2:4ff. is a particularization of day 6 of Genesis 1. The reason is simple: the verse provides a different picture of the circumstances at the beginning of day 6. As Meredith Kline comments, "Verse 5 itself describes a time when the earth was without vegetation."[82] Since, according to Genesis 1:11–12, vegetation was created on day 3, then there is discord between the two accounts. Consequently, some scholars conclude that Genesis 1 is not sequential but topical, and Genesis 2, by contrast, is the historical, chronological account of the creation of mankind, vegetation, and animals.[83]

But the incongruity between Genesis 1 and Genesis 2:5 is not as sharp as some commentators would have us believe. First, the text does not say there was no vegetation on the earth at this time; it declares that every plant (*'eseb*) of the field simply had not yet sprouted (*yitsmakh*). In

---

82 Kline, "Because It Had Not Rained," 149.

83 Futato, "Because It Had Rained," 1–21, goes as far as to argue that neither chapter 1 nor chapter 2 are to be understood as chronological.

other words, plants were there, but they simply had not blossomed or budded.[84] The verb *tsamach* ("to sprout") is not used of the vegetation in Genesis 1:11–12. Second, this verse refers to only two categories of plant life, and not to all vegetation.[85] As a result, a preferable explanation is that some plant life existed on the earth prior to the description of Genesis 2:5 and, therefore, this verse is not an insurmountable obstacle to the generalization-particularization view.

The reason the plants had not sprouted yet is twofold: the Lord had not brought rain, and there was "no man" to cultivate the ground. The Hebrew negative particle *'eyn* employed in the last clause of verse 5 ("there was no man to work the ground") is a particle of nonexistence.[86] The use of this particle indicates that no human beings yet existed, and thus argues against a sequential understanding of Genesis 1–2, in which mankind was created in Genesis 1:26–27 and then Adam and Eve were elected out of the existing human population to be representatives in the garden. We need to be careful here because, while the Hebrew particle of nonexistence can be used to negate the existence of something completely, it can also negate the presence of something in a particular location. This text, however, does not seem to localize the nonexistence to the garden, because verse 5 precedes God's planting of a garden in Eden (2:8) and, therefore, it likely refers to the circumstances of the entire earth: "There was no man."

Genesis 2:7 also affirms the nonsequential nature of Genesis 1–2. The text declares that Yahweh "formed the man, dust from the ground." Verbs of forming often require two accusatives, an object accusative (the thing made) followed by a material accusative (the material from which the thing is made).[87] This signifies that the material composition

---

84 Ludwig Koehler, Walter Baumgartner, and Johann J. Stamm, *The Hebrew and Aramaic Lexicon of the Old Testament* (HALOT), trans. and ed. under the supervision of Mervyn E. J. Richardson, 5 vols. (Leiden: Brill, 1994–2000), 807.

85 Futato, "Because It Had Rained," 4–5; and Cassuto, *Commentary on the Book of Genesis*, 101–3.

86 See the discussion of this particle in Paul Joüon, *A Grammar of Biblical Hebrew*, vol. 2 (Rome: Pontifical Biblical Institute, 2005), 576, 604–5.

87 Arnold and Choi, *Guide to Biblical Hebrew Syntax*, 21; and B. K. Waltke and M. O'Connor, *An Introduction to Biblical Hebrew Syntax* (Winona Lake, IN: Eisenbrauns, 1990), 174.

of the man Adam was dust; the Hebrew term for "dust" (*'aphar*) simply means "the dry, fine crumbs of the earth."[88] The man who is placed in the garden did not descend from previous humans but was formed directly from the material earth.

C. *Toledoth* Formula ("These Are the Generations of . . .")

The clause "These are the generations of . . ." is a repetitive formula that is a structural device for the entire book of Genesis. It appears eleven times in the book (2:4; 5:1; 6:9; 10:1; 11:10, 27; 25:12, 19; 36:1, 9; 37:2). Many interpreters understand this expression as a caption or heading for the section that is to follow. In fact, this understanding is so prevalent that several translations do not translate the Hebrew phrase as "These are the generations of," but as "This is the account of," showing it to be a heading for what follows (this is the translation of Genesis 2:4 used in the NIV, NASB, NET, NLT, and CSB, for example).

John Walton claims that sometimes this *toledoth* formula "functions as an introduction to the next sequential time period."[89] He concludes that *toledoth* in Genesis 2:4 is just such an introduction, and there it is transitional and conjunctive. The verse, therefore, transitions one narrative to another, and the second narrative would be later in time than the first. Based on this literary analysis, Walton suggests "that the text is not making an overt claim that Adam and Eve should be identified as the people of the first account if it presents the second account as sequential to the first."[90]

But the evidence that *toledoth* serves as a transitional marker between two narratives in sequence is quite thin. The only instance of the eleven appearances of the formula that Walton cites as bridging two narratives in this way is Genesis 6:9, "These are the generations of Noah. Noah was a righteous man, blameless in his generation. Noah walked with God." However, a close reading of that verse indicates it is introductory

---

88 HALOT, 723.
89 Walton, "Historical Adam: Archetypal Creation View," 109.
90 Ibid., 110.

to a concise genealogy in the next verse: "And Noah had three sons, Shem, Ham, and Japheth" (Gen. 6:10). Therefore, this verse fits into a pattern in which the formula frequently introduces genealogies in Genesis, but these cases do not require that the following passage be historically sequential to the previous one.

In fact, the preponderance of the usages of the *toledoth* formula is disjunctive, indicating that a new topic is being discussed, not that the subsequent material will be a sequence that follows from the previous material. It introduces a new topic in two ways: first, the formula regularly introduces a genealogy in Genesis and elsewhere in the Old Testament (see Gen. 10:1; 11:10, 27; 25:12; 36:1, 9; Num. 3:1; Ruth 4:18; 1 Chron. 1:29). Genealogies by nature are disjunctive, and they disrupt the flow of sequential narrative. Second, *toledoth* is a common heading in the book of Genesis announcing a new block of significant writing (see Gen. 2:4; 5:1; 25:19; 37:2). The term itself, *toledoth* ("generations"), derives from the Hebrew root *yld*, and it means "beginnings, births." The *toledoth* formula is, therefore, a caption or heading of what is to come and not a sequential bridge from what went before.[91]

For several reasons, then, Walton's proposal that Genesis 2 reports events long after Genesis 1 is not persuasive as a legitimate interpretation of what is actually in the text.

V. ETIOLOGY AS METHODOLOGY

One of the ways in which some scholars today view the account of creation is through the lens of etiology. "Etiology" in Old Testament studies means claiming that a biblical story was written for the purpose of explaining the existence of some feature in the known world—even if the explanatory story itself does not record any true historical facts. The etymology of the Greek word "etiology"

---

91 Some commentators have argued that Genesis 2:4 is a summation of Genesis 1 rather than a caption to Genesis 2. In response, see J. Brinktrine, "Gn 2, 4a, Überschrift oder Unterschrift?" *Biblische Zeitschrift* 9 (1965): 277.

indicates that it means simply "to give a reason for something."[92] The interpretive method of etiology has been practiced in the field of biblical studies for a long time.[93] M. P. Nilsson provides a classic definition of etiological narrative in Greek mythology: ". . . a narrative which seeks to explain why something has come to be, or why it has become such and such."[94]

Critical Old Testament scholars have commonly used etiology as a means to interpret a biblical text and to define why a certain narrative may have been written. I will first provide a couple of examples from other parts of the Old Testament for clarity.

A. Etiology Used to Deny the Historicity of Some Old Testament Events

1. Genesis 19: The Destruction of Sodom and Gomorrah

The Dead Sea region plays a prominent geographical role in parts of the Abrahamic narratives (Genesis 13–14 and 18–19). This area is barren and largely devoid of flora and fauna. The Dead Sea itself lies 1,300 feet below sea level, and its salt concentration is seven times as dense as seawater. No fish are able to live in it. Now, according to some biblical commentators, the writer(s) of Genesis sought to explain the saltiness and barrenness of the Dead Sea area in his(their) day by spinning a tale about the destruction of Sodom and Gomorrah (Gen. 19:24–25). Then, for literary emphasis, the author(s) added a yarn of Lot's wife turning into a pillar of salt (Gen. 19:26). Gerhard Von Rad comments that "it is quite probable that an old aetiological motif is present in the strange death of Lot's wife, i.e., that a bizarre rock formation was the reason for this narrative."[95]

92 It derives from the Greek *aitia*, "cause, reason."

93 The champions of the etiological perspective were German scholars of the first half of the twentieth century. Classic examples are: Albrecht Alt, *Kleine Schriften*, I (Munich: Beck, 1953); Hermann Gunkel, *Die Sagen der Genesis*; and M. Noth, *Das Buch Josua* (Tubingen: J. C. B. Mohr, 1938).

94 M. P. Nilsson, *Geschichte der griechischen Religion*, vol. 1 (Munich: Beck, 1941), 25. Quoted in B. O. Long, *The Problem of Etiological Narrative in the Old Testament*, Beihefte zur Zeitschrift für die alttestamentliche Wissenschaft 108 (Berlin: de Gruyter, 1968), 1.

95 Gerhard Von Rad, *Genesis* (Göttingen: Vandenhoeck & Ruprecht, 1949), 221.

2. Joshua 8:28–29: The Conquest of Ai as an Explanation for a Pile of Rubble

Another example appears in Joshua 8:28–29, and it is what can be called a "double etiology." At the close of the story of Israel's conquest of the city of Ai, two monuments are mentioned in the text. The first memorial is the city of Ai itself in its post-destruction state. Israel has burned it down and it has become "forever a heap of ruins" (v. 28). The biblical writer then comments that this heap remains "to this day"—a reference to the time of the composition of the story. At face value, the ruins of Ai attest to the victory of Israel over the city of Ai during the time of Joshua. However, numerous commentators believe that the biblical author was, in fact, trying to explain why a large, ruined mound existed in the central highlands, and so he created a fictitious account (with perhaps a kernel of historical validity).[96] Such stories, written by Israelites living in the land of Canaan, were purposefully written to provide justification and explanation for their presence in the land. This reconstruction is commonly accepted in modern biblical scholarship.

The second monument at Ai, in addition to the city itself, is a large, distinctive pile of stones. This is described as "a great heap of stones" that the people of Israel placed over the body of Ai's king at the gate of the city. This memorial serves as a warning, and it also remains "to this day" (Josh. 8:29). Again, many biblical interpreters argue that the heap of stones preceded the narrative and that it (not any real historical event) was the reason that the narrative was composed. Thus, rather than the heap reflecting a prior historical incident, the narrative was invented to give meaning to the heap.

B. Etiology Used to Deny the Events of the Creation Account

Etiological methodology in biblical studies has also had a recent, strong impact on the interpretation of the Hebrew creation account.

---

96 See, e.g., the comments of Carolyn Pressler, *Joshua, Judges, and Ruth* (Philadelphia: Westminster/John Knox, 2002), 63; and Hartmut Rosel, *Joshua* (Louvain: Peeters, 2011), 130–31.

Notre Dame professor Joseph Blenkinsopp, in his major work on the Pentateuch, makes a case that a parallel exists between Adam and Eve in the garden and the history of Israel as a nation.[97] He claims that the story of Adam and Eve was not intended to recount actual historical events but was created sometime after Israel's exile (after 586 BC) as an etiological explanation for the exile. He understands that Israel, like mankind in Genesis 2–3, was placed in a favorable environment, namely, the Land of Promise that was a veritable garden of Eden. In this "paradise," Israel is required to obey God's law, and if Israel fails then a curse will descend upon them. This sanction comes to pass when Israel is thrown out of the land into exile, in much the same way as Adam and Eve are expulsed from the garden. Blenkinsopp's argument extends beyond a mere general similarity between the accounts. For instance, he argues that Canaanite cult practices that lure Israel to fall may be compared to the serpent in the garden who tempts Eve. He says, "Behind the figure of the seductive serpent we also detect the cults practiced by the native inhabitants of the land, and behind the words he utters the promises which they hold out for their practitioners."[98] He goes so far as to suggest that the role of Eve in the temptation account may parallel women as a catalyst for adopting pagan cults in the history of Israel (e.g., as in the time of Solomon; 1 Kings 11:1–8).[99]

Blenkinsopp's conclusion is clear and pointed: "One would therefore think that the pattern of events in the history has generated a reflective recapitulation, recasting the national experience in universal terms by the learned use of familiar mythic themes and structures, and placing it at the beginning as a foreshadowing of what was to follow."[100] In other words, the Eden episode is to be "read as a sapiential reflection in narrative form on the historical experience of Israel."[101]

---

97 Blenkinsopp, *Pentateuch*.

98 Ibid., 66.

99 For further parallels, see Martin Emmrich, "The Temptation Narrative of Genesis 3:1–6: A Prelude to the Pentateuch and the History of Israel," *Evangelical Quarterly* 73, no. 1 (2001): 3–20.

100 Blenkinsopp, *Pentateuch*, 66.

101 Ibid., 67; in Old Testament studies, "sapiential" literature is writing that gives wise insight into some aspect of life.

But now at least one Old Testament scholar from the evangelical world has adopted Blenkinsopp's position on the Edenic episode, and his position is promoted as a legitimate view on the BioLogos website. In a white paper hosted by the BioLogos Foundation, Peter Enns writes, "Israel's history happened first, and the Adam story was written to reflect that history. In other words, the Adam story is really an Israel story placed in primeval time."[102] Consequently, the Adam and Eve episode is to be viewed as etiology. It is a symbolic, even a mythic, account used to explain the origin of Israel. Adam is, therefore, "proto-Israel."[103]

The consequences of this etiological position in respect to the Hebrew creation account are enormous and far-reaching. Enns gets at the heart of it when he says in the BioLogos white paper that the Adam story "is not a story of human origins but of Israel's origins." In other words, the Adamic episode is not an account of the creation of mankind but is "really an Israel story placed in primeval time." If that be the case, then what follows is astounding: according to Enns, "if the Adam story is not about absolute human origins, then the conflict between the Bible and evolution cannot be found there."[104]

Thus, in one full etiological swoop, the ages-long tension between science and the Bible in regard to human origins is solved. Genesis 2–3 is, therefore, a backward projection of Israel's history that is to be read symbolically, and certainly not as a historical account that gives true insight into human origins. Blenkinsopp sums up this kind of position well when he comments, "The impulse to trace the course of history backward to human origins arose not only from a natural curiosity about the remote past, but also a need to validate the present social and political order."[105]

---

102 Available at Peter Enns, "Understanding Adam," *BioLogos*, https://biologos.org/uploads/projects /enns_adam_white_paper.pdf.

103 Scot McKnight, in Venema and McKnight, *Adam and the Genome*, uncritically accepts Enns's interpretation and then concludes that Genesis 1–3 "is far more about *Adam and Eve as Israel* than about the historical, biological, and genetic Adam and Eve" (144, emphasis original).

104 Enns, "Understanding Adam."

105 Blenkinsopp, *Pentateuch*, 54.

C. Response to Etiological Interpretations

1. The Assumption That Genesis 2–3 Was Written after Israel's Exile

When one considers the validity of an interpretation, it is critical to uncover the various presuppositions that are foundational to the position. No one comes to the biblical material without such presuppositions. At the heart of the etiological interpretation of Genesis 2–3 is the belief that these chapters were composed after the written history of Israel that appears in the historical literature of Judges through Esther. This is a critical point. The exile of Judah in 586 BC, for example, must have occurred before the writing of Genesis 2–3 because, according to this view, the content of these two chapters is dependent on the exile already having taken place: Adam's exile from the garden is written as a retroactive reflection of Judah's exile from the Promised Land. This etiological chronology, however, is a titanic assumption that is far from certain.

The assumption of such a late date of composition for Genesis 2–3 has been foundational to higher critical theories of the Old Testament for many decades.[106] However, there is little agreement among scholars regarding the specific century in which they think this material was written. The early source critics believed that Genesis 2–3 was part of what they called the "J" (Jehovist) source that dated to the time of the United Monarchy (tenth century BC), and this position is held by some more recent commentators as well.[107] Others, to the contrary, argue that this postulated "J" source was a person living in the exilic period (that is, that it was written after 586 BC).[108] R. N. Whybray correctly judges the current state of affairs when he says,

> There is at the present moment no consensus whatever about when, why, how, and through whom the Pentateuch reached its present

---

106 See, for instance, John Van Seters, *Abraham in History and Tradition* (New Haven, CT: Yale University Press, 1975); and T. L. Thompson, *Historicity of the Patriarchal Narratives: The Quest for the Historical Abraham* (Berlin: de Gruyter, 1974).

107 See, e.g., T. E. Fretheim, *Creation, Fall, and Flood* (Minneapolis: Augsburg, 1969).

108 Van Seters, *Abraham in History*, 125–53; and R. N. Whybray, *Introduction to the Pentateuch* (Grand Rapids, MI: Eerdmans, 1995).

form, and opinions about the date of composition of its various parts differ by more than five hundred years.[109]

The reality is that an etiological explanation for the Genesis account of human origins is on shaky chronological footing. The assumption that all of Israel's history until the exile occurred prior to the composition of Genesis 2–3, and that the description of human origins is merely a reflective echo, is exactly that . . . merely an assumption.

2. The Assumption That Earlier Events Were Fabricated

A second major presupposition of the etiological method is that the connection between the given phenomenon and its explanation must be artificial and nonhistorical.[110] In other words, a story is fabricated in order to explain, describe, and give meaning to an existing phenomenon. Albrecht Alt and others conclude that etiology is a creative force. The present incident or scene is the causal antecedent of the story/tale.

One problem with this presupposition is the reality that, in Israel's writings, an actual historical event can be the reason for something like the name of a city or location, and thus a "genuinely historical tradition might assume an etiological form."[111] So, for instance, after the Israelites cross into the Land of Promise, Joshua commands that the people be circumcised. It is done at the site of Gibeath-haaraloth: "So Joshua made flint knives and circumcised the sons of Israel at Gibeath-haaraloth" (Josh. 5:3). The Hebrew name Gibeath-haaraloth significantly means "the hill of the foreskins." Its name is an example of a genuine historical etiology, in which the site receives a name based on the incident that occurred there.[112]

---

109 Whybray, *Introduction to the Pentateuch*, 12–13.

110 Brevard S. Childs, "The Etiological Tale Re-Examined," *Vetus Testamentum* 24, no. 4 (October 1974): 387–97.

111 Brevard S. Childs, "A Study of the Formula 'Until This Day'," *Journal of Biblical Literature* 82, no. 3 (September 1963): 279–92.

112 The Midrash Rabbah agrees by saying that Gibeath-haaraloth is named this because, "It was the place, said R. Levi, which they had made into a hill by means of foreskins." See H. Freedman and M. Simon, *The Midrash Rabbah*, vol. 3 (London: Soncino, 1977), 422.

Another example from the book of Joshua is the common expression "until this day," or "to this day," as in the story of the death of Achan: "And they raised over him a great heap of stones that remains to this day. Then the LORD turned from his burning anger. Therefore, to this day the name of that place is called the Valley of Achor" (Josh. 7:26). The phrase "to this day" occurs several other times (e.g., Josh. 4:9; 5:9; 8:28, 29; 9:27), and it always is a reference by the biblical writer to the time of the composition of that particular story and not to the time of the episode's occurrence. Many critical scholars believe the phrase "to this day" reflects a nonhistorical etiology in which the author has formulated a story in order to account for a natural phenomenon. But Yale professor Brevard Childs, to the contrary, has demonstrated that the expression "seldom has an etiological function of justifying an existing phenomenon, but in the great majority of cases is a formula of personal testimony added to, and confirming, a received tradition."[113] And, therefore, it is true that biblical writers employ etiology, but much of it is their attempt to explain a real and genuine chronology of events.

In regard to the etiological explanation for Genesis 2–3, Blenkinsopp argues that the biblical writers recast Israel's national experience "in universal terms by the learned use of familiar mythic themes and structures."[114] This judgment assumes that Israel's writers accepted the use of nonfactual myth to tell the story of the people and the nation. However, it ignores Israel's deep resistance to anything mythological. In regard to Genesis 1, the immediately preceding chapter, critical scholars have argued for a long time that the biblical writer demythologized the account. In other words, the Hebrew creation account is essentially an ancient Near Eastern myth that has been "cleansed" of its myth by a biblical author. But surely it would be paradoxical if the biblical writer would employ a familiar ancient Near Eastern myth to describe creation and then proceed to demythologize the account. Consequently, the foundational point of the etiological position when it comes to the

---

113 Childs, "Study of the Formula," 292.
114 Blenkinsopp, *Pentateuch*, 66.

Hebrew creation account is an "unwarranted mythologizing of Israel's historical tradition."[115]

3. Adam as an Actual Historical Prototype of Israel

Certainly there are thematic parallels between the history of Israel and the Edenic episode of Genesis 2–3. But the most natural way to read the material is *chronologically* and not in a reversal of the sequence of the two events. Adam serves as a genuine historical person who also serves as an archetype or prototype of Israel, and not vice versa.

Therein is the great theological lesson: as Adam was exiled from the garden for not obeying God's word, so Israel, a second Adam, is expelled from the Land of Promise for its failure to keep God's commands. There is, therefore, a need for a true second Adam to come (see 1 Cor. 15:45), to obey God's word, and to secure an inheritance—a true Promised Land (see Heb. 11:15–16)—for the people of God. When understood in this historical, sequential framework, then the question of human origins cannot be swept away by the mere brushstroke of etiology.

VI. CONCLUSION

As can be seen in these various approaches to the issue of origins, and human origins in particular, the landscape in the field of biblical studies has changed dramatically in recent years. In evangelical Old Testament scholarship especially, several scholars who confess to orthodox, historic, evangelical Christianity also support evolutionary creation.[116] At the forefront of this movement is the BioLogos Foundation, whose mission is to invite "the church and the world to see the harmony between

---

115 Childs, "Etiological Tale," 396.

116 The acceptance of evolutionary creation *and* the view that Adam and Eve were not individual, historical, genetic persons from whom all humanity descended has some possible grave, sorrowful consequences. One of these is evident in the recent publication of Venema and McKnight, *Adam and the Genome*, in which McKnight clearly and brazenly denies the historical doctrine of original sin (see, in particular, 139, 145, 183–87). Pelagianism is almost an inevitable result of the denial of the historical Adam and Eve.

science and biblical faith as we present an evolutionary understanding of God's creation."[117] At a recent national meeting of the Evangelical Theological Society (Atlanta, 2015), the BioLogos Foundation maintained a booth to promote its evolutionary creation views.

The shape of the debate on origins, and on human origins in particular, will no doubt continue to change. This will happen on both sides of the issue, with science and biblical interpretation. Science, of course, is a continuing process, and new data and theories will emerge. I further suppose that new interpretations of Scripture will appear, but I also think it is likely that the more traditional interpretations will increasingly prevail in the church. At base level, the issue is the same as it has been for more than a hundred and fifty years: does one hold to the complete truthfulness of the facts reported for us in Genesis 1 and 2, and especially in the immediate creation of Adam and Eve as the first humans, or not? This is the question that thundered during the time of the James Woodrow controversy, and it still thunders today.

At least for Presbyterians who affirm the Westminster standards, and I would hope for countless others who believe the Bible, the Westminster Larger Catechism, question 17, satisfactorily summarizes the correct position:

> How did God create man? After God had made all other creatures, he created man male and female; formed the body of the man of the dust of the ground, and the woman of the rib of the man, endued them with living, reasonable, and immortal souls; made them after his own image, in knowledge, righteousness, and holiness; having the law of God written in their hearts, and power to fulfill it, and dominion over the creatures; yet subject to fall.

117 This mission statement appears on the website biologos.org.

Theistic Evolution Is Incompatible with the Teachings of the New Testament

Guy Prentiss Waters

Summary

This chapter claims that theistic evolution is incompatible with the teachings of the New Testament. It surveys the passages in the New Testament that address Adam and Eve (as reported in Genesis 1–3) and also passages that reflect on the period of history covered in Genesis 4–11. It shows that the New Testament writers regarded the entirety of Genesis 1–11 in fully historical terms. The chapter also gives closer attention to two of the most extended New Testament expositions of Adam: 1 Corinthians 15:20–22, 44–49; and Romans 5:12–21. Paul understands Adam to be as historical a figure as Jesus of Nazareth, and the biological parent of the entire human race. He also attributes the entrance of sin and death into the human race to the first sin of Adam, and shows that Adam's one sin is imputed to his natural posterity. The chapter finally shows the ways in which leading proponents of theistic evolution depart from the New Testament writers' testimony to Adam and Eve, thereby calling into question the historical underpinnings of the gospel.

Introduction

At first glance, it might appear that the testimony of the New Testament lies at the periphery of discussions concerning the detailed historicity of Adam. The New Testament, after all, makes sparing explicit mention of Adam (Luke 3:38; Rom. 5:14; 1 Cor. 15:22, 45; 1 Tim. 2:13–14; Jude 14; cf. Acts 17:26; 1 Cor. 11:8). These passages, furthermore, add little by way of historical detail to the narratives of Genesis 1–2.

The New Testament's witness to Adam, however, must sit at the very center of these discussions for at least two reasons. First, Christians properly recognize the New Testament as the final and climactic installment of God's inscripturated revelation to his people (Heb. 1:1–2). As such, New Testament revelation is possessed of a clarity and fullness that, relatively speaking, is lacking in Old Testament revelation. This progressive character of special revelation requires that "the Old Testament . . . be read in light of the New," and not vice versa.[1]

Special revelation is also organic in character.[2] One implication of Scripture's organic character is that the New Testament writers' statements about Old Testament people, events, or texts are true to the intention of the original Old Testament authors.[3] We are therefore not in a position to dismiss the statements of Jesus or the apostles concerning the early chapters of Genesis. On the contrary, such statements are faithful expositions of the meaning of those earlier passages. Therefore, when the New Testament authors speak to the historicity or theological significance of Adam, that speech is regulative of our readings of Old Testament passages that speak about Adam.

---

1   Richard B. Gaffin Jr., *No Adam, No Gospel: Adam and the History of Redemption* (Phillipsburg, NJ: P&R, 2015), 9.

2   The organic character of Scripture has been likened to the growth of a tree, from seed to mature plant: "the organic progression is from seed-form to the attainment of full growth; yet we do not say that in the qualitative sense the seed is less perfect than the tree" (Geerhardus Vos, *Biblical Theology: Old and New Testaments* [Edinburgh: Banner of Truth, 1975], 7).

3   The subject of the New Testament's use of the Old Testament is a complex and debated one in contemporary scholarship. For a helpful overview in relation to recent discussions, see G. K. Beale, *The Erosion of Inerrancy in Evangelicalism: Responding to New Challenges to Biblical Authority* (Wheaton, IL: Crossway, 2008).

A second reason for the importance of the New Testament's witness to Adam concerns the content of that witness. The apostle Paul offers two extended reflections on the person and work of Adam in relation to the person and work of Christ (1 Cor. 15:20–22, 44–49; Rom. 5:12–21). As we will see, the ways in which Paul tethers Adam to Christ has necessary implications for how we are to understand Adam's historicity and the relationship of Adam to the human race. Paul's reflections, furthermore, reveal a macrostructure not only to the history of redemption (Rom. 5:12–21) but also to the whole of human history itself (1 Cor. 15:20–22, 44–49). One is therefore not in a position to relegate Adam to the periphery of the apostle's theology. Furthermore, one is not able to extract Adam's historicity, his relationship with the human race, or his historical work from Paul's teaching without destroying the fundamental integrity of that teaching.

In this chapter, we will first survey the passages in the New Testament that address Adam (and Eve). In addition, in response to attempts to understand much or all of Genesis 1–11 in nonhistorical or semihistorical terms, we will also consider some of the New Testament's reflections on the period of history covered in Genesis 4–11.

Second, we will look at the two most extended expositions of Adam in the New Testament—1 Corinthians 15:20–22, 44–49, and Romans 5:12–21. Here we will see that the apostle Paul understood Adam to be a figure as historical as Jesus of Nazareth, and to be the biological parent of the entire human race. We will also see that Paul attributes the entrance of sin and death into the human race to the first sin of Adam, and that Adam's one sin is imputed to his natural posterity. These New Testament teachings are incompatible with the views of contemporary advocates of theistic evolution.

Third, we will survey the way in which some proponents of theistic evolution have read these New Testament passages, especially Paul's statements concerning Adam in 1 Corinthians and Romans. We will conclude that these readings fail to satisfy the demands of the text. We will also see that these readings effectively undermine Paul's authority as an apostle of Jesus Christ, and call into question the historical underpinnings of the gospel that Paul preached.

I. ADAM AND EVE IN THE NEW TESTAMENT

What is the testimony of the New Testament to Adam and Eve? We will first consider what the New Testament writers explicitly say about Adam and Eve. We will then broaden our horizon of study to explore the New Testament's testimony to the events recorded in Genesis 4–11.

A. Adam and Eve in the New Testament

1. Luke 3:38

In one of the two New Testament genealogies of Jesus, Luke identifies Jesus as "the son (as was supposed) of Joseph, the son of Heli" (Luke 3:23). Luke proceeds to trace Jesus's descent back to "Adam, the son of God":

> Jesus, when he began his ministry, was about thirty years of age, being the son (as was supposed) of Joseph, the son of Heli, the son of Matthat, the son of Levi, the son of Melchi, the son of Jannai, the son of Joseph. . . . the son of Jacob, the son of Isaac, the son of Abraham, the son of Terah, the son of Nahor, . . . the son of Cainan, the son of Arphaxad, the son of Shem, the son of Noah, the son of Lamech, the son of Methuselah, the son of Enoch, the son of Jared, the son of Mahalaleel, the son of Cainan, the son of Enos, the son of Seth, the son of Adam, the son of God. (Luke 3:23–38)

Setting aside the exegetical questions attending this passage, and the challenges of harmonizing this genealogy with that of Matthew, we may draw a few observations about the way in which Luke presents Adam in this genealogy.[4]

---

4   For a recent and brief survey of the interpretive issues attending the genealogies in Matthew and Luke, see James R. Edwards, *The Gospel according to Luke*, Pillar New Testament Commentary (PNTC) (Grand Rapids, MI: Eerdmans, 2015), 123–24; and D. R. Bauer, "Genealogy," in

First, Adam appears among dozens of figures whom the biblical writers regard as fully historical ("Jacob . . . Isaac . . . Abraham . . . Noah . . . Seth . . . Adam . . . God"). There is no basis for exempting Adam from this grouping as a nonhistorical or semihistorical figure.[5]

Second, Adam is placed at the head of a linear genealogical sequence. Each of the human beings in Luke 3:23c–38a traces his descent from Adam. Part of Luke's objective in presenting this genealogy is to show that Jesus, who traces his descent from Adam, is thereby qualified to be the Redeemer of all kinds of people.[6] Back of this message is Luke's conviction that all human beings trace their descent from Adam.[7]

Third, Adam, as a historical person and genealogical progenitor, is the first man. Luke recognizes no progenitor of Adam and thereby exempts him from the normal sequence of biological parentage that follows Adam. The reason for this unique circumstance is that Adam is descended from no man. Adam is, rather, "the son of God," a reference to his special creation in Genesis 1–2. All human beings trace their descent from Adam, while Adam traces his descent from no human.

In view of these observations, it is surprising to see Old Testament professor Peter Enns, an advocate of theistic evolution, claim that "the

---

Dictionary of Jesus and the Gospels, ed. Joel B. Green, Jeannine K. Brown, and Nicholas Perrin, 2nd ed. (Downers Grove, IL: InterVarsity Press, 2013), 299–302. A venerable and satisfying harmonization understands Matthew's genealogy to document Jesus's legal line of descent and Luke's genealogy to document Jesus's biological line of descent.

5   "The name of Adam is on a line with all other names. Given the character of the genealogies and the accuracy with which they are attended, it is inconceivable that Luke would have thought about Adam other than as a historical person" (J. P. Versteeg, *Adam in the New Testament: Mere Teaching Model or First Historical Man?*, trans. Richard B. Gaffin Jr., 2nd ed. [Phillipsburg, NJ: P&R, 2012], 33).

6   Darrell L. Bock, *Luke 1:1–9:50*, Baker Exegetical Commentary on the New Testament (BECNT) (Grand Rapids, MI: Eerdmans, 1994), 359–60; Edwards, *Gospel according to Luke*, 124. The Greek word translated "as was supposed" likely is intended to exempt Jesus from biological descent from Joseph (Robert W. Yarbrough, "Adam in the New Testament," in *Adam, the Fall, and Original Sin: Theological, Biblical, and Scientific Perspectives*, ed. Hans Madueme and Michael Reeves [Grand Rapids, MI: Baker, 2014], 40); Edwards, *Gospel according to Luke*, 122. As Bock notes, "the genealogical line is Joseph's, despite the virgin birth. It is merely a legal line" (*Luke 1:1–9:50*, 352).

7   In view of this conviction, which Luke states at the outset of his Gospel, we may concur with Yarbrough's assessment that "Adam is a dominant if unspoken presence in the redemptive narrations of the Gospels and Acts" ("Adam in the New Testament," 41).

issues raised by these genealogies (i.e., Luke 3:38 and Jude 14) add little to the conversation" about the historicity of Adam.[8]

Wheaton College professor John H. Walton, on the other hand, acknowledges the theological significance of Luke's genealogy, but dismisses it as a testimony either to the historicity of Adam or to Adam as progenitor of the entire human race.[9] He says that we are simply meant to understand Adam as "the first *significant* human," who, by virtue of his "very particular role" as "federal head" and "priest," had a special "connection to God."[10] He admits that Luke may well have understood Adam to be "the first human being," but says that God merely "use[d] [Luke's] contemporary concepts as a framework for communication."[11]

This viewpoint, that Adam was not the first human but the first *significant* human, allows Walton to avoid any conflict with current evolutionary theory, which affirms that the current genetic diversity in the human race does not go back to just one or two human beings but can best be explained by descent from a very early population of approximately ten thousand genetically diverse humans.[12]

The problem with Walton's analysis is that Luke is founding a theological claim upon a historical foundation. If Adam is merely the first *significant* human and not the first human being and the progenitor of all human beings, then Luke's claim that Jesus, by virtue of his genealogy, is qualified to be the Redeemer of all human beings is void. To separate the historical and the theological in Luke's genealogy is to forfeit them both.[13]

---

8   Peter Enns, *The Evolution of Adam: What the Bible Does and Doesn't Say about Human Origins* (Grand Rapids, MI: Baker, 2012), 150n9.

9   John H. Walton, *The Lost World of Adam and Eve: Genesis 2–3 and the Human Origins Debate* (Downers Grove, IL: InterVarsity Press, 2015), 188.

10 Ibid., 188–89, emphasis added.

11 Ibid., 188.

12 See Francis Collins, *The Language of God* (New York: Free Press, 2006), 126; see also 207.

13 G. B. Caird has articulated the point positively: "By calling Adam son of God [Luke] makes a link between the baptism and God's purpose in creation. Man was designed for that close filial relationship to God which was exemplified in Jesus, and which Jesus was to share with those who became his disciples" (*The Gospel of Saint Luke*, Pelican New Testament Commentaries [*Harmondsworth*, Middlesex, UK: Penguin 1963], 77–78, cited in Edwards, *Gospel according to Luke*, 124n86).

2. Acts 17:26

A second reference to Adam in Luke's writings appears in his account of Paul's address to the Areopagus in Athens (Acts 17:26):

> And he made from one man every nation of mankind to live on all the face of the earth, having determined allotted periods and the boundaries of their dwelling place.

Although Paul does not mention Adam by name, he testifies to the universal descent of humanity from a single man, whom Paul knew to be "Adam" (Rom. 5:12–21; 1 Cor. 15:20–22, 44–49).[14]

The Greek text underlying this translation does not explicitly use the word "man." It reads literally "from one" (*ex henos*), but since the Greek word *henos* is a masculine singular form, the translation "from one man" is legitimate. Some proponents of theistic evolution have argued that Paul is not referring to Adam in this expression. Walton argues that the referent is Noah.[15] He concludes that Paul's concern in this speech is "national origins" not "biology or human origins."[16] Paul is therefore said to be referencing the Septuagint translation of Genesis 10:32, in which "the nations" of the earth are said to originate from the three sons of Noah.

Paul, however, must be referring to Adam. David Peterson rightly concludes that the phrase "on all the face of the earth" "echoes the teaching of Genesis 1:28–29," thereby identifying the "one man" as Adam.[17] Furthermore, the conclusion of Paul's speech centers upon the

---

14 F. F. Bruce, *The Acts of the Apostles: The Greek Text with Introduction and Commentary*, 3rd ed. (Grand Rapids, MI: Eerdmans, 1990), 382; C. K. Barrett, *The Acts of the Apostles*, International Critical Commentaries (ICC), vol. 2 (Edinburgh: T&T Clark, 1998), 842; David Peterson, *The Acts of the Apostles*, PNTC (Grand Rapids, MI: Eerdmans, 2009), 497.

15 John H. Walton, "A Historical Adam: Archetypal Creation View," in *Four Views on the Historical Adam*, ed. Matthew Barrett and Ardel B. Caneday (Grand Rapids, MI: Zondervan, 2013), 105; Walton, *Lost World of Adam and Eve*, 186–87. In addition to Walton, see Denis Alexander, *Creation or Evolution: Do We Have to Choose?*, 2nd ed., rev. and updated (Oxford: Monarch, 2014), 234.

16 Walton, *Lost World of Adam and Eve*, 186.

17 Peterson, *Acts of the Apostles*, 497. In Genesis 1:28–29, God gives Adam and Eve dominion "over every living thing that moves on the earth" and every plant yielding seed "on the face of all the earth."

"man" whom God raised and who will judge "the world" at the end of the age (Acts 17:31). The one man, Adam, is a natural and expected counterpoint to the one man, Christ Jesus.[18] As from a man the world has been populated, so by a man the world will be judged. The "one" of Acts 17:26, then, must refer to Adam, the ancestor of every human being. Walton's proposal about Noah is simply not persuasive.

3. Romans 5:12–21

This significant passage begins by saying,

> Therefore, just as sin came into the world through one man, and death through sin, and so death spread to all men because all sinned . . . (Rom. 5:12)

Paul then continues with an extended discussion of the parallels between Adam and Christ. I will treat this passage in more detail in the second section of this chapter.

4. 1 Corinthians 11:8–9

> For man was not made from woman, but woman from man. Neither was man created for woman, but woman for man.

Although Paul does not mention Adam and Eve by name in 1 Corinthians 11:8–9, these verses summarize the biblical account of the creation of Adam and Eve in Genesis 1–2.[19] Specifically, Paul recounts the special creation of Eve from Adam (1 Cor. 11:8; cf. Gen. 2:21–23).

---

18 So, rightly, E. Jerome Van Kuiken, "John Walton's *Lost Worlds* and God's Loosed Word: Implications for Inerrancy, Canon, and Creation," *Journal of the Evangelical Theological Society* 58, no. 4 (2015): 687. Van Kuiken has also suggestively proposed that "one man" (Acts 17:26) may echo Deuteronomy 4:32 (ibid.).

19 David Garland has observed that "Paul interprets Gen. 1:27 . . . through the creation account in Gen. 2" (*1 Corinthians*, BECNT [Grand Rapids, MI: Eerdmans, 2003], 522). Gordon Fee sees Genesis 2:23, 18–20 as the verses that Paul especially has in view (*The First Epistle to the Corinthians*, rev. ed. [Grand Rapids, MI: Eerdmans, 2014], 572). In particular, Fee notes a verbal reference to the Septuagint translation of Genesis 2:23 in 1 Corinthians 11:8, 12 ("from man") (ibid., 572n106).

Paul furthermore observes that Eve was created "for man," that is, in the words of Genesis, to be "a helper fit for him" (1 Cor. 11:9; cf. Gen. 2:18). On the basis of the creation account, Paul issues a command concerning the deportment in public worship of the wives in the Corinthian church (1 Cor. 11:10).

This passage sheds light on Paul's understanding of Adam and Eve in at least two respects. First, Paul regards Adam and Eve to have been historical persons, and the account of Genesis 1–2 to be a historical account. Second, Paul understands, with Genesis, Eve to have been specially created by God from Adam. Paul's words exclude any scenario in which Eve may be said to have descended from a previously existing human being or humanoid.

5. 1 Corinthians 15:20–22 and 44–49

This long discussion about the resurrection includes significant parallels and differences between Adam and Christ, such as this:

> For as by a man came death, by a man has come also the resurrection of the dead. For as in Adam all die, so also in Christ shall all be made alive. (1 Cor. 15:21–22)

I will treat this passage, as well, more extensively in section 2 of this chapter.

6. 2 Corinthians 11:3

> But I am afraid that as the serpent deceived Eve by his cunning, your thoughts will be led astray from a sincere and pure devotion to Christ.

In this passage, Paul is concerned about the spiritually destructive influences of false teachers in Corinth. These teachers are "false apostles, deceitful workmen, disguising themselves as apostles of Christ" (2 Cor. 11:13). Paul likens their strategies to those of Satan. Just as "Satan disguises himself as an angel of light," so these false teachers "disguise themselves as servants of righteousness" (2 Cor. 11:14, 15). Paul assures the Corinthians that the false teachers' "end will correspond to their deeds" (2 Cor. 11:15). That is to say, they will fall under the judgment of God.[20] Just as Satan fell under God's judgment for his role in enticing Eve to sin, so also these false teachers will be held to account for their Satan-like activities.

In 2 Corinthians 11:3, Paul draws a more direct connection between these false teachers and Satan. Paul likens the church in Corinth to Eve. He fears that, just as "the serpent deceived Eve by his cunning," these teachers will lead the Corinthians' thoughts "astray from a sincere and pure devotion to Christ." In the words of Murray Harris, "just as Eve was deceived in her thinking (Gen. 3:1–6) and so lost her innocence (Gen. 3:7), so too the Corinthian church was at risk of being deluded in thought . . . and so losing her virginity."[21]

This extended analogy in 2 Corinthians 11 assumes readers' awareness of the account in Genesis 3. There are verbal echoes of Genesis 3 in 2 Corinthians 11:3, namely, "deceived" and "cunning."[22] Moreover, Paul regards this account to be a thoroughly historical account. Satan is a historical personage who poses no less a threat to the Corinthians than he did to Eve.[23] Furthermore, Eve is no less a historical person than the Corinthians are historical people—Paul's warning, in fact, requires the full historicity of Eve.

Not only does Paul understand the narrative of Genesis 3 to be historical, but his argument in 2 Corinthians 11 also assumes the historicity of the previous two chapters of Genesis. Paul's analogy predicates the uprightness and sinlessness of Eve when Satan approached her to tempt her to sin (see 2 Cor. 11:2–3). Eve's moral rectitude, according to the testimony of Genesis 1:26–31, was concreated. That is to say, God created her a righteous person. That Paul should assume the historicity

---

20 Paul Barnett, *The Second Epistle to the Corinthians*, New International Commentary on the New Testament (NICNT) (Grand Rapids, MI: Eerdmans, 1997), 527n22.

21 Murray J. Harris, *The Second Epistle to the Corinthians*, New International Greek Testament Commentary (NIGTC) (Grand Rapids, MI: Eerdmans, 2005), 740.

22 See Genesis 3:13; 3:1 ("crafty") (ibid., 740, 741–42).

23 Understanding Satan to be the "cause of any enticement toward disloyalty among the Corinthians" (so, rightly, ibid., 741).

of this one detail in Genesis 1 confirms his confidence in the historicity of the whole of Genesis 1–2.

7. 1 Timothy 2:11–14

> Let a woman learn quietly with all submissiveness. [12] I do not permit a woman to teach or to exercise authority over a man; rather, she is to remain quiet. [13] For Adam was formed first, then Eve; [14] and Adam was not deceived, but the woman was deceived and became a transgressor.

Paul speaks explicitly about Adam and Eve in 1 Timothy 2:11–14. In the larger context (1 Tim. 2:1–15), Paul is giving the church instructions about public worship. In the course of these instructions, Paul says that he does not permit "a woman to teach or to exercise authority over a man; rather, she is to remain quiet" (1 Tim. 2:12). The ground for this command follows in verse 13: "For Adam was formed first, then Eve."[24] To this ground, Paul appends the observation in verse 14, "and Adam was not deceived, but the woman was deceived and became a transgressor."[25] Both statements treat very specific details of Genesis 2–3 as historical fact, not as parts of a myth or a parable or an allegorical or figurative story.

It is outside the scope of this chapter to address precisely how these statements explicate the command that precedes, or the way in which these verses apply to the church,[26] but we may specifically address what

---

24 For an extended, syntactical defense of our saying that verse 13 supplies grounds for verse 12 and is not merely an illustration of verse 12, see William D. Mounce, *The Pastoral Epistles*, Word Biblical Commentary (WBC), vol. 46 (Nashville: Thomas Nelson, 2000), 131–33.

25 Commentators debate the place of 1 Timothy 2:14 in Paul's argument of 1 Timothy 2:11–15, on which see I. H. Marshall, *The Pastoral Epistles*, ICC (Edinburgh: T&T Clark, 1999), 460–61. George W. Knight has argued that "Paul argues not from creation and fall but from creation, and then illustrates this argument, albeit negatively, from the fall . . ." (Knight, *The Pastoral Epistles: A Commentary on the Greek Text*, NIGTC [Grand Rapids, MI: Eerdmans, 1992], 144). While Knight may put matters too strongly here, he is surely correct to highlight the primacy of creation for Paul's argument in 1 Timothy 2:11–15.

26 For detailed exegetical treatments of this text, see especially Douglas Moo, "What Does It Mean Not to Teach or Have Authority over Men?," in *Recovering Biblical Manhood and Womanhood*, ed. John Piper and Wayne Grudem (Wheaton, IL: Crossway, 1991), 179–93; Thomas R. Schreiner,

Paul says here about Adam and Eve. In verse 13, Paul appeals to the creation of Adam and Eve, observing the sequence in which each was formed: "Adam was formed first, then Eve," referring to Genesis 2:7, 22: "then the LORD God formed the man of dust from the ground. . . . And the rib that the LORD God had taken from the man he made into a woman and brought her to the man."[27]

In 1 Timothy 2:14, Paul reflects upon the deception and transgression of Eve when he says, "and Adam was not deceived, but the woman was deceived and became a transgressor." This statement is based on Genesis 3:13: "The woman said, 'The serpent deceived me, and I ate.'" Paul cited these specific details in the life of Adam and Eve only because he took Genesis 2–3 as literal history, not as mythological, figurative, or allegorical stories.

In addition, Paul understands the creation of Adam prior to Eve to ground his command to the church in Ephesus. What follows in 1 Timothy 2:14 shows "by a negative example the importance of heeding the respective roles established by God in the creation of Eve from Adam."[28] Paul is treating the accounts of the creation and the fall as historical accounts that serve as the norm for the way in which human beings subsequent to Adam and Eve are to relate to one another.[29] The historical details of the creation, including the creation of Adam and Eve, provide the basis upon which Paul expects all Christians to order their lives.

Walton has argued that Paul "is using Adam and Eve as illustrations for the Ephesians," and nothing more.[30] He dismisses an "ontological"

"An Interpretation of 1 Timothy 2:9–15: A Dialogue with Scholarship," in *Women in the Church: An Analysis and Application of 1 Timothy 2:9–15*, ed. Andreas J. Köstenberger and Thomas R. Schreiner, 2nd ed. (Grand Rapids, MI: Baker, 2005), 85–120; and Wayne Grudem, *Evangelical Feminism and Biblical Truth* (Sisters, OR: Multnomah, 2004), 279–328.

27 Note the expressly temporal language that Paul uses: "first," "then" (so Moo, "What Does It Mean?," 190). For a fuller statement of the ways in which Genesis 2 lies behind Paul's claim in verse 13, see Mounce, *Pastoral Epistles*, 130–31.

28 Knight, *Pastoral Epistles*, 144. As Schreiner rightly observes, "the appeal to Genesis 3 serves as a reminder of what happens when God's ordained pattern is undermined" ("An Interpretation of 1 Timothy 2:9–15," 115).

29 Knight, *Pastoral Epistles*, 142, 143.

30 Walton, *Lost World of Adam and Eve*, 95.

understanding of Paul's words on the basis that such an understanding would require Paul to say not only "that man by his created nature is first," but also that "woman by her created nature is deceivable."[31] Since, however, "that vulnerability [i.e., "susceptibility to deception"] is not ontological to only one gender," Paul's words cannot be ontologically referential.[32]

But Paul does not say here or elsewhere that women are inherently gullible.[33] Having affirmed that Eve, like Adam, was created (1 Tim. 2:13), Paul proceeds to rehearse the historical account of the deception of Eve, and the subsequent transgression of both Eve and Adam (2:14). Paul recognizes that Eve's deception was subsequent to her creation, but he nowhere ascribes Eve's deception *to* her creation, much less her creation as a woman.[34] What undergirds Paul's injunction in verse 12 is the historical fact that Eve, on this particular occasion, was deceived, not that Eve was created as a gullible person. This circumstance, Paul reasons, served to upend the order that God had established for human beings at the creation (2:13).[35]

Paul, then, is treating the account of Genesis 1–3 as fully historical narrative. He regards Adam and Eve as specially created by God. He regards Eve's deception as a historical event with implications for the way in which, after the fall, her descendants are to relate to one another.[36] Paul's argument in 1 Timothy 2:13–14 requires Adam and Eve to have been

---

31 Ibid.

32 Ibid.

33 For a partial listing of commentators who have read Paul to say that women are more prone to deception than men, see Schreiner, "An Interpretation of 1 Timothy 2:9–15," 225n210. For fuller discussion, see Daniel Doriani, "Appendix 2: History of the Interpretation of 1 Timothy 2," in *Women in the Church*, ed. A. J. Köstenberger, T. R. Schreiner, and H. S. Baldwin (Grand Rapids, MI: Baker, 1995), 215–69.

34 Furthermore, to say that women are ontologically more gullible than men counters Paul's earlier affirmation of the ontological equality of men and women (1 Cor. 11:11–12).

35 For support of this view, see Moo, "What Does It Mean?," 190.

36 As Philip Towner has observed, Paul, in addressing women in Ephesus who were "influenced to think that they were free from the constraints and limitations brought on by the fall, reminds [them] of their role in the fall and of the present unfinished nature of Christian existence" ("1–2 Timothy and Titus," in *Commentary on the New Testament Use of the Old Testament*, ed. G. K. Beale and D. A. Carson [Grand Rapids, MI: Baker, 2007], 897, as cited in Yarbrough, "Adam in the New Testament," 50). In this respect, as Towner also notes, Paul's argument in 1 Timothy 2 is of a piece with his broader argument in this letter that Christians live within the callings, norms, and boundaries established by God for all humanity at creation (ibid.).

the first man and woman and, as such, to be the parents of every human being. This is why the command of 1 Timothy 2:12 is not provisional but universal.[37] It is not restricted to time, circumstance, or geography, but is for all kinds of people.[38] Were Paul to have regarded "Adam and Eve" as "mere mythological symbols of the timeless truth that men pre-exist women," then "Paul's argument would collapse into nonsense."[39]

8. Jude 14

In the midst of a warning (Jude 3–16) about false teachers who are threatening the churches of which Jude's readers are a part, Jude reminds his audience that these false teachers were the concern of earlier prophecy. Specifically,

> Enoch, the seventh from Adam, prophesied, saying, "Behold, the Lord came with ten thousands of his holy ones . . ." (Jude 14)

Jude here identifies "Enoch" as descended from Adam, in the seventh generation from Adam. He treats Enoch as a historical personage, who utters the prophesies documented in verses 14–15. The fact that Enoch is identified as "the seventh from Adam" not only confirms Enoch's historicity but also assumes Adam's historicity.

The citation in verses 14–15 has been the subject of considerable academic attention.[40] Many scholars have observed the similarities between the words that Jude records here and *1 Enoch* 1:9, a pseudepigraphical book, authored between the third and first centuries BC, that has a

---

37 See further Moo, "What Does It Mean?," 188ff.; Grudem, *Evangelical Feminism and Biblical Truth*, 280–88, 296–302.

38 This is not to say, of course, that local circumstances or conditions did not occasion Paul's teaching in these verses. As Moo argues, "local or cultural issues may have provided the *context* of the issue, [but] they do not provide the *reason* for his advice" ("What Does It Mean?," 190). The reason that Paul gives, rather, "is the created role relationship of man and woman" (ibid.).

39 Michael Reeves, "Adam and Eve," in *Should Christians Embrace Evolution? Biblical and Scientific Responses*, ed. Norman C. Nevin (Phillipsburg, NJ: P&R, 2009), 44.

40 For overviews, see representatively Richard J. Bauckham, *Jude, 2 Peter*, WBC, vol. 50 (Waco, TX: Word, 1983), 93–101; Thomas R. Schreiner, *1, 2 Peter, Jude*, New American Commentary, vol. 37 (Nashville: B&H, 2003), 468–73; Peter H. Davids, *The Letters of 2 Peter and Jude*, PNTC (Grand Rapids, MI: Eerdmans, 2006), 75–80.

complicated literary history.[41] Scholars have differed over how to account for these similarities.[42] Most now agree that Jude has quoted from some version of *1 Enoch* available to him.[43] Some have argued that Jude quotes from a book that his opponents regarded as authoritative, but that Jude did not. Others more plausibly have suggested that Jude regarded these words as a historically accurate, authentic utterance of the prophet Enoch, an utterance that, in the providence of God, was preserved in *1 Enoch*.[44]

Walton has characterized the words of Jude 14–15 as a "*literary* factuality (yes, this is how the familiar story goes)" rather than a "*historical* factual[ity] (yes, this is what really happened in time and space)."[45] Jude, then, is quoting a myth or story that is part of the common cultural vocabulary of his audience. To take Jude as historically factual, Walton reasons, requires one to conclude that the (historical) Enoch was the "author of the intertestamental book of *Enoch*."[46]

But this is surely an unnecessary inference. One may cogently argue that *1 Enoch* preserves some authentic statements of the historical Enoch, the seventh from Adam, without attributing the whole of *1 Enoch* to the historical Enoch. That Jude identifies Enoch with a precise genealogical marker and quotes him in the train of a host of historical Old Testament references (Jude 5–11) indicates Jude's understanding of Enoch in Jude 14–15 as a historical person.[47] That Enoch is said to be "the seventh from Adam" furthermore requires the conclusion that Jude understood Adam to be no less a historical person than

41 On which, see Davids, *Letters of 2 Peter and Jude*, 77.

42 For what follows, see D. A. Carson, "Jude," in *Commentary on the New Testament Use of the Old Testament*, 1078.

43 On the particular text that Jude used, see the discussion at Bauckham, *Jude, 2 Peter*, 94–96. Bauckham concludes that Jude "*knew* the Greek version, but made his own translation from the Aramaic" (96, emphasis original).

44 Schreiner, *1, 2 Peter, Jude*, 469. This observation need not commit one to the conclusion that the entirety of *1 Enoch* is genuine prophecy, or that *1 Enoch* has a warranted claim to belong to the canon of Scripture; see Schreiner, ibid., and Carson, "Jude," 1078.

45 Walton, *Lost World of Adam and Eve*, 100, emphasis added.

46 Ibid.

47 The Old Testament references include "disobedient Israelites (v. 5); rebellious angels (v. 6); residents of Sodom and Gomorrah (v. 7); and an unholy trio consisting of Cain, Balaam, and Korah (v. 11)" (Yarbrough, "Adam in the New Testament," 35).

Enoch. Versteeg rightly notes, "When [Jude] calls Enoch 'the seventh from Adam,' he sees a specific historical distance between Enoch and Adam."[48] Jude makes this statement because he regards the narratives about both Adam and Enoch in Genesis 1–5 as historically accurate.

Jude's identification of Enoch as "the seventh from Adam" points to an important but distinct strand of the New Testament's testimony to the historicity of Adam. It is that the New Testament writers do not separate the events of the first two chapters of Genesis from conventional space-time history. The creation of Adam and Eve is as qualitatively historical as any other event documented in biblical history. It is neither mythological nor semihistorical. For this reason, then, Jude without qualification or defense yokes Enoch to Adam. Both men are fully and equally historical persons.

Both Adam and Enoch, furthermore, occupy the same historical space as other events that Jude mentions from the Pentateuch: the exodus (Jude 5, "Jesus who saved a people out of the land of Egypt . . ."); the destruction of Sodom and Gomorrah (Jude 7, "just as Sodom and Gomorrah and the surrounding cities, which likewise indulged in sexual immorality and pursued unnatural desire, serve as an example by undergoing a punishment of eternal fire"); Cain's murder of Abel, the prophetic activity of Balaam, and Korah's rebellion (Jude 11, "Woe to them! For they walked in the way of Cain and abandoned themselves for the sake of gain to Balaam's error and perished in Korah's rebellion"). This conjunction of events in the letter indicates that Jude did not understand the events of Genesis 1–11 as a semihistorical or mythological prologue to the events documented in Genesis 12ff. He understood Genesis 1–11 to be fully historical.

B. Other Texts about Genesis 1–11 in the New Testament

1. Matthew 1:1

The book of the genealogy of Jesus Christ, the son of David, the son of Abraham . . .

---

48 Versteeg, *Adam in the New Testament*, 43.

Many commentators have observed how the opening line of Matthew's Gospel intentionally echoes portions of the book of Genesis. Specifically, Matthew's opening words ("the book of the genealogy") are identical with the Septuagint translation of Genesis 2:4 ("These are the generations of the heavens and the earth when they were created, in the day that the LORD God made the earth and the heavens") and of Genesis 5:1 ("This is the book of the generations of Adam"). Since, as R. T. France has observed, "the phrase occurs nowhere else in the [Septuagint]," Matthew must be intentionally connecting the opening of his Gospel with "the opening chapters of Genesis."[49]

What is the significance of this Matthean literary connection with Genesis? First, Matthew intends for his readers to understand his historical account of the birth, life, death, and resurrection of Jesus Christ in light of the biblical narrative of Genesis. Matthew's genealogy explicitly situates the life and ministry of Jesus within the larger "history of the people of God from its very beginning with Abraham, the ancestor of Israel."[50] Matthew's phrase "the book of the genealogy" furthermore compels readers to place the life and ministry of Jesus in the wider history narrated in the first chapters of Genesis.

Second, this connection shows that Matthew understands the narrative of Genesis to be as fully historical as the narrative of Jesus Christ that follows Matthew 1:1–17. Matthew thus regards Adam and Eve to be fully historical persons. He regards the details of their creation in Genesis 2:4b–25 to be fully historical. He does not situate either the persons or the origins of Adam and Eve in a mythological or prehistorical past. For Matthew, history is a seamless garment running from creation through Abraham and Jesus Christ to "the end of the age" (Matt. 28:20).[51]

---

49 R. T. France, *The Gospel of Matthew*, NICNT (Grand Rapids, MI: Eerdmans, 2007), 26n1.
50 Ibid., 29.
51 On Matthew's word "end" (28:20) as an echo of Matthew's word "genealogy" (1:1), see John Nolland, *The Gospel of Matthew*, NIGTC (Grand Rapids, MI: Eerdmans, 2005), 71.

2. Matthew 19:4–6

> He answered, "Have you not read that he who created them from the beginning made them male and female, and said, 'Therefore a man shall leave his father and his mother and hold fast to his wife, and the two shall become one flesh'? So they are no longer two but one flesh. What therefore God has joined together, let not man separate."

Jesus addresses the institution of marriage at the creation in Matthew 19:4–6 (citing Gen. 2:24). We are not at liberty to say, with Denis O. Lamoureux, that Jesus "was accommodating to the Jewish belief of the day that Adam was a real person."[52] The distinction that Jesus draws between the grant of the certificate of divorce through Moses and "the beginning" (Matt. 19:8) is a fundamentally historical one. Jesus therefore understands the institution of marriage (Gen. 2:24) and the subsequent giving of the law through Moses to exist on a single historical continuum. Furthermore, Jesus's statement, "but from the beginning it was not so," independently testifies to the fall of humanity in Adam as marking a decisive shift in the human experience of marriage.[53] Jesus's words assume the universal ramifications of Adam's one sin for the entire human race.[54]

3–4. Matthew 23:35 and Luke 11:51

> . . . so that on you may come all the righteous blood shed on earth, from the blood of righteous Abel to the blood of Zechariah the son of Barachiah, whom you murdered between the sanctuary and the altar. (Matt. 23:35)

> . . . from the blood of Abel to the blood of Zechariah, who perished between the altar and the sanctuary. Yes, I tell you, it will be required of this generation. (Luke 11:51)

---

52 Denis O. Lamoureux, "No Historical Adam: Evolutionary Creation View," in Barrett and Caneday, *Four Views on the Historical Adam*, 60.

53 France, *Gospel of Matthew*, 720.

54 Yarbrough, "Adam in the New Testament," 41; C. John Collins, *Did Adam and Eve Really Exist?: Who They Were and Why You Should Care* (Wheaton, IL: Crossway, 2011), 77.

In this statement, Jesus references Cain's murder of Abel (Genesis 4). He places that event on the same historical continuum as the martyrdom of "Zechariah the son of Barachiah" (Matt. 23:35), recorded at 2 Chronicles 24:21. Scholars dispute the precise identification of "Zechariah the son of Barachiah," but many have plausibly identified him with the prophet Zechariah mentioned in 2 Chronicles 24:20–22.[55] Assuming that this identification is correct, Jesus is speaking about the range of martyred prophets across the Old Testament Canon (Genesis–Chronicles).[56] Jesus's words are not only a testimony to the historicity of Abel but also a testimony to the historicity of the entirety of Genesis.[57] We have no reason to doubt, then, that Jesus regarded the entirety of the events of Genesis to be fully historical. But if someone claims that the early chapters of Genesis are mythological or merely allegorical fiction, does this claim not imply that Jesus was mistaken in his belief?

5–6. Matthew 24:37–38 and Luke 17:26–27

For as were the days of Noah, so will be the coming of the Son of Man. For as in those days before the flood they were eating and drinking, marrying and giving in marriage, until the day when Noah entered the ark, . . . (Matt. 24:37–38)

Just as it was in the days of Noah, so will it be in the days of the Son of Man. They were eating and drinking and marrying and being given in marriage, until the day when Noah entered the ark, and the flood came and destroyed them all. (Luke 17:26–27)

---

55 See the discussion at Nolland, *Gospel of Matthew*, 946–47.

56 As France has observed, "the death of Zechariah in the late ninth century BC was of course not the last martyrdom in historical sequence, but because it is recorded toward the end of 2 Chronicles, the last book of the Hebrew canon, it suitably rounds off the biblical record of God's servants killed for their loyalty" (France, *Gospel of Matthew*, 880). "The scope is mapped," Nolland argues, "by the choice of the first and last pertinent murders in the Hebrew Bible" (Nolland, *Gospel of Matthew*, 947).

57 That is to say, had there been a martyred prophet prior to Abel in Genesis, we fully expect that Jesus would have mentioned him, and mentioned him as a historical person.

Jesus here predicts the sudden character of his return in glory to judge the world. Unbelievers will not be prepared for his return and will be taken by surprise when it happens. Jesus likens this state of affairs to "the days of Noah." People went about their daily activities until they were overtaken by the divine judgment of the flood. Noah escaped this judgment because he heeded God's Word and "made advance preparation."[58] The same principle applies to humanity in anticipation of the return of Christ—those who heed Christ's Word and prepare will be spared the judgment that will fall upon human beings. Jesus's warning employs an analogy that requires Jesus's acceptance of the historicity of Noah and of the biblical narrative about Noah (Genesis 6–9). It is further indication that Jesus regarded the opening chapters of Genesis as fully historical.

7. Romans 8:18–23

> For I consider that the sufferings of this present time are not worth comparing with the glory that is to be revealed to us. For the creation waits with eager longing for the revealing of the sons of God. For the creation was subjected to futility, not willingly, but because of him who subjected it, in hope that the creation itself will be set free from its bondage to corruption and obtain the freedom of the glory of the children of God. For we know that the whole creation has been groaning together in the pains of childbirth until now. And not only the creation, but we ourselves, who have the firstfruits of the Spirit, groan inwardly as we wait eagerly for adoption as sons, the redemption of our bodies.

In these verses, Paul contrasts the "sufferings of this present time" with "the glory that is to be revealed to us." The revelation of this glory is something that even the creation eagerly anticipates. The creation does so because it "was subjected to futility," is presently in "bondage to corruption," and now "groan[s] together in the pains of childbirth until

---

58 France, *Gospel of Matthew*, 940.

now." That creation "was subjected to futility" means two things. First, the present state of affairs here described by Paul did not characterize creation at its inception. Second, creation did not choose, as it were, its present condition. God has consigned the creation to its present condition.[59] We have, then, an "obvious reference to the Gen. 3 narrative," and a "commentary on Genesis 3:17, 18."[60] The "hope" appended to this subjection, then, must refer to the hope offered in the divine promise of Genesis 3:15—"the very decree of subjection was given in the context of hope."[61] Paul, then, regards the opening chapters of Genesis to be fully historical. The world that God created has, in light of the fall of Adam into sin, been subjected to the curse of God. This subjection, however, was attended by a promise that the creation would become at the consummation a fit and glorious habitation for the children of God. This state of affairs constitutes no small part of the hope that the gospel holds out to suffering Christians in the present. Were the opening chapters of Genesis anything less than fully historical, then the hope that Paul sets before Christians in these verses would be illusory.

8. Hebrews 11:1–7

Now faith is the assurance of things hoped for, the conviction of things not seen. [2] For by it the people of old received their commendation. [3] By faith we understand that the universe was created by the word of God, so that what is seen was not made out of things that are visible.

[4] By faith Abel offered to God a more acceptable sacrifice than Cain, through which he was commended as righteous, God commending him by accepting his gifts. And through his faith, though he died, he still speaks. [5] By faith Enoch was taken up so that he should not see death, and he was not found, because God had taken him. Now before he was taken he was commended as having pleased God. [6] And without faith it is impossible to please him, for whoever

---

59 Taking "God" as the implied agent of the passive verb, "was subjected," on which see Douglas J. Moo, *The Epistle to the Romans*, NICNT (Grand Rapids, MI: Eerdmans, 1996), 516.

60 Ibid., 515; John Murray, *Epistle to the Romans*, cited at ibid.

61 Ibid., 516.

would draw near to God must believe that he exists and that he rewards those who seek him. [7] By faith Noah, being warned by God concerning events as yet unseen, in reverent fear constructed an ark for the saving of his household. By this he condemned the world and became an heir of the righteousness that comes by faith.

The writer to the Hebrews presents a table of examples of persevering faith (Heb. 10:39) in Hebrews 11:1–40. Beginning with the creation (Heb. 11:1–3), the writer draws examples of faith from Abel (11:4, "by faith Abel offered to God a more acceptable sacrifice than Cain, through which he was commended as righteous, God commending him by accepting his gifts"; cf. Genesis 4); Enoch (11:5, "by faith Enoch was taken up so that he should not see death, and he was not found, because God had taken him"; cf. Genesis 5); Noah (11:7, "by faith Noah, being warned by God concerning events as yet unseen, in reverent fear constructed an ark for the saving of his household"; cf. Genesis 6); Abraham (11:8–19); Isaac (11:20); Jacob (11:21); Joseph (11:22); Moses (11:23–29); and multiple judges and prophets, some named and some unnamed (11:32–38). While the writer has clear exhortatory purposes in this catalog (11:39–12:1), the very nature of the writer's exhortations to persevere in faith requires that each of the individuals named be flesh and blood human beings.[62] Nonhistorical figures could not persuasively model persevering faith for historical

---

62 There are other considerations, noted by C. John Collins, including Hebrews's reference to the individuals of Hebrews 11 as "the people of old" (Heb. 11:2); the fact that "the list begins with an affirmation about the creation of the universe, which is taken to be an actual event"; and the fact that "these people [will] be 'made perfect' along with himself and his audience (v. 40) . . ." (*Did Adam and Eve Really Exist?*, 91). F. F. Bruce argues that the "catalog of spiritual heroism" of Hebrews 11 falls in a "literary genre" attested elsewhere in Jewish literature (*Sir.* 44:1–50:21; *1 Macc.* 2:51–60; cf. *4 Macc.* 16:20ff., 18:11ff.) (*The Epistle to the Hebrews*, NICNT [Grand Rapids, MI: Eerdmans, 1990], 278). The Jewish catalogs that Bruce mentions all commend *historical* figures to readers' attention. See the fuller listings at Paul Ellingworth, *The Epistle to the Hebrews: A Commentary on the Greek Text*, NIGTC (Grand Rapids, MI: Eerdmans, 1993), 560–61; and Peter T. O'Brien, *The Letter to the Hebrews*, PNTC (Grand Rapids, MI: Eerdmans, 2010), 395. O'Brien also notes that Hebrews sets the historical exemplars of this chapter in their historical, narrative sequence: "our author's examples, like many Jewish lists, create a sustained account of Israel's history" (ibid.).

people. The writer evidences no categorical distinction of historicity between, for example, the account of Abel and the account of Moses. Each person occupies the same historical space. The very way in which the writer crafts his argument in this chapter, then, indicates his understanding of the entirety of biblical narrative, extending back to its earliest beginnings, as fully and conventionally historical.[63]

9. Hebrews 12:24

. . . and to Jesus, the mediator of a new covenant, and to the sprinkled blood that speaks a better word than the blood of Abel.

In the previous chapter, the writer to the Hebrews references Abel as a historical person. In this chapter, the writer once again references Abel in the same fashion. Here, Abel is brought into relation with Jesus Christ. Abel is in view as the righteous sufferer, martyred by his brother, Cain. The writer likely references God's words to Cain in Genesis 4:10 that "the voice of your brother's blood is crying to me from the ground." The blood of Abel called for "vengeance against Cain," but Christ's blood brings salvation to sinners.[64] In placing Abel and Jesus in the relation that he does, the writer understands Abel to be as historical a figure as he understands Jesus to be. That is to say, the writer understands Genesis 4 to be a record of fully historical persons and events.

10. 1 Peter 3:20

. . . because they formerly did not obey, when God's patience waited in the days of Noah, while the ark was being prepared, in which a few, that is, eight persons, were brought safely through water.

In this verse, Peter crisply summarizes the events narrated in Genesis 6–9. Noah prepared the ark that he, his wife, his three sons, and

---

63 As C. John Collins has rightly observed, "if . . . the author of Hebrews assumes the historicity of these characters from Genesis 4–5, there is no reason to exclude Adam and Eve from the same assumption" (*Did Adam and Eve Really Exist?*, 91).

64 Ellingworth, *Hebrews*, 682.

their wives entered. God stayed his hand of judgment until Noah had finished building the ark. Having entered the ark, these eight persons were delivered from that judgment, having been "brought safely through water." Peter proceeds to draw a comparison between these events and the experience of Christians with the sacrament of baptism (1 Pet. 3:21). Peter understands the waters of judgment in Genesis 6–9 to be typological of the judgment that Christ has undergone for his people.[65] It is of this eschatological judgment that Christian baptism is a sign. Like Noah, believers, united with Christ in his death and resurrection, have been delivered through judgment. In these verses, Peter treats the narrative of Genesis 6–9 as fully historical in character. The comparison that Peter draws between Noah and the new covenant community, furthermore, assumes that God's dealings with Noah are as fully and as truly historical as his dealings with Christ in Christ's death and resurrection.

11. 2 Peter 2:5

. . . if he did not spare the ancient world, but preserved Noah, a herald of righteousness, with seven others, when he brought a flood upon the world of the ungodly; . . .

Peter again appeals to Noah with reference to the judgment of the flood of Genesis 6–9. God spared Noah "with seven others" from the "flood" that he "brought . . . upon the world of the ungodly," that is, "the ancient world." He infers from God's actions in the distant past God's ability "to rescue the godly from trials . . ." (2 Pet. 2:9). The "trials" that are facing Peter's readership are occasioned by the presence and activity of false teachers in their midst (2:1–3). Peter encourages his readers by appealing to God's preservation of his people in times past. If God was willing to preserve his people then, Peter reasons, he is no less willing to preserve his people now. That Peter makes such an

---

65 Schreiner, *1, 2 Peter, Jude*, 193. Schreiner further notes, "The waters of baptism, like the waters of the flood, demonstrate that destruction is at hand, but believers are rescued from these waters in that they are baptized with Christ . . ." (194).

argument indicates his conviction that the events of Genesis 6–9 are fully historical in nature.

12. 1 John 3:12

> We should not be like Cain, who was of the evil one and murdered his brother. And why did he murder him? Because his own deeds were evil and his brother's righteous.

This reference to Cain constitutes the sole explicit "reference to the [Old Testament] in 1 John."[66] Cain here is said to be "of the evil one," that is, one who is spiritually allied to Satan. He shows his allegiance to Satan by his heinous act of fratricide, his murder of Abel. John further specifies what motivated Cain to do this "evil" deed. It was that his brother's "deeds" were "righteous." John proceeds to broaden his concern from Cain specifically to "the world" generally.[67] As righteous Abel, allied with God against Satan, was hated by Cain, so those who have been "born of God" will be hated by the world (3:9, 13). On the other hand, John warns believers not to "be like Cain," who hated his brother (3:12, 15). John's argument treats the account of Cain and Abel in Genesis 4 as relating fully historical events. The nature of the analogy that John draws between Cain and the "world," and the warning in verse 15 (". . . you know that no murderer has eternal life abiding in him") undergirded by that analogy require, furthermore, that Cain be a fully historical personage.

13. Jude 11

> Woe to them! For they walked in the way of Cain and abandoned themselves for the sake of gain to Balaam's error and perished in Korah's rebellion.

Jude warns his readers at length about false teachers who "pervert the grace of our God into sensuality and deny our only Master and

---

66 Stephen S. Smalley, *1, 2, 3 John*, WBC, vol. 51 (Waco, TX: Word, 1984), 183.
67 Ibid., 185.

Lord Jesus Christ" (Jude 4). Here Jude pronounces a word of judgment ("Woe to them!") upon these false teachers and proceeds to offer reasons ("for") why they are subject to this judgment. Jude first says that "they walked in the way of Cain," that is, "they have followed in Cain's footsteps by imitating his sin."[68] In saying this, Jude "hint[s] that to follow in Cain's path will lead to Cain's fate."[69] Jude immediately follows this comparison with Cain with two further comparisons, Balaam (Numbers 22–24) and Korah (Numbers 16). As we have observed above, the fact that Jude conjoins these three persons indicates his belief that they are equally and fully historical. One is not in a position, then, to understand Cain in mythological or subhistorical terms. Furthermore, Scripture records that each of these three persons came under the judgment of God for his sin. Jude is able to pronounce a word of judgment on false teachers in his own generation because God brought his own opponents under judgment in past generations. Jude's word of woe, in other words, requires that all three men (Cain, Balaam, and Korah) be fully historical persons.

II. THE SIGNIFICANCE OF ADAM IN THE NEW TESTAMENT

We have surveyed the testimony of multiple New Testament authors to the historicity of Adam and Eve. And they affirm much more than the mere fact that there once existed two individuals named Adam and Eve. Without exception, the New Testament writers uphold the full historicity of both Adam and Eve, affirming many specific details about their lives as recorded in Genesis 1–3. They clearly regard Adam and Eve to be the first human beings, having been specially created by God. They affirm both the order in which they were created (Adam, then Eve) and the fact that Eve was specially created from Adam. They understand every human being to be descended from Adam. They recognize that Eve was deceived by Satan. They confess Adam to be

---

68 Richard Bauckham, *Jude, 2 Peter*, WBC, vol. 50 (Waco, TX: Word, 1983), 80.
69 Ibid., 81.

the man through whom sin entered into the world, and the occasion of the creation's subjection to futility.

The New Testament writers' affirmations about Adam and Eve occur in the context of an unswerving and uncompromising commitment to the full historicity of the events recorded in Genesis 1–11, and the full trustworthiness of the record of those events, that is, the Old Testament Scripture. We should furthermore appreciate the wide range of the New Testament authors who testify to the historicity of Adam and Eve. Matthew, Luke, John, Paul, the author of Hebrews, Peter, and Jude all concur in their testimony to the historicity of the events recorded in the opening chapters of Genesis. We should finally register the fact that no New Testament author mounts an apologetic for the historicity of the events under review.[70] The reason that they mount no apologetic is that none was needed in the first-century church. We have no record from the New Testament of any early Christian denying the historicity of Adam, Eve, or any person or event from the opening chapters of Genesis. In light of these considerations, we must pause to ask, were the New Testament authors incorrect in these beliefs?

The apostle Paul offers two extended reflections on Adam, in 1 Corinthians and in Romans, and I will now consider these passages in more detail. In these passages, Paul not only affirms the historicity of Adam but also reflects at length on the significance of Adam's person and work. In both places, Paul tethers Adam's person and work to the person and work of Christ. In light of this conjunction, we will consider what implications questioning the historicity of the details from Genesis 1–3 about the life of Adam may have for the historical integrity of the gospel that Paul preached.

A. 1 Corinthians 15:20–22, 44–49

Paul's argument in 1 Corinthians 15 is in three parts. In 1 Corinthians 15:1–11, Paul defends the bodily resurrection as an essential part

---

70 In fact, Peter appeals both to the fact of the creation of the world and to the judgment of the world by the flood to prove an event that false teachers in his day were denying—the future and glorious return of Christ in judgment (see 2 Pet. 3:1–7).

of "the gospel I preached to you" (15:1, cf. v. 2, "the word I preached to you"); in verses 12–34 he addresses the "that" of the bodily resurrection; and in verses 35–58 he addresses the "how" of the bodily resurrection.[71]

Paul addresses "Adam" in the latter two sections of the argument of the chapter. The section that is most relevant for our purposes is this:

> But in fact Christ has been raised from the dead, the firstfruits of those who have fallen asleep. For as by a man came death, by a man has come also the resurrection of the dead. For as in Adam all die, so also in Christ shall all be made alive. (1 Cor. 15:20–22)

In verse 22, Paul sets in antithetical parallel "Adam" and "Christ": "for as in Adam all die, so also in Christ shall all be made alive." Adam is the "man" of the previous verse—"for as by *a man* came death, by *a man* has come also the resurrection of the dead" (v. 21). The two men are similar in that they are representative persons. Death comes to "all" those who are "in Adam"; resurrection life comes to "all" those who are "in Christ."[72] Each is "a man" whose actions come into the possession of those human beings whom they represent. The two men are different with respect to their actions as representative persons. Adam has brought "death," so that "in Adam all die" (vv. 21, 22). Christ has brought the "resurrection of the dead," so that "in Christ . . . all [are] made alive" (vv. 21, 22). The phrase "of the dead" (v. 21) has reference to the "death" of verse 21 and "die" of verse 22. Christ, by his resurrection, reverses and overcomes for his people the death that is theirs in Adam. The death that Christ has overcome, we should note, is not

---

71 Herman Ridderbos, *Paul: An Outline of His Theology*, trans. John Richard de Witt (Grand Rapids, MI: Eerdmans, 1975), 540.

72 That these respective outcomes belong to those and only those who are "in" each respective person suffices to eliminate universalism as a legitimate reading of this verse. Paul is not saying that every human being will be saved, that is, receive resurrection life in Christ. He is saying that all those who are united with Christ will receive the resurrection life that he has won on their behalf (Gordon Fee, *The First Epistle to the Corinthians*, rev. ed., NICNT [Grand Rapids, MI: Eerdmans, 2014], 832).

merely spiritual death. Christ has also overcome the physical death that came to human beings because of Adam's sin.

We may draw two important implications from Paul's statements in these verses. First, the parallel that Paul establishes between Adam and Christ not only requires that each be a representative figure, but also that each be a representative *man* (v. 21). To question or to compromise the humanity of the one is necessarily to question or to compromise the humanity of the other. Second, Paul's claims about Adam and Christ in these verses lie not on the periphery but at the heart of his gospel. The resurrection is among the matters "of first importance" that Paul delineates at verses 3–4. Since Paul explicates the resurrection of the man Christ in terms of the death that the man Adam has brought to the human race, Paul inseparably yokes the historicity of each man to the resurrection of Christ. The historicity of Adam, then, is not a disposable element of Paul's teaching concerning the resurrection of Christ.

Paul continues his comparison of Adam and Christ in verses 44b–49:

> If there is a natural body, there is also a spiritual body. Thus it is written, "The first man Adam became a living being"; the last Adam became a life-giving spirit. But it is not the spiritual that is first but the natural, and then the spiritual. The first man was from the earth, a man of dust; the second man is from heaven. As was the man of dust, so also are those who are of the dust, and as is the man of heaven, so also are those who are of heaven. Just as we have borne the image of the man of dust, we shall also bear the image of the man of heaven.

In 1 Corinthians 15:44–49, Paul maintains his focus on the two men, Adam and Christ, but he broadens that horizon beyond the scope of verses 21–22. As Richard B. Gaffin Jr. has observed, "in 1 Corinthians 15:44b–49 [Paul's] perspective is the most comprehensive possible, covering nothing less than the whole of human history from its beginning to its end, from the original creation to its consummation."[73] In 1 Corinthians 15:44–49, both Adam and Christ are representative persons.[74] Adam is "the first man Adam" (v. 45) and "the first man" (v. 47). Christ is "the last Adam" (v. 45) and "the second man" (v. 47).

One difference from Paul's argument earlier in the chapter is that the apostle here enumerates each man. Adam is "first"; Jesus is "second" and "last." This enumeration conveys how sweeping the reach of the work of each man is. That Christ is the "second man" indicates that there is no representative person that stands between Adam and Christ. That Christ is the "last Adam" indicates that there is no representative person or age that will follow Christ. That Adam is "first" indicates that there is no representative person who precedes Adam. The "contrast between Adam and Christ" here "is not only pointed but also comprehensive and exclusive."[75]

There is another difference between Paul's presentation of Adam in 1 Corinthians 15:21–22 and his presentation of Adam in verses 44–49. In the earlier verses, Adam is the one through whom "death" comes to his posterity. In view is the sin of Adam and its consequences for himself and for humanity. In the latter verses, however, Paul's perspective on Adam is decidedly on Adam before he sinned. That is to say, Adam is in view as created but not (yet) fallen. The citation of Genesis 2:7 at 1 Corinthians 15:45a ("The first man Adam became a living being") confirms Paul's interest in Adam prior to his fall into sin.

When Paul speaks of Adam as "the man of dust" (15:48), then, this description has reference to Adam-as-created. When Paul goes on to speak of human beings as "of the dust" and as those who "have borne the image of the man of dust," he has in view humanity, outside of Jesus Christ, represented by Adam.[76] The sole alternative to being "of

---

73 Gaffin, *No Adam, No Gospel*, 9. See further Richard B. Gaffin Jr., *Resurrection and Redemption: A Study in Paul's Soteriology*, 2nd ed. (Phillipsburg, NJ: P&R, 1987), 78–92.

74 I have drawn the material that follows from my "1–2 Corinthians," in *A Biblical-Theological Introduction to the New Testament*, ed. Michael Kruger (Wheaton, IL: Crossway, 2016), 212–14.

75 Gaffin, *Resurrection and Redemption*, 85.

76 Even though human beings continue to bear the Adamic image (James 3:9), it has been profoundly defaced, although not completely effaced, in consequence of the fall.

the dust" is to be "of heaven," to "bear the image of the man of heaven" (vv. 48, 49). This descriptor is true of those who have been brought from union with Adam to union with Christ, who is "the man of heaven" (vv. 48, 49).

We are now in a position to draw some implications from these observations for the historicity of several important details about Adam. First, the comprehensiveness of Paul's discussion of Adam precludes any human ancestry that does not trace its ultimate biological origin to Adam, "the first man." Adam is not "the 10,000th man on the earth" (as a proponent of theistic evolution might claim); he is "the first man." That is to say, for Paul, Adam is not simply one historical man among 10,000 human beings who existed at the same time. Adam, rather, is the ancestor of *every* human being. Every human being, according to Paul, bears, as one naturally descended from Adam, the image of the man of dust. The sole alternative, for Paul, is the Christian who, by grace, "shall also bear the image of the man of heaven" (v. 49). As far as Paul is concerned, there is no alternative. Every human being in every time and place falls into one or the other of these two categories.

Second, for Paul, those who "shall also bear the image of the man of heaven" are those who once "have borne the image of the man of dust" (v. 49). The Christian is one who has been transferred from Adam to Christ. Gaffin rightly notes, "It is quite foreign to this passage, especially given its comprehensive outlook . . . , to suppose that some not in the image of Adam will bear the glory-image of Christ."[77] Were there a human being not descended from Adam, he would not be eligible for redemption. Only those who have borne Adam's image may bear Christ's image. In light of the fact that the New Testament writers insist that the gospel is to be proclaimed to every human being without exception, we are thereby bound to conclude that every human being in every time and place of the world traces his genealogical descent from Adam.

---

77 Gaffin, *No Adam, No Gospel*, 12.

Third, Paul presents the ministry of Christ in a particular light. Christ's work of death and resurrection was not designed to destroy or eliminate our humanity. Neither was it designed so that we might transcend our humanity. It was designed to perfect and to advance our humanity. For this reason, Paul repeatedly refers to Adam and to Christ, in parallel, as "man" (1 Cor. 15:47, 48, 49). If the omega point of our redemption is an eschatologically consummate humanity, then Paul's alpha point in this chapter is the pre-eschatological humanity of Adam (v. 45, citing Gen. 2:7). To call into question the humanity of Adam or to challenge the universal descent of humans from Adam therefore has dire implications for the gospel as Paul outlines it in this chapter. Absent either a historical Adam or the universal descent of humanity from Adam, Paul's gospel is incoherent.

B. Romans 5:12–21

The other place in Paul's correspondence where he offers an extended reflection on Adam and Christ is Romans 5:12–21. These verses raise many issues that range widely across Paul's theology.[78] We will confine our attention to the implications of what Paul says here for Adam's historicity.

As in 1 Corinthians 15, Paul sets Adam and Christ in parallel. On the one hand, there is "Adam" (Rom. 5:14, twice), or, as Paul prefers to refer to him in this passage, the "one man" (vv. 12, 15, 16, 17 [twice], 19). On the other hand, there is "Jesus Christ" (vv. 15, 17, 21), who is also referred to as "one man" (vv. 15, 17, 19). Each is a representative person. The destinies of many hang upon the actions of Adam and Christ. For this reason, Paul says, "many died through one man's trespass," while "the free gift by the grace of that one man Jesus Christ abounded for many" (v. 15).

The parallel between Adam and Jesus, as in 1 Corinthians 15, is an *antithetical* parallel. This antithesis emerges as Paul details both the

---

78 For helpful exegetical and theological overviews of Paul's teaching in these verses, see John Murray, *The Imputation of Adam's Sin* (Phillipsburg, NJ: P&R, 1992); and Thomas R. Schreiner, "Original Sin and Original Death," in *Adam, the Fall, and Original Sin*, 271–88.

work that each representative has done on behalf of the represented, and the consequences or results of that work for the represented.[79] By the one trespass (Rom. 5:16, 18; cf. v. 14) of Adam has come "condemnation" (vv. 16, 18) and "death" (vv. 17, 21). But by the "one act of righteousness" or "obedience" (vv. 18–19) of Jesus has come "justification" vv. 16, 18) and "life" (vv. 17–18, 21).[80] Adam and Christ differ, then, in the nature and outcome of their respective actions. Their work also differs with respect to scope ("much more," v. 17; "all the more," v. 20). The "life" that Christ has won far surpasses the reign of death inaugurated by Adam's sin (v. 17).[81] Because it is Christ's righteousness alone that has secured "life" for his people, they may be assured that they will "reign in life through the one man Jesus Christ" (v. 17; cf. v. 21).

How does Paul's argument inform our understanding of Adam? First, Paul identifies Adam in verse 14 as "a type [Greek *typos*] of the one who was to come," that is, Jesus. Adam, then, is a "type" of Jesus. At the very least, the word "type" denotes correspondence. As a representative man whose action is imputed to those whom he represents, Adam corresponds to Jesus as his "prefiguration."[82] But this prefigurative correspondence is *fundamentally historical* in nature.[83] As Versteeg aptly summarizes the denotation of this word, "a type always stands at a particular moment in the history of redemption and points away to another (later) moment in the same history."[84] That

---

79 Material in this paragraph has been drawn from my "Romans," in *Biblical-Theological Introduction to the New Testament*, ed. Michael Kruger (Wheaton, IL: Crossway, 2016), 186–87.

80 The mode of the transfer of the work of the representative to the represented is rightly termed "imputation," on which see further Murray, *Imputation of Adam's Sin*.

81 "Adam's transgression introduced death as the king of human beings, but the grace of God brooks no rivals, conquering both sin and death" (Schreiner, "Original Sin and Original Death," 284).

82 Versteeg, *Adam in the New Testament*, 10.

83 Ibid, citing H. N. Ridderbos, *Aan de Romeinen* (Kampen: J. H. Kok, 1959), 116, "in a previously established redemptive-historical correlation" (in *een tevoren vastgestelde heilshistorische correlatie*); and L. Goppelt, *Typos: The Typological Interpretation of the Old Testament in the New* (Grand Rapids, MI: Eerdmans, 1982), 130, "Adam is not only an illustrative figure. [Paul] views Adam through Christ as a type in redemptive history, as a prophetic personality placed in Scripture by God."

84 Versteeg, *Adam in the New Testament*, 11.

is to say, "type" denotes a *fundamentally historical relationship*. Paul's application of this term to the correspondence between Adam and Christ confirms the essentially historical relationship between these two men. Adam and Christ are historical men who occupy the same plane of history. This historical plane, furthermore, finds its meaning and integration in the "redemptive plan of God."[85] The relationship that Paul expresses between Adam and Christ therefore carries necessary implications for our understanding of Adam's person. Adam is a historical person, no less a historical person than Jesus Christ. One is not free to maintain, then, that Adam is a mythical or semihistorical figure while Jesus Christ is a fully historical figure. Affirming the historicity of Jesus Christ requires affirming the historicity of Adam. It bears reiterating that this Adam, for Paul, is the Adam of whom Genesis 1–3 speaks in detail, the first human being, whom God specially created and from whom the entirety of the human race is biologically descended.

Second, Paul represents Adam as a historical person in yet another way. In Romans 5:13–14, Paul speaks of a bounded period in human history "before the law was given" (v. 13), that is, "from Adam to Moses" (v. 14). This historical window ranges from Adam to the giving of the Mosaic law at Sinai (Exodus 19ff.). As Versteeg has rightly observed, "as surely as a historical terminus is in view in the case of Moses, a historical starting point is in view in the case of Adam."[86] Adam can be no less historical a person than Moses.

Third, Paul argues in this passage that sin and death are not perennial features of the human experience. They are not essential to human nature. They have a particular point of entry into humanity. This alpha point is the "one man's trespass" (Rom. 5:15)—not the lifetime of Adam's sinning, but the single sin of disobeying God's command not to eat of the fruit of the tree of knowledge of good and evil.[87]

---

85 Ibid., 13.
86 Ibid., 24.
87 Note how in the following verse Paul contrasts the "one trespass" with the "many trespasses" (Rom. 5:16).

Death is not a given of human life, but the judicial consequence of the one sin of the one man (5:12; cf. Eccles. 7:29, "See, this alone I found, that God made man upright, but they have sought out many schemes"). Because Adam's one sin has been transferred to all those whom he represents, death is the universal penalty that they justly bear in consequence of that one sin (Rom. 5:12). Therefore, Paul attributes the reign of "death" to "the one man's trespass" (v. 17) and can speak of "sin reign[ing] in death" (v. 21). For Paul, "death" in the experience of those who are "in Adam" is inescapably judicial or penal in character.

Fourth, Paul's statements about Adam, the work of Adam, and the conveyance of Adam's work to those whom Adam represents provide the framework for the gospel of Jesus Christ. Jesus Christ is a *representative* man. His obedience and death were undertaken on behalf of his people (v. 19; cf. vv. 6–11). That obedience and death are so transferred or imputed to his people that they are now justified or declared righteous through faith in him (vv. 16–19). Because of the work of Christ, they have passed from "death" to nothing less than "eternal life through Jesus Christ our Lord" (v. 21). Each of these propositions about Jesus parallels a comparable proposition about Adam in verses 12–21. To compromise or to deny the historicity of the person and work of Adam, therefore, is not without consequence for the gospel. Paul does not give us the liberty of extracting the gospel from the redemptive-historical framework within which the gospel exists and has its meaning.

Fifth, and similarly to his argument in 1 Corinthians 15:20–22, 44–49, Paul understands the gospel solution to correspond to the Adamic plight. For Paul, as "all" human beings share in the Adamic plight, so "all" human beings who are represented by Christ receive the salvation that Christ has won for his people (Rom. 5:18).[88] This plight-solution

---

88 In Romans 5:18, Paul is not teaching universalism, that is, the salvation of all human beings. The "all" in the latter part of 5:18 refers to all people who are represented by the one man, Jesus Christ, just as the "all" in the former part of verse 18 refers to all people who are represented by Adam. That this is Paul's understanding of these two uses of the term translated "all" is in part confirmed by his use of the term "many" twice in the following verse (v. 19).

framework is comprehensive of all humanity. Paul recognizes no individual person or group of persons that is exempt from this framework.

III. THEISTIC EVOLUTIONARY READINGS OF PAUL (1 COR. 15:20–22, 44–49; ROM. 5:12–21)

How have proponents of theistic evolution approached and understood the apostle Paul's two extended reflections on the person and work of Adam (1 Cor. 15:20–22, 44–49 and Rom. 5:12–21)? We may answer that question by exploring what three proponents, Denis Alexander, John H. Walton, and Peter Enns have argued from these passages. Because Alexander, Walton, and Enns are not altogether agreed upon these passages' meaning, we will address each separately.

A. Denis Alexander on Paul's Understanding of Adam

Denis Alexander has argued that the biblical writers speak of "three types of death: physical death; spiritual death here and now; and eternal spiritual death."[89] According to Alexander, the Old Testament writers do not view "death per se [as] caused by sin."[90] He says that the New Testament writers, by contrast, conceived "physical death" as "an enemy to be overcome," which in fact has happened in the resurrection of Jesus from the dead.[91] The difference between the Testaments with respect to physical death, then, is that the Old Testament sees physical death "as the normal lot of humankind," whereas the New Testament "transforms [physical death] into something that has no place in the future kingdom of God."[92]

Spiritual death refers to "alienation from God caused by sin."[93] In the New Testament, spiritual death and physical death are so closely related that it is difficult to "distinguish" the two in many instances.[94]

---

89 Alexander, *Creation or Evolution*, 306.
90 Ibid., 310.
91 Ibid., 311.
92 Ibid., 312.
93 Ibid.
94 Ibid., 313.

Eternal, spiritual death is "the spiritual death that continues on after this life" and is "permanent."[95]

This understanding of death informs Alexander's readings of Romans 5 and 1 Corinthians 15. Paul's concern in Romans 5 is said to be spiritual death, brought about by sin.[96] Paul understood Adam to be "a real person," a "historical figure," no less than Jesus himself was.[97] Paul also sees Adam in "corporate solidarity" and "federal headship" with the people who follow him. Adam's sin has somehow resulted in the humans after him having "a propensity to sin," even as "each person is responsible for his or her own sin."[98]

Alexander is unwilling to say from Romans 5 that physical death originated with Adam. He makes this point explicit in his exposition of 1 Corinthians 15.[99] According to Alexander, Paul sees "physical death" in 1 Corinthians 15 as ". . . the normal state of humankind and always has been. This is the status of earthly men (v. 48); it's what you expect."[100] The cross and the resurrection, however, have conquered not only spiritual death but also physical death. With death so comprehensively nullified, we are therefore qualified to enter the kingdom (vv. 48–49).

What, then, may be said of Adam's disobedience and its implications for humanity? Alexander denies that Adam and Eve are the "genetic progenitors of the entire human race."[101] We do not inherit *guilt* from Adam, "but *a propensity to sin*, so that . . . everyone does in a sense repeat the sin of Adam."[102] Part of Alexander's reticence in affirming that we inherit the sin of Adam is that the idea "implies some kind of genetic transmission."[103] In some fashion, which Alexander acknowledges he

---

95 Ibid., 315.
96 Ibid., 329.
97 Ibid., 330.
98 Ibid., 331.
99 "1 Corinthians 15 does not actually address the question as to whether physical death began with Adam's sin—nowhere is this mentioned" (ibid., 332).
100 Ibid., 333.
101 Ibid., 343.
102 Ibid., 344, emphasis added.
103 Ibid., 345.

is unable satisfactorily to articulate, every human has a "propensity to sin" and "repeats the sin of Adam" but does not "inherit" sin from his "parents in any genetic sense."[104]

What may be said of the person of Adam himself? Adam and Eve were "real historical people . . . the progenitors of God's new family on earth, comprising all those who would enter into a personal relationship with God by faith."[105] These two people were "a couple of Neolithic farmers in the Near East" or even a "community of farmers, to whom [God] chose to reveal himself in a special way."[106] This call of God did not render them human, for they were already human. Prior to this call, people, presumably including Adam and Eve, "sought after God or gods in different parts of the world, offering their own explanations for the meaning of their lives."[107] What the call did was to bring them to spiritual life "in fellowship with God."[108] Adam and Eve furthermore stood in "federal headship in relation to the rest of humanity."[109] By virtue of the divine choice, Adam and Eve come to represent, then, presumably all human beings, even those who are "not descended genetically" from them.[110]

How are we to assess Alexander's understanding of Adam from the perspective of Paul's writings? First, the distinction that Alexander presses between physical and spiritual death is alien to Paul's thought. For Paul, death is not a given of human nature. It is an intruder. Its entrance into human experience came with the first sin of the first man, Adam.[111] Paul cannot conceive of death, furthermore, apart from its penal character (cf. 1 Cor. 15:54–57). Believers, who continue to experience the evil of death, do not experience death as the penalty for their sin only because Christ, in his death, bore that penalty for them.

---

104 Ibid. Alexander, on the following page, wishes to set his view apart from that of Pelagius, even as he sets his view apart from that of Augustine.

105 Ibid., 317–18.

106 Ibid., 290.

107 Ibid.

108 Ibid.

109 Ibid., 291.

110 Ibid., 292.

111 For a perceptive critique of Alexander's allowance for pre-Adamic "sin," see Reeves, "Adam and Eve," 48–49.

Second, Alexander's proposal that Adam and Eve were selected from an existing group of human beings and appointed as federal representatives over all human beings, whether descended from them or not, runs counter to the testimony of Paul. Paul affirms that all human beings, Christ excepted, by nature bear the "image" of Adam (1 Cor. 15:49). They do so as they are naturally descended from Adam, the "first man" (v. 45). As Gaffin has observed, "*image bearers of Adam* is hardly an apt, much less valid or even intelligible, description of human beings who are held either to have existed before Adam or subsequently not to have descended from him."[112] Paul knows no mode of Adamic representation that is not conjoined to and predicated upon genetic descent from Adam.

Third, Alexander acknowledges a difficulty in affirming two propositions. On the one hand, all human beings have a universal propensity to sin that is traceable to the first sin of Adam. On the other hand, we may not use the language of "inheritance" to explain this state of affairs, nor may we explain any process of transmission in terms of or in light of a genetic relationship between Adam and his posterity. One may appreciate Alexander's stated insistence to distance himself from the Pelagian denial of the transmission of Adam's sin to his posterity. The question remains, however, in what precise sense Alexander has affirmed Adamic representation. We are said to derive from Adam not guilt but a "propensity to sin," but we are not told how that propensity comes into our possession.[113] A person's guilt is said to commence when he or she personally commits sin.[114] Alexander's statements do not adequately safeguard Paul from the "personal self-determination" that characterizes Pelagian readings of Paul.[115] If, for Alexander, Adam

---

112 Gaffin, *No Adam, No Gospel*, 12, emphasis original.

113 "It is not guilt that is inherited from Adam but a propensity to sin, so that as a matter of fact everyone does in a sense repeat the sin of Adam. Exactly how that propensity is transmitted is a moot point and a matter of much theological speculation. . . . [T]he propensity is part of that dark theological cloud of sin, which affects the whole of humanity. But irrespective of how we precisely define that propensity, we can agree that people become guilty when they then proceed to sin . . ." (Alexander, *Creation or Evolution*, 344).

114 See the quote in the previous note.

115 Reeves, "Adam and Eve," 52.

is more than a bad exemplar for the human beings who followed him, it is difficult to discern just in what sense that is so.

The liabilities attending this position advocated by Alexander are illuminated in a recent publication by another proponent of theistic evolution, Scot McKnight.[116] McKnight has argued that "the Adam of Paul was not the historical Adam."[117] For Paul, McKnight insists, Adam is "literary" and "genealogical," that is, "the entire history of Israel is built" upon Adam in the Old Testament.[118] In company with other Second Temple Jewish writers, Paul is said to conceive of Adam as an "archetypal" and "moral" figure.[119]

In the course of making this argument, McKnight advances some troubling claims regarding the relationship between the sin of Adam and the sinful condition of human beings. He claims that "original sin and damnation for all humans by birth is not found in Paul."[120] No one sins "in Adam"; rather, "each person is *Adamic in that each person sins in the way Adam sinned.*"[121] To be sure, each person sins in the wake of the "cosmic death" that Adam "unleash[ed]" by his own sin, but, for Paul, "each of us [is] an Adam or Eve generating our own death."[122] "Humans have been impacted by Adam's sin, but individuals are not accountable until they sin themselves."[123]

This understanding of Adam and human beings has implications for the way that McKnight understands the relationship between Christ and his people. McKnight explains Romans 5:18–19 in these terms: "*just as one must act—believe—in order to benefit from the one act of Christ's obedience in order to inherit eternal life, so we need to act—sin or disobey—in order to accrue to ourselves death.*"[124] Adam "is the para-

---

116 Dennis R. Venema and Scot McKnight, *Adam and the Genome: Reading Scripture after Genetic Science* (Grand Rapids, MI: Brazos, 2017).
117 Ibid., 191.
118 Ibid., 176.
119 Ibid., 180.
120 Ibid., 183.
121 Ibid., 183, 184, emphasis original.
122 Ibid., 184.
123 Ibid., 186.
124 Ibid., emphasis original.

digmatic human who failed to live according to God's demand and so becomes the paradigmatic moral (or immoral) man, leaving the haunting question that runs right through the whole Bible: Will we follow Adam or will we follow Christ?"[125]

This understanding of sin and redemption is indisputably semi-Pelagian and arguably Pelagian (the unorthodox view that we are not born with a sinful nature, but are able to choose by our own moral strength to obey God). These formulations follow directly on McKnight's denial of the full historicity of Adam. They confirm that one's understanding of the historicity of Adam has serious implications for the integrity of the biblical gospel.

To conclude our discussion of the way in which Alexander understands Adam in Paul, Alexander's proposal conflicts in fundamental ways with Scripture's testimony about Adam, sin, death, and the work of Christ. Alexander not only denies that all human beings are biologically descended from Adam; he also fails to offer a clear and coherent account of the relationship between Adam's sin and his posterity. Alexander, furthermore, fails adequately to account for Scripture's understanding of death, on the one hand, and of the work of Christ to deliver sinners from death, on the other. In an attempt to accommodate Scripture to evolutionary theory, Alexander's proposal, at best, dilutes the testimony of Scripture concerning matters that lie at the heart of Scripture's teaching about sin and salvation.

B. John H. Walton on Paul's Understanding of Adam

Although John Walton has concentrated his attention on the Old Testament witness to Adam, he has also addressed what Paul had to say about Adam in 1 Corinthians 15 and Romans 5. Walton argues that in both Testaments Adam appears as an *archetype*. An archetype, as Walton has defined the term, "refers to *a representative of a group* in whom all others in the group are embodied. As a result, all members of the group are included and participate with their representative."[126]

125 Ibid., 188.
126 Walton, *Lost World of Adam and Eve*, 240, emphasis added.

Walton distinguishes the *historical existence* of such a figure as Adam from his *archetypal significance* in the biblical literature. The recognition that "the New Testament authors believe Adam and Eve to be real individuals in a real past (as do I)" is distinct from the "theological" or "archetypal" "use that is made of them."[127] It is as an archetype that the New Testament writers are said to have interest in Adam.

What implications does Walton's distinction have for the way in which he approaches the Pauline material? Romans 5:12–21 is said to represent Adam archetypally in two ways: "first, he is seen as a pattern of Christ; second, Adam represents all people in Paul's treatment (through him all sinned)."[128] Paul is not interested in committing his readers to the proposition that "Adam was the first human being or that we all must be related biologically or genetically to Adam"; or that "sin [is] passed through biological relationship."[129] Paul does commit us, however, to "the reality of sin and death entering human experience in an event," with the implication that there is "a historical Adam."[130]

Walton draws similar conclusions from 1 Corinthians 15:22, 45. Although Adam is the "first" man, he cannot be the "first biological specimen" because "Christ was not the last biological specimen."[131] Furthermore, since Paul terms Jesus both "second" and "last," these two terms must be the "same" and must "not focus on actual numeration value."[132] Paul's interest in the two men is as archetypes, "contrast[ing] and compar[ing] Adam to Jesus and our relationship to both." Paul has no interest in "genetic relationships" of human beings with Adam or "material origins" other than saying that "we share the 'dust' nature of the archetype."[133]

---

127 Walton, "Historical Adam: Archetypal Creation View," 105.

128 Ibid., 106.

129 Ibid. "Here [i.e., Rom. 5:12–21] the archetypal use is connected to the fall, not to his forming" (*Lost World of Adam and Eve*, 93).

130 Walton, "Historical Adam: Archetypal Creation View," 106.

131 Ibid., 107.

132 Walton, *Lost World of Adam and Eve*, 93.

133 Walton, "Historical Adam: Archetypal Creation View," 107. Elsewhere, Walton concludes "that all of Paul's treatment of Adam pertains to the issues of sin, death and the theological archetypal

What, then, may be positively affirmed of Adam and his work in relation to humanity? Walton argues that Adam and Eve were drawn from a larger human population (all of whom, as human beings, were in the "image of God") and these two were appointed "representative priests for humanity."[134] Adam and Eve are not "de novo creations." They are, rather, "positioned as fountainheads of humanity even if we are not all their direct descendants."[135]

Walton states, furthermore, that in the pre-Adamic "earliest populations . . . there was never a time when sinful (= at least personal evil) behavior was not present."[136] Appealing to Romans 5:13, Walton argues that, prior to Adam and Eve, when "law or revelation" was first given, "there was no sin (no consciousness of relationship, no immorality)."[137] They were behaving badly and committing evil, but they were not morally accountable to God for their actions, nor were they in "a personal, conscious relationship" with God.[138]

This state of affairs changed when Adam and Eve sinned. They brought "sin to the entire human race by bringing accountability."[139] Furthermore, their sin "made the antidote to death inaccessible." How particularly does Adam's sin reach subsequent generations of human beings? Walton suggests that "the world . . . got polluted because of that first act (disorder let loose and run amok)," and that we are thereby "infected" from this world.[140] We are "born into [a] toxic environment," and "suffer the consequences both universally and particularly." And we are not only "victims" of this state of affairs, but "we all contribute to it."[141] It was this "disorder" that "brought the need for resolution through the work of Christ," who alone brings order

---

roles of both Adam and Jesus. His patently theological comments do not address the issues of science" (*Lost World of Adam and Eve*, 168).

134 Walton, *Lost World of Adam and Eve*, 159.

135 Ibid., 206.

136 Ibid., 154.

137 Ibid., 155.

138 Ibid.

139 Ibid.

140 Ibid., 157.

141 Ibid., 158.

into disorder.[142] The "historicity of Adam," Walton concludes, "finds its primary significance in the discussion of the origins of sin rather than in the origins of humanity."[143]

How may we assess Walton's reading of Paul? First, Walton insists that Paul's interest is not the "forming accounts" of the Old Testament but "the accounts of the fall."[144] But we have argued from 1 Corinthians 15:20–22, 44–49, that Paul displays sustained interest in Adam *prior to any sin*. His identification of Adam as the "first man" and of human beings as bearing Adam's "image" shows that, for Paul, Adam is both the first human being and the genetic ancestor of all human beings. Adam's representative role in 1 Corinthians 15 and Romans 5 is therefore tethered to his historical place as the first man and the ancestor of the human race. Paul has so woven these two strands together that we may not retain the former while jettisoning the latter.

Second, Walton's formulations on sin and accountability part ways with the way in which Paul understands sin and accountability. Walton identifies pre-Adamite human beings as image-bearers, and describes their behavior as "evil." Even so, appealing to Romans 5:13, he refrains from characterizing this behavior as "sin." He does so because "sin" is said to require the moral accountability that commenced in human history only with Adam and Eve. Paul's words in Romans 5:13–14, however, are far removed from Walton's construction, for Paul says,

> . . . for sin indeed was in the world before the law was given, but sin is not counted where there is no law. Yet death reigned from Adam to Moses, even over those whose sinning was not like the transgression of Adam, who was a type of the one who was to come. (Rom. 5:13–14)

Paul's words concern the narrow historical window between the sin of Adam and the giving of the Mosaic law; Paul predicates the prevalence of sin in humanity even before the Mosaic law. For all of the complexi-

---

142 Ibid., 159.
143 Ibid., 203, emphasis removed.
144 Ibid., 95. He notes 1 Corinthians 15:47–48 as "one exception" (ibid.).

ties of Paul's argument in Romans 5:13–14, there is no reason to think that, at any point in human history, Paul conceived of human beings who were "engaged in activity that would be considered sin [but who were] not . . . held accountable for it."[145]

One may also fairly ask by what standard Walton characterizes pre-Adamite human beings' behavior as "evil"? Is their behavior intrinsically evil, or is this a judgment after the fact? If such behavior merits the wrath of God presently (see Rom. 1:18–32), would one say that pre-Adamite humans did not suffer divine displeasure for their own evil actions? These questions underscore the impossibility of Walton's position and return us to Paul's contention that sin commenced with the one act of disobedience of the first man and progenitor of the entire human race, Adam.

Third, Walton employs the metaphor of pollution to explain how Adam and Eve's sin affected subsequent humanity. The metaphor, however, is imprecise and fails to explain exactly how it is that Adam and Eve's sin is passed along to other human beings. Walton does not exonerate these other human beings—they are said to be both victims of and contributors to the toxic environment in which people find themselves. At the same time, it remains unclear exactly *how* or even *if* human beings enter the world guilty of sin, or if they are merely disposed to commit sin.

Such a view of man's nature, to put it mildly, is considerably less pessimistic than that of the apostle Paul. It fails to reckon with the specificity with which Paul speaks of the imputation of Adam's sin to his posterity and the radical universality of the "reign" of "sin . . . in death" in Romans 5:12–21.

Walton's proposal counters Scripture's testimony to the person and work of Adam, to the nature of sin, and to the way in which Adam's sin was passed on to his posterity. It denies the universal, biological descent of humanity from Adam. It fails to adequately account for the Bible's

---

145 Ibid., 155. We are not saying that Walton understands Paul to be speaking of pre-Adamite human beings in Romans 5:13. We are saying, rather, that the principle he articulates is not found in Romans 5:13 and, therefore, may not legitimately be applied to any segment of the human population.

understanding of sin, of moral accountability, and of the origin and transmission of sin among human beings. In the interest of reconciling Scripture with evolutionary theory, Walton's proposal stands against the teaching of Scripture in matters that are central to that teaching, namely, sin and redemption.

C. Peter Enns on Paul's Understanding of Adam

Old Testament professor Peter Enns argues that previous generations have not adequately reckoned with Paul as a first-century reader of Old Testament Scripture. When we do so, we will necessarily have to adjust our "understanding of Adam."[146] Decisive for Paul's reading of the Old Testament was "his experience of the risen Christ."[147] This experience "drive[s] . . . his reading of the Old Testament in general," a reading that is "creative."[148]

What, then, were the contours of this reading? Paul had a "high view of Christ," which required his "recast[ing]" of "Israel's story, specifically Adam . . . to account for Christ." For this reason, Paul "invests Adam with capital he does not have either in the Genesis story, the Old Testament as a whole, or the interpretations of his contemporary Jews."[149] "Paul's understanding of Adam is shaped by Jesus, not the other way around."[150]

Critical for Enns's readings of 1 Corinthians 15 and Romans 5, then, is that Paul's statements about Adam are reflective of his experience of Christ. Therefore, Paul gives us "not a plain reading of Genesis but a transformation of Genesis." Paul's statements about Adam do not "settle what Adam means in Genesis itself, and most certainly not the question of human origins as debated in the modern world."[151]

---

146 Peter Enns, *Evolution of Adam: What the Bible Does and Doesn't Say about Human Origins* (Grand Rapids, MI: Baker, 2012), xiii.

147 Ibid., 135. "Paul's reading of the Adam story was conditioned by his experience of the risen Christ" (142).

148 Ibid., 135.

149 Ibid.

150 Ibid., 122.

151 Ibid., 117.

What, then, does Paul say about Adam, and how are these statements said to stem from his prior experience of the risen Christ? Adam is both a "theological and *historical* figure for Paul."[152] Paul assumed that Adam was "the first man created by God . . . from whom the human race descended and from whom all inherited sin and death."[153] Not only does Paul affirm the historicity of Adam as the first man and as the progenitor of every human being, but these realities, for Paul, are what "makes [Adam] such a vital theological figure."[154] In other words, these historical convictions were integral, as far as Paul was concerned, to Adam's theological importance in 1 Corinthians 15 and Romans 5.

And yet, Paul did not come to these convictions about Adam independently. His point of entry to them was his experience of the crucified and risen Christ. In light of "the cross and resurrection of Christ," Paul and other Christians saw "grace."[155] No longer did Gentiles have to become Jews in order to be part of God's people. "The resurrection of the Son of God is a game changer: gentiles can now be part of the family of God as gentiles."[156] Jew and Gentile are "on an even footing" now. It is in light of this solution ("Jesus's death and resurrection") that Paul came to the conclusion that Jew and Gentile "are both saved from the same plight (sin and death)."[157]

Paul's handling of Adam in Romans 5:12–21 is in service of advancing a solution to the human plight. Because the solution had "such earth-shattering significance, there must have been a corresponding 'problem' it was designed to address."[158] This plight is not failure to "keep the law," but "death."[159] Paul "trace[d]" the "cause of death . . .

---

152 Ibid., 120.

153 Ibid. Enns mentions efforts "to preserve an 'Adam' who is not the first human as Paul has it but is the first 'spiritual' hominid (or group of hominids) endowed with a soul and so forth, who acts as a 'representative head' of humanity," but he concludes that "any such creature is as foreign to Paul as any other solution that is trying to bring Paul and evolution into conversation" (*Evolution of Adam*, 123).

154 Ibid., 120.

155 Ibid., 129.

156 Ibid., 130.

157 Ibid.

158 Ibid., 131.

159 Ibid.

to the trespass of Adam, understood as the first man."[160] Adam was responsible for bringing "sin and death . . . into the world," antecedently to "the law."[161] Not only did Adam introduce sin into the world, but his "trespass somehow is responsible for putting all of humanity under the power of sin."[162] Therefore, Adam's first sin, "the cause of death, was handed on . . . [to] *all* humans . . . somehow."[163]

For Paul, Enns continues, Christ has the effect of displacing the Mosaic law as the solution to the human plight. The Adamic plight (sin and death) was "at work before the law," therefore, "Christ's resurrection—death's reversal—was clearly a solution to a much deeper problem than the law."[164] The plight of the first Adam required for its solution not the law but the work of the second Adam.[165]

Enns insists that if we "take Paul's *theology* with utmost seriousness [we] are not also bound to accept Paul's view of Adam *historically*."[166] Why is this? All that is essential to the gospel is that we accept "the reality of the human plight of sin and death" and "of God's unexpected, universal solution."[167] The "universal and self-evident problem[s]" of "death" and "sin" (along with "the historical event of the death and resurrection of Christ") are what are said to be the three "core elements of the gospel."[168] Paul's explanations of sin and death are not necessary to the retention of the plight that makes up a core element of the gospel. For Enns's part, we are free to say that "Adam is not the historical first man" and thereby "leav[e] behind Paul's understanding of the *cause* of the universal plight of sin and death."[169] "The need for a Savior does not require a historical Adam."[170]

160 Ibid.
161 Ibid., 133.
162 Ibid.
163 Ibid., 134.
164 Ibid., 135.
165 Ibid.
166 Ibid., emphasis original.
167 Ibid.
168 Ibid., 123.
169 Ibid.
170 Ibid., 143.

What are we to make of Enns's proposals concerning Paul and Adam? We may, as a preliminary observation, note an important difference between Enns, on the one hand, and Alexander and Walton, on the other. Alexander and Walton claim a shared belief with the apostle Paul concerning the existence and activity of a historical Adam. Their conception of Adam, however, is markedly different from that of most Christians and, we have argued, from that of Paul himself. Enns, however, argues for a *Pauline* understanding of Adam that more closely approximates classical understandings of the person of Adam. Unlike Alexander and Walton, however, Enns senses a freedom explicitly to disagree with and to shed that Pauline understanding of Adam.

Critical for Enns's proposal is that the person and activity of Adam do not constitute a core element of the gospel. That is to say, we are free to shed Paul's statements about Adam without jeopardizing the integrity of the gospel that Paul preached. What Paul has done is to "appropriat[e] an ancient way to address pressing concerns of the moment. That has no bearing whatsoever on the truth of the gospel."[171]

In point of fact, however, Paul places his testimony to the historicity of Adam at the core of his gospel. For Paul, Adam and Christ stand or fall together as historical persons occupying the same plane of history. Adam is a "type" of Christ (Rom. 5:14). Adam is the "first man," while Christ is the "second man" and "last Adam" (1 Cor. 15:47, 45).[172] Christ's work *in history* remedies the work of Adam *in history*. The sins for which Christ has died (vv. 3–4) are sins that follow in the train of our Adamic plight—the imputation of his sin to us, and the transmission of his corrupt nature to his posterity by natural generation. To jettison the historicity of Adam's person or actions necessarily calls into question the historicity and effectiveness of the saving work of Christ and, therefore, of the gospel that proclaims that saving work.

---

171 Ibid., 102.

172 We are therefore not free to say, with Enns, that Paul's statements about Adam are "a *cultural* assumption that Paul makes about *primordial* time," while his statements about the resurrection reflect "*present*-time reality, an actual *historical event*," even as Enns acknowledges that Paul understood the "historical Adam" to be "an unquestioned historical reality *for him*" (*Evolution of Adam*, 126, emphasis original).

But what of Enns's contention that one may hold on to the universal plight of sin and death without holding on to Paul's Adamic explanation of that plight? May we not set to the side "original sin" while maintaining "sin of origin," that is, the "absolute inevitability of sin that affects every human being from *their* beginnings, from birth"?[173] May we not be content to say "*that* all humans are born in sin (sin of origin)" while "remain[ing] open on the ultimate origins of *why* all humans are born in sin (original sin)"?[174]

Decisively against this distinction, as Enns employs it, is its refusal to affirm, in the words of Gaffin, "that sin entered human history at a point subsequent to its beginnings." As Gaffin goes on to explain, Enns's view would have us believe that sin "is not a matter of human *fallenness* but of human *givenness*. Whatever else being human may mean, it entails being sinful or at least being naturally and inalterably disposed to sin."[175]

The gospel, however, does not treat sin as a constituent part of our humanity. It is something that has entered human experience after the creation of humanity. It is, therefore, something that may be removed from human experience by divine grace. Apart from this understanding of sin, redemption, at least on any biblical terms, is meaningless. Paul's gospel simply has nothing to say to the kind of human condition that Enns describes.

Enns's explanation of sin and, correspondingly, redemption stands at odds with the testimony of Scripture. In an effort to reconcile Scripture's teaching about Adam, sin, and salvation with evolutionary theory, Enns effectively dehistoricizes a core element of the biblical gospel, namely, its testimony about sin. To undertake such a project, we have seen, not only parts ways with the Bible's understanding of sin but also renders meaningless the Bible's teaching about redemption. Enns's proposal raises serious and foundational questions about the integrity of the biblical gospel.

---

173 Ibid., 124, emphasis original. Enns has drawn this distinction from Lutheran theologian George L. Murphy.
174 Ibid., 125, emphasis original.
175 Gaffin, *No Adam, No Gospel*, 16, emphasis original.

IV. CONCLUSION

The New Testament authors speak with one voice about the person and work of Adam. Adam is a historical man, not mythological or semihistorical. Adam is the first man, specially created by God. Adam is the progenitor of the human race. All people (except for Jesus Christ) descend from Adam by natural generation. Adam is, furthermore, a representative man. His first sin has been imputed to his natural posterity. As a result, we are all guilty of Adam's first sin. We are all justly subject to death, and sin now reigns in death. The reigning depravity and corruption of sin and the consequence of sin, death, are the norm for all those who are "in Adam."

Some proponents of theistic evolution have attempted to reconcile modern evolutionary theory with the teaching of the New Testament. These efforts are not uniform, but we have observed certain patterns emerging. First, what we have summarized as the united testimony of the New Testament concerning Adam is rejected. Some see Adam as a human being, chosen from among other already existing human beings to undertake a special calling from God. Enns sees Adam, for Paul at least, as a culturally appropriate way of articulating the depth of the human plight in light of his experience of Christ and his corresponding conviction that the death and resurrection of Christ provided the solution to that plight. Each proponent surveyed refuses to affirm the biological descent of all human beings from a common and first ancestor, Adam. Each refuses to affirm that the transgression of Adam marked the alpha point of sin and evil into humanity. Each functionally understands sin and evil to be a given of human existence. Each declines to understand death on the judicial and penal terms on which the New Testament writers, and especially the apostle Paul, understand death.

Second, the proponents of theistic evolution whom we have surveyed advance understandings of sin and death that strike at the integrity of the biblical gospel. All agree that sin pervades present human experience, and some will find ways to trace the universality of human sin to Adam. Such explanations, however, are invariably vague and imprecise.

We are left wondering how and under what circumstances a person becomes a sinner. Furthermore, death is presumed to be a standing and perennial part of the human experience. At the very least, the biblical connection between sin and death is left without adequate explanation.

Such imprecision concerning sin and death cannot bode well for the gospel. The gospel, we have observed, comes to us in a particular redemptive-historical framework. The work of Christ is set forth and explicated in light of the work of the representative man, Adam. Christ presents the solution to our Adamic plight. But if our plight is other than what the New Testament writers represent it to be, then how can the gospel solution proffered by the New Testament writers be a solution to our genuine plight? On what basis can the church proclaim to the world a gospel that poses a solution to a nonexistent problem?

These questions underscore the fact that the New Testament writings cannot be accommodated to theistic evolution apart from transforming their teachings in a fundamental fashion. This observation in no way militates against Christians undertaking the hard and necessary work of participating in and engaging the broader scientific community. It is simply to say that underlying this engagement is a deep and perennial hermeneutical question: Will the regnant scientific consensus determine what the Bible may or may not say, or will the Bible be permitted to speak for itself?[176] We may be grateful that on the important matters before us—human origins, sin, death, and salvation—the Bible is not silent, and it speaks with clarity a message that is truly good news to the perishing.

---

176 See here the brief but perceptive hermeneutical reflections, to which I am indebted, of Gaffin, *No Adam, No Gospel*, 8–9.

4

Theistic Evolution Is Incompatible with Historical Christian Doctrine

Gregg R. Allison

Summary

Church leaders have historically been called upon to embrace and guard the orthodox position of the church on creation. This chapter develops the specific components of sound doctrine in the area of creation. It articulates the church's historical perspective and demonstrates how theistic evolution is incompatible with the consensus viewpoint. It briefly discusses the views of several more recent evangelical writers.

———

The thesis of this chapter is that theistic evolution is incompatible with doctrinal standards that have been required for church leadership, as those doctrinal standards have been developed throughout church history. At the heart of this matter is the conviction that church leaders are required to embrace sound doctrine, in accordance with Paul's insistence for an elder: "He must hold firm to the trustworthy word as taught, so that he may be able to give instruction in sound doctrine and also to rebuke those who contradict it" (Titus 1:9). Church leaders must steadfastly cherish sound doctrine for themselves, be competent to communicate sound doctrine to others through preaching and teaching (1 Tim. 3:2; 5:17), and be able to expose and refute false doctrine and silence its purveyors. While it is certainly true that all Christians bear the responsibility "to contend for the faith that was once for all delivered to the saints" (Jude 3), that grave duty falls especially on the shoulders of church leaders. Furthermore, as Jude noted in his day, the sound doctrine that is enjoined on leaders today comports well with the historical faith of the church.[1]

Held to doctrinal standards and responsible for the teaching and defense of those sound doctrines, church leaders are called upon to embrace and guard the orthodox position on creation. This chapter will develop the identity of that sound doctrine by articulating the church's historical perspective on creation and by demonstrating how theistic evolution is incompatible with this consensus view.

A. The Doctrinal Standard on Creation in the Early Church

The particular doctrinal standard that is at stake with regard to theistic evolution is the creedal affirmation or confessional statement in the first sentence of what is now commonly known as the Nicene Creed:

> I/We believe in one God, the Father Almighty, *maker of heaven and earth, and of all things visible and invisible.*[2]

Explicit in this credo is monotheism, divine omnipotence, and creation of all that exists (outside of God, of course), specifically the present world

---

1   Indeed, as argued elsewhere, such theological consensus should enjoy presumptive authority in the church (Gregg R. Allison, "The *Corpus Theologicum* of the Church and Presumptive Authority," in *Revisioning, Renewing, and Rediscovering the Triune Center: Essays in Honor of Stanley J. Grenz,* ed. Derek J. Tidball, Brian S. Harris, and Jason S. Sexton (Eugene, OR: Wipf & Stock, 2014), 319–42.

2   More precisely, this is identified as the Nicene-Constantinopolitan Creed (381). This formulation combined into one affirmation the two affirmations of the Creed of Nicaea (325). This earlier creed had affirmed that God the Father is "maker of all things *visible and invisible.*" It had further affirmed that the Son is the one "*by whom all things were made,* both which be in *heaven* and in *earth*" (emphases added).

but not limited to it, including all that is seen (e.g., dry land, seas, vegetation and trees of all kinds, the sun and the moon, fish and sea creatures and birds, amphibians and reptiles and land mammals, and human beings; Gen. 1:3–31) and all that is unseen (e.g., angels). It is this belief that the church from its earliest days has confessed as being the truth in regard to creation. The phrase "maker of heaven and earth" is a clear echo of Genesis 1:1, "In the beginning, God created the heavens and the earth," and the added specification that God is the "maker" of "all things visible" was uniformly understood in the early church to affirm God's direct creation of all the varieties of plants and animals on the earth. Yet this creedal affirmation contradicts the claim of theistic evolution that God was the "maker" only of the initial inanimate matter in the universe and that that matter, apart from divine guidance or intervention, eventually developed by purely natural processes into "all things visible."

Certainly, this early creed did not specifically address the issue of evolution in general or theistic evolution in particular. At the same time, it was not articulated in a vacuum. Indeed, it was formulated within a biblical-theological framework and against philosophical theories that challenged the belief.

Theologically, creation ex nihilo was affirmed over against the Platonic idea of the eternality of matter. Tatian underscored, "Matter is not, like God, without beginning, nor, as having no beginning, is of equal power with God; rather, it is begotten, and not produced by any other being, but brought into existence by the Framer of all things alone."[3] Theophilus reasoned,

> If God is uncreated and matter is uncreated, God is no longer, according to the Platonists' own thinking, the Creator of all things, nor, so far as their opinions hold, is the monarchy [God is the first and only principle] established. And what great thing is it if God made the world out of existing materials? For even a human artist, when he gets material from someone, makes out of it whatever he pleases.

3 Tatian, *Address to the Greeks* 5, in *Ante-Nicene Fathers* (*ANF*) 2:67.

> But the power of God is manifested in this, that out of things that are not, he makes whatever he pleases.[4]

Irenaeus expressed the church's belief in creation ex nihilo, explaining that God "himself called into being the substance of creation, when previously it had no existence."[5] Undergirding this belief was the divine character: God is self-sufficient; therefore "It cannot be said that God made the world for his own sake, since he can exist without the world, as he did before it was made."[6] Furthermore, he is omnipotent and wise; indeed, "The God of hosts . . . by his invisible and mighty power and by his great wisdom created the world."[7] And God is sovereign; thus, "he created all things not influenced by anyone but according to his own free will."[8] The early church thus appealed to divine aseity (God's self-sufficiency or independence), omnipotence, wisdom, and sovereignty in its affirmation of creation ex nihilo.

Biblically, the silence of Scripture on how God created the heavens and the earth implied creation ex nihilo. Noting that in Genesis 1, "whenever anything is made out of anything, [the Holy Spirit] mentions both the thing that is made and the thing of which it is made,"[9] Tertullian concluded,

> God, when producing other things out of things which had been already made, indicates them by the prophet [Moses], and tells us what he has produced from such and such a source. . . . If the Holy Spirit took upon himself so great a concern for our instruction, that

---

4   Theophilus, *Theophilus to Autolycus* 2.4, in *ANF* 2:95.

5   Irenaeus, *Against Heresies* 2.10.4, in *ANF* 1:370; cf. Tertullian, *The Prescription against Heretics*, 13, in *ANF* 3:249.

6   Lactantius, *Divine Institutes* 7.4, in *ANF* 7:198.

7   Shepherd of Hermas, *Vision* 1.3 (3.4), in *ANF* 1:10.

8   Irenaeus, *Against Heresies* 2.1.1, in *ANF* 1:359. Cf. Clement's "the sheer exercise of his [God's] will" (Clement of Alexandria, *Exhortation to the Heathen* 4, in *ANF* 2:189–90).

9   Examples include Genesis 1:11–12 (the land brought forth vegetation, plants, and fruit trees after their own kinds), Genesis 1:20–21 (the seas brought forth living creatures and the sky brought forth living creatures according to their own kinds), and Genesis 1:24 (the earth brought forth living creatures according to their own kinds).

we might know from what everything was produced, would he not in like manner have kept us well informed about both the heaven and the earth, by indicating for us what it was that he made them of, if their original consisted of any material substance? . . . He confirms (by that silence our assertion) that they were produced out of nothing. "In the beginning," then, "God made the heaven and the earth."[10]

Furthermore, Christian writers often affirmed (though never put into creedal confession) that this creation out of nothing took place in six literal days in the not too distant past. For example, Methodius affirmed that God created "heaven and earth, and the things which are in them, in six days," and that "the creation of the world in six days was still recent."[11] Though not all early Christians interpreted Genesis 1 literally (Origen, for example, did not[12]), most did, taking the six days of creation as also indicative of how long the created world would exist. Relying on the biblical phrase "a day with the Lord is like a thousand years" (2 Pet. 3:8), Irenaeus calculated, "In as many days as this world was made, in so many thousand years it shall be concluded. . . . For the day of the Lord is as a thousand years; and in six days created things were completed. It is evident, therefore, that they will come to an end at the sixth thousand year [mark]."[13] From this reasoning, many in the early church considered the creation to be not very old, having taken place in the not too distant past.[14]

10 Tertullian, *Against Hermogenes* 22, in *ANF* 3:490.

11 Methodius, *The Banquet of the Ten Virgins* 8.11 and 7.5, in *ANF* 6:339 and 6:333. Basil the Great understood the days of creation as twenty-four-hour periods (Basil the Great, *The Hexaemeron*, Homily 2.8, in *Nicene and Post-Nicene Fathers*, Series 2 [*NPNF²*] 8:64).

12 Origen, *First Principles* 4.1.16, in *ANF* 4:365. Rather than embracing a literal interpretation of Genesis 1, Origen spiritualized the creation account (as he did the rest of Scripture) and promoted the strange idea that God originally created an invisible spiritual world (Gen. 1:1). Following the fall of rational creatures that inhabited this spiritual world, God created the material, visible world (Gen. 1:2–31).

13 Irenaeus, *Against Heresies* 5.28.3, in *ANF* 1:557. Cf. *Letter of Barnabas* 15, in *ANF* 1:146–47; Hippolytus, *Fragments from Daniel* 2.4–5, in *ANF* 5:179. Some early Christians tacked on the Sabbath day to these calculations, resulting in the conviction that the span of the world's existence was seven thousand years (Cyprian, *Treatise* 11.11, in *ANF* 5:503).

14 This literal, historical reading of Genesis 1 stands at odds with Denis Alexander's position: "Figurative and theological understandings of Genesis 1 were the dominant approach to the text

This doctrine of creation, formulated within this biblical-theological framework, was set in opposition to several prevailing philosophical theories that challenged the belief.[15] Important for our discussion was the challenge of the atomic theory: This was the view that all life had originated by the chance collision of atoms in the unlimited void of the universe.[16] Origen described Celsus's version of this theory as affirming that

> a certain fortuitous concurrence [an accidental collision] of atoms gave birth to qualities so diverse that it was owing [due] to chance that so many kinds of plants, trees, and herbs resemble one another, that no disposing reason [the infinite mind of God] gave existence to them, and that they do not derive their origin from an understanding that is beyond all admiration.[17]

---

among both Jewish and Christian commentators until at least into the fourteenth century" (Denis Alexander, *Creation or Evolution: Do We Have to Choose?*, 2nd ed., rev. and updated (Oxford and Grand Rapids, MI: Monarch, 2014), 185. In support of his view, Alexander appeals to Origen and Augustine. Certainly, Origen applied an allegorical hermeneutic to Genesis 1, but this approach also led him to postulate the creation of an invisible, spiritual world prior to the creation of this present spatio-temporal world, a position that no one in the church's history has embraced. Augustine also used a figurative hermeneutic in interpreting Genesis 1, but again, Alexander's appeal to this approach neglects another important matter. Like (nearly?) all the pastors and theologians of the early church, Augustine "believed in a fairly recent creation and explicitly warned against accepting the view that the world is old": "They are deceived, too, by those highly untrue documents that profess to give the history of many thousand years. If we calculate by the sacred writers, however, we find that not six thousand years have already passed" (Augustine, *The City of God*, 12.10, in *Nicene and Post-Nicene Fathers*, Series 1, 2:210; cited in Gregg R. Allison, *Historical Theology: An Introduction to Christian Doctrine* (Grand Rapids, MI: Zondervan, 2011), 259). In other words, while adopting figurative and spiritual applications for the early chapters of Genesis, Augustine did not deny that the events recorded in Genesis actually happened. He simply added figurative and spiritual applications to the historical record.

15   The Platonic idea of the eternality of the universe has already been discussed above. Another false theory involved the idea of a demiurge, an emanation from God that possessed sufficient spiritual nature to bring something into existence and sufficient material nature to create a material world. By means of this demiurge, the supreme deity, being spiritual and thus good, was able to create the world, which is material and thus evil (Irenaeus, *Against Heresies* 2.1.5, in *ANF* 1:360).

16   The concept of "atoms" as used in these theories was not the scientifically developed idea—the smallest unit of a chemical element, consisting of neutrons, protons, and electrons—common today. Rather, "atoms," as the basic elements of life, were the smallest, solid, distinct, indivisible, and invisible entities that existed.

17   Origen, *Against Celsus* 4.75, in *ANF* 4:531.

This atomic theory postulated that the accidental collision of small elements resulted in the world as it is today, completely apart from the infinite mind of God directing those atoms. The early church stood firmly against this theory: "We Christians, however, who are devoted to the worship of the only God, who created these things, feel grateful for them to him who made them."[18] This atomic theory that the church rejected bears striking similarities to some aspects of contemporary theistic evolution theories.

From this brief survey of the early church's development of its doctrine of creation, several themes stand out:

1. There is only one God who alone is eternal, self-sufficient, omnipotent, wise, and sovereign. This affirmation contradicts the idea of the eternality of matter.
2. This God created the universe and everything in it out of nothing. Scripture at least implies creation ex nihilo. The extensiveness of divine creation is all-encompassing: all visible things, including the sun, moon, stars, land, seas, trees, fish, birds, animals, and human beings; and all invisible things, like the angelic realm.
3. Divine creation took place in six literal days in the not too distant past.
4. The notion of an undirected process—a random collision of already existing elements—fortuitously resulting in the origin and development of the vast diversity of living beings currently in existence was strongly denounced and considered absurd.

This was the doctrine of creation that the early Christians embraced and defended. It was enshrined in the first article of one of its earliest

---

18 Ibid. Cf. Minucius Felix, who considered the atomic theory to be rationally absurd: "they who deny that this furniture [existing reality] of the whole world was perfected by the divine reason, and assert that it was heaped together by certain fragments casually adhering to each other, seem to me not to have either mind or sense, or, in fact, even sight itself. For what can possibly be so manifest, so confessed, and so evident, when you lift your eyes up to heaven, and look into the things which are below and around, than that there is some deity of most excellent intelligence, by whom all nature is inspired, is moved, is nourished, is governed?" (Minucius Felix, *The Octavius* 17, in *ANF* 4:182).

and most widely influential creeds, popularly known as the Nicene Creed: "maker of heaven and earth, and of all things visible and invisible."

But there is more.

Another important aspect of this creed is what its second article affirms. It expresses belief in the

> Lord Jesus Christ, the only begotten Son of God . . . *by whom all things were made*; who for us men and for our salvation came down from heaven and was incarnate of the Holy Spirit and of the Virgin Mary and made man; was crucified . . . suffered and was buried . . . rose again . . . and ascended into heaven . . . and shall come again . . .

Formulated against the Arian heresy, which denied the divinity of the second person of the Trinity, this article offered compelling evidence for the Son's deity: his role as agent in the creation of the world. As Creator along with the Father, the Son is fully God, as is the Father. Moreover, the Son's work of creation and his work of salvation go hand in hand. As Creator of the universe and Savior of humanity, the Son is fully God. The Creator-Savior link is crucial: "The one who became incarnate to save the world was none other than the one who had created the world in the first place."[19] Thus, the church warned, "A man is altogether irreligious and a stranger to the truth if he does not say that Christ the Savior is also the Maker of all things."[20] Accordingly, to the above summary of the early church's doctrine of creation is added,

5. The creation of the world and "all things" in it is evidence for the deity of the Son of God, whose work of creation and work of salvation are linked together. The Creator is also the Savior, and vice versa.

---

19 Allison, *Historical Theology*, 259.

20 Amphilochius, *Fragment* 16, cited in Jaroslav Pelikan, *The Christian Tradition: A History of the Development of Doctrine*, 5 vols. (Chicago and London: University of Chicago Press, 1971–1991), 1:204–5.

Thus, the early church affirmed that God the Father created, out of nothing, the heavens and the earth and all that is visible and invisible, through God the Son, in six days, a few thousand years ago.[21]

In addition to the doctrine of creation, the early church affirmed its belief in divine providence, or God's continuous operation to sustain in existence and direct everything that he created. Divine providence applies to the physical universe, as Clement of Rome affirmed:

> The heavens move at God's direction and obey him in peace. Day and night complete the course assigned by him, neither hindering the other. The sun and the moon and the choirs of stars circle in harmony within the courses assigned to them, according to his direction, without any deviation at all. . . . The seasons, spring and summer and autumn and winter, give way in succession, one to the other, in peace.[22]

The same providence applies to the angelic and human realms.[23] Such control means, according to Origen,

> Of those events that happen to men, none occur by accident or chance, but in accordance with a plan so carefully considered, and so stupendous, that it does not overlook even the number of hairs on a person's head. . . . And the plan of this providential government extends even to caring for the sale of two sparrows for a penny.[24]

Thus, the early church affirmed both God's creation of "all things visible and invisible" and his providential sustaining and ordering of

---

21 As for the relative silence of Scripture on the role of the Holy Spirit in creation, see Gregory of Nyssa, *On the Holy Spirit against the Followers of Macedonius*, NPNF[2] 5:319–20.

22 Clement of Rome, *Letter of the Romans to the Corinthians* 20, cited in Michael Holmes, *The Apostolic Fathers: Greek Texts and English Translations* (Grand Rapids, MI: Baker, 1999), 53; cf. *ANF* 1:10.

23 Irenaeus, *Against Heresies*, 5.22.2, in *ANF* 1:551.

24 Origen, *First Principles*, 2.11.5, in *ANF* 4:299. The text has been changed to make it clearer. His biblical allusions are to Matthew 10:29–30.

the creation. But it never collapsed or confused these two divine works, as do some contemporary versions of theistic evolution.

B. The Later Catholic and Protestant Developments of the Doctrinal Standards on Creation

This doctrine of creation (along with the doctrine of providence) continued to be the belief of the church in the medieval era and in the Reformation and post-Reformation periods.

Additions to this basic framework included the role of the Holy Spirit in the work of creation,[25] continuing rejection of theories that creation came about by chance,[26] ongoing affirmation of exhaustive divine providence,[27] strengthening the biblical basis for creation ex nihilo,[28] and application of the doctrine in terms of the proper human use of created things.[29] For example, influential Catholic theologian Thomas Aquinas affirmed that God alone creates, and he rejected the idea that the creation itself possesses the ability to create or develop other living realities:

> [S]ome have supposed that although creation is the proper act of the universal cause [God], still some inferior cause acting by the power of the first cause, can create. And thus [the philosopher] Avicenna asserted that the first separate substance created by God created another after itself, and the substance of the world and its soul; and that the substance of the world creates the matter of inferior bodies [creatures]. And in the same manner [Peter Lombard] says . . . that

---

25 Thomas Aquinas, *Summa Theologica*, pt. 1, q. 45, art. 6; Martin Luther, *Lectures on Genesis: Chapters 1–5*, in *Luther's Works*, ed. Jaroslav Pelikan, Hilton C. Oswald, and Helmut T. Lehmann, 55 vols. (St. Louis: Concordia, 1955–1986), 1:1–9.

26 Thomas Aquinas, *Summa Theologica*, pt. 1, q. 1, art. 2. For Aquinas, if the world came about by chance, the existence of God could not be proven by the cosmological argument, which demonstrates God's existence by cause (God) and effect (the world).

27 Ibid., pt. 1, q. 22; q. 103; q. 104.

28 John Calvin, *Commentaries on the First Book of Moses Called Genesis*, vol. 1, trans. John King (repr., Grand Rapids, MI: Baker, 2005), 70.

29 John Calvin, *Institutes of the Christian Religion*, 3.10.1–2, in *Library of Christian Classics* 20:719–21.

God can communicate to a creature the power of creating, so that the latter can create ministerially, not by its own power.[30]

Aquinas rejected this idea because only the first cause, God, as absolute being, possesses the power of creating, which is impossible for created things. His position stands against theistic evolution views that attribute creative power to matter and its development by purely natural processes.

In the Protestant churches after the Reformation, while the confessions of faith and catechisms carefully articulated the many differences between Protestant doctrines and Roman Catholic doctrines (e.g., Scripture and Tradition, justification, Mary), the doctrine of creation (and providence) was not one of those fault lines. The Augsburg Confession of Faith,[31] the Heidelberg Catechism,[32] and the Second Helvetic Confession,[33] for example, briefly restate the traditional view, which was not a matter of controversy.

At the same time, these Protestant confessions and catechisms expanded to include specific affirmations not previously incorporated into the church's doctrinal standards. These detailed confessional elements included angels, Adam and Eve, the fall, original sin, death, and more about divine providence.

1. The Creation of Angelic and Human Beings

To the general profession of divine creation of all things, Protestant doctrinal standards added details about the types of created beings. The Belgic Confession of Faith, for example, affirmed,

---

30 Thomas Aquinas, *Summa Theologica*, pt. 1, q. 45, art. 5. Aquinas's reference to Peter Lombard is *Sentences* 4.D.5.

31 Augsburg Confession, pt. 1, art. 1: God is "the creator and preserver of all things, visible and invisible."

32 Heidelberg Catechism, q. 26: The confession "I believe in God the Father, Almighty, Maker of heaven and earth" means "the eternal Father of our Lord Jesus Christ . . . of nothing made heaven and earth, *with all that is in them* . . . [and] likewise upholds and governs the same by his eternal counsel and providence."

33 Second Helvetic Confession, 7: "GOD CREATED ALL THINGS. This good and almighty God created *all things*, both *visible* and *invisible*, by his co-eternal Word, and preserves them by his co-eternal Spirit."

We believe that the Father, by the Word, that is, by his Son, has created of nothing, the heaven, the earth, *and all creatures*, as it seemed good unto him, *giving unto every creature its being, shape, form*, and several offices to serve its Creator. . . . He also created the angels good. . . . We believe that God *created man out of the dust of the earth*, and made and formed him after his own image and likeness, *good, righteous, and holy*, capable in all things to will, agreeably to the will of God.[34]

Though the church had always believed that "all things in heaven and earth, visible and invisible" were created by God, this belief was specified as including the angels, all of whom were originally created good, and the first man, Adam, who was created out of the dust of the ground (Gen. 2:7) in the divine image and likeness (Gen. 1:26–27) and endowed with uprightness. Similarly, the Westminster Confession of Faith expressed the historical doctrine: "It pleased God the Father, Son, and Holy Spirit, . . . in the beginning, to create, or make of nothing, the world, *and all things therein*, whether visible or invisible, in the space of six days; and all very good."[35] It continued,

After God had made all other creatures, he created man, male and female, with reasonable and immortal souls, endued with knowledge, *righteousness, and true holiness*, after his own image; having the law of God written in their hearts, and power to fulfill it: and yet under a possibility of transgressing, being left to the liberty of their own will, which was subject unto change. Beside this law written in their hearts, they received a command, not to eat of the tree of the knowledge of good and evil; which while they kept, they were happy in their communion with God, and had dominion over the creatures.[36]

34 Belgic Confession of Faith, 12, 14. Italics added to emphasize differences with theistic evolution.
35 Westminster Confession of Faith, 4.1. Italics added to emphasize differences with theistic evolution.
36 Ibid., 4.2. Italics added to emphasize differences with theistic evolution. Cf. Second Helvetic Confession, 7.

This doctrinal standard specified belief in God's creation of Adam and Eve in the divine image as complex moral beings (consisting of both body and soul, and endowed with a sense of right and wrong) who were created righteous and holy and given the responsibility to obey the Edenic command. Many advocates of theistic evolution do not affirm these beliefs about Adam and Eve.

2. The Creation of Adam and Eve versus the Pre-Adamite Theory

The post-Reformers were even more specific about the beginning of the human race as a divine act, affirming the creation of Adam and Eve as the first human beings and as the progenitors of the entire human race. This declaration was necessary as a response to the "pre-Adamite" theory, first articulated in 1655–1656 by Isaac Le Peyrère in his *Prae-Adamitae* and *Men before Adam*.[37] His theory asserted that Adam was not the first human being created by God, but the first person of the Jewish people. Indeed, he claimed that the Gentiles existed long before Adam and the Jewish race:

> The Gentiles are diverse from the Jews in race and origin; the Jews were formed by God in Adam, the Gentiles were created before, on the same day as other animate beings. . . . [T]he origin of the *latter* [the Gentiles] is described in Gen. 1, that of the former [the Jews] in Gen. 2. . . . Gentiles are many ages before the Jewish nation, and, by race and nature, diverse from the same, and survivors of the Noachian flood of the Jews. . . . [Accordingly], the epoch of the creation of the world should not be dated from that beginning, which is commonly imagined in Adam, but must be sought for still further back, and from ages very remote in the past.[38]

---

37 Isaac Le Peyrère, *Prae-Adamitae sive exercitatio . . . capitis quinti Epistolae D. Pauli ad Romanos* (Latin, 1655) and *A Theological Systeme upon That Presupposition That Men Were before Adam* (English, 1656).

38 Isaac Le Peyrère, quoted by John Andrew Quenstedt, *Theologia Didactico-Polemica*, 2 vols. (1685), 1:543, in Schmid, *Doctrinal Theology of the Evangelical Lutheran Church,* trans. Charles Hay and Henry Jacobs (Minneapolis: Augsburg, 1961 [1875]), 165. Quenstedt cites a section of Le Peyrère's *Prae-Adamitae*.

In this way, Isaac Le Peyrère challenged the historical view that Adam and Eve were the precursors of the entire human race.

The post-Reformers vigorously refuted this pre-Adamite theory. Positively, the influential Lutheran theologian John Quenstedt explained, "Adam, framed by God on the sixth day of the first hexahemeron [six-day creation], is the first of all men, and the parent of the entire human race, throughout the whole globe."[39] Biblical support included Genesis 2:7; Luke 3:23–38; Acts 17:26; Romans 5:12; and 1 Corinthians 15:22, 45–48. Further support, according to Reformed theologian Francis Turretin, was the "constant opinion thus far not only among Christians, but also among the Jews (yea even among the Mohammedans [Muslims] themselves) . . . that Adam was created in the beginning of the world and was the first man, the father not only of the Jews, but also of all men universally."[40]

Negatively, the pre-Adamite theory was critiqued from several angles: First, Turretin argued,

> if innumerable men had been created before Adam, there would have been no need of a repeated creation of men from the dust (since ordinary generation would have been abundantly sufficient). And it cannot be said that there could not have been found for man a help-meet [helper, i.e., Eve] similar to himself, if myriads of women already existed; nor would man have been alone, as is said in Gen. 2:18.[41]

Second, the theory failed in regard to the first woman created, Eve (Gen. 2:18–25), "so named because she was 'the mother of all living' (Gen. 3:20), which would be untrue if only the Jewish nation sprang from her."[42]

Thus, the leading theologians of the church had a ready answer to Le Peyrère's pre-Adamite theory, and they defended the traditional

---

39 Quenstedt, in ibid.

40 Francis Turretin, *Institutes of Elenctic Theology*, ed. James T. Dennison Jr., trans. George Musgrave Giger, 3 vols. (Phillipsburg, NJ: P&R, 1997), 1:457.

41 Ibid., 1:460.

42 Ibid., 1:458. Cf. Caspar Brochmann, *Universae Theologiae Systema* (1633), 239; in Schmid, *Doctrinal Theology of the Evangelical Lutheran Church*, 165.

view that Adam and Eve were the parents of the entire human race.[43] This dismissed pre-Adamite theory bears similarities to the view of theistic evolutionists today that there were human beings on Earth for thousands of years before Adam and Eve.

3. The Relationship between Creation, Death, and the Fall

In its wrestling with this wrong view, the church also had to face the issue of natural death before Adam and Eve's fall into sin. Le Peyrère had made a distinction between natural sin and death, on the one hand, and legal sin and death, on the other hand. The former existed among "the Gentile Preadamites who were liable to sin and natural death from their innate corruptible and mortal nature."[44] The latter was introduced only after Adam and Eve, to whom God had given the prohibition in the garden of Eden, disobeyed that law, thus falling into legal sin and death.

Turretin roundly denounced Le Peyrère's novel idea:

> [S]in cannot be called natural without impinging upon God himself the author of nature; nor ought death to be called natural, as if man was necessarily to die even if he had not sinned. . . . False also is the pretense that there can be any sin which is not against law, since it is nothing else than lawlessness (*anomia*). It is also false that there can be a death which is not legal, since from no other source than from the power of the law and by its sanction was it ordained that man should die once.[45]

Accordingly, the Reformers and post-Reformers emphasized the origination of the human race with Adam and Eve and their tragic fall into sin.

43 To take a contemporary example, the Reformation rejection of the pre-Adamite theory is still reflected in Wheaton College's Statement of Faith: "WE BELIEVE that God directly created Adam and Eve, the historical parents of the entire human race." Available at "Statement of Faith and Educational Purpose," *Wheaton College*, accessed September 12, 2016, http://www.wheaton .edu/About-Wheaton/Statement-of-Faith-and-Educational-Purpose.

44 Le Peyrère, quoted in Turretin, *Institutes of Elenctic Theology*, 1:459–60.

45 Turretin, *Institutes of Elenctic Theology*, 1:460.

To this was added the belief that original sin is passed down from Adam and Eve to their posterity, the entirety of the human race. Not only were Adam and Eve the first human beings; they were also those whose disobedience wreaked havoc for all human beings after them.

The Belgic Confession exemplifies this doctrinal standard. It first treats Adam's disobedience to the Edenic law:

> [T]he commandment of life, which he had received, he transgressed; and by sin separated himself from God, who was his true life, having corrupted his whole nature; whereby he made himself liable to corporal and spiritual death. And being thus become wicked, perverse, and corrupt in all his ways, he has lost all his excellent gifts.[46]

It then addresses original sin:

> Through the disobedience of Adam, original sin is extended to all mankind; which is a corruption of the whole nature, and a hereditary disease, wherewith infants themselves are infected even in their mother's womb, and which produces in man all sorts of sin, being in him as a root thereof; and therefore is so vile and abominable in the sight of God, that it is sufficient to condemn all mankind."[47]

Similarly, the Westminster Confession of Faith addressed the originating sin of Adam and Eve—"our first parents, being seduced by the subtlety and temptations of Satan, sinned, in eating the forbidden fruit"—and the original sin that devastates their progeny, the human race:

> By this sin they fell from their original righteousness and communion with God, and so became dead in sin, and wholly defiled in all the parts and faculties of soul and body. They being the root of all

46 Belgic Confession of Faith, 14.
47 Ibid., 15.

mankind, the guilt of this sin was imputed; and the same death in sin, and corrupted nature, conveyed to all their posterity descending from them by ordinary generation.[48]

The Lutheran theologians concurred, with David Friedrich Hollaz representing their view:

> Adam and Eve were substitutes for the whole human race, inasmuch as they ought to be regarded as both the *natural* (i.e., *seminal*) and also the *moral* source of the human race, namely, of the entire progeny in nature and grace. . . . For our first parents were then considered not only as the first individuals of the human race, but also as the true root, stock, and source of the whole human race, which in them could both stand and fall.[49]

Accordingly, the post-Reformation Protestant church insisted on the introduction of both sin and death into the originally good creation through Adam and Eve, and the transmission of original sin from them to their progeny, all subsequent human beings. This position refutes a view similar to the theistic evolution proposal by John Walton that, prior to Adam and Eve, human beings were committing sinful deeds and were dying but "they were not being held accountable" for their sin.[50]

4. The Creation and Divine Providence

Like the early church and the medieval church, Protestant churches continued to affirm God's ongoing providential care of all that he created, yet the acts of initial creation and subsequent providential care were continually distinguished. Thomas Aquinas earlier had formulated

---

48 Westminster Confession of Faith, 6.2–3. Cf. New Hampshire Confession of Faith, 3.
49 Quenstedt, *Theologia Didactico-Polemica*, 2.53; in Schmid, *Doctrinal Theology of the Evangelical Lutheran Church*, 240, emphasis original.
50 John H. Walton, *The Lost World of Adam and Eve: Genesis 2–3 and the Human Origins Debate* (Downers Grove, IL: InterVarsity, 2015), 155.

the basic idea of divine government, or God's rulership and direction of the creation in accordance with his eternal purpose:

> In government there are two things to be considered; the design of government, which is providence itself; and the execution of the design. As to the design of government, God governs all things immediately; whereas in its execution, he governs some things by means of others.[51]

The Westminster Confession of Faith continued this idea. Specifically, it linked God's meticulous, exhaustive providence to his wisdom, holiness, omniscience, and sovereign decree ("the free and immutable counsel of his own will"; Eph. 1:11) while acknowledging that such divine direction and government occurs "according to the nature of second causes." Thus, God uses means (e.g., the laws of physics and genetic codes) to carry out his providential care of all things. Still, one of the effects of divine providence is that God's image-bearers praise his glorious "wisdom, power, justice, goodness, and mercy"; that is, the character of God is revealed and recognized from his creative handiwork.[52] The Belgic Confession emphasized the comfort supplied by such providence:

> We believe that the same God, after he had created all things, did not forsake them, or give them up to fortune or chance, but that he rules and governs them according to his holy will, so that nothing happens in this world without his appointment. . . . This doctrine affords us unspeakable consolation, since we are taught thereby that nothing can befall us by chance, but by the direction of our most gracious and heavenly Father; who watches over us with a paternal care, keeping all creatures so under his power, that not a hair of our head (for they are all numbered), nor a sparrow, can fall to the ground, without the will of our Father, in whom we do entirely trust; being

---

51 Thomas Aquinas, *Summa Theologica*, pt. 1, q. 103, art. 6.
52 Westminster Confession of Faith, 5.1–3.

persuaded, that he so restrains the devil and all our enemies, that without his will and permission, they cannot hurt us. And therefore we reject that damnable error of the Epicureans, who say that God regards nothing, but leaves all things to chance.[53]

In this way, divine providence, by which God sustains in existence everything that he created and directs all things toward his eternal goal, was given detailed attention in the Reformation and post-Reformation period. But, in contrast to contemporary theories of theistic evolution, this providential work of God, by which he maintains the properties of all created things, was never confused with or used as the explanation for the initial work of God in creating all things.

With these details spelled out, it is now possible to summarize the Protestant doctrinal standards as specifying belief in the following tenets:

1. God created ex nihilo all things in heaven and earth, both visible and invisible, including human beings in the divine image and angels.

2. Adam and Eve were created as the first human beings and as the progenitors of the entire human race.

3. As originally created, Adam and Eve were upright moral beings governed by the Edenic command and charged with the responsibility to exercise dominion over the rest of the created order.

4. By disobeying this Edenic command, Adam and Eve fell into sin. They became guilty before God and thoroughly corrupted in nature, and their punishment included both spiritual and physical death, the first incidence of such death in the human race.

5. Because of solidarity with Adam and Eve, their progeny—each and every member of the human race—enters into life loaded down with guilt and characterized by corruption of nature. This is the state of original sin.

---

53 Belgic Confession of Faith, 13. The biblical allusions are to Matthew 10:29–30.

6. Not only did God initially create all things in heaven and earth, both visible and invisible; he also exercises providential care and control over all created things. Such meticulous, exhaustive providence does not allow for randomness, accident, chance, fortune, luck, and fate. On the contrary, while using secondary means to accomplish his eternal purpose, God directs all created things teleologically, ruling out all notions of undirected processes at work in this world.

C. Contemporary Doctrinal Standards on Creation

Ever since the outset of the modern period, the doctrinal standards that have been widely, if not unanimously, held by churches have come under fierce attack. The doctrine of creation is no exception; indeed, it can be argued that this belief has been the target of extreme criticism. Moreover, many churches/denominations that have formulated or reformulated their doctrinal standards in the modern period have expressed their beliefs without great detail. Again, the doctrine of creation exemplifies this trend. It means that the doctrinal standards about creation of many contemporary churches/denominations are very minimal affirmations, if they even appear.

For example, the Baptist Faith and Message (2000) of the Southern Baptist Convention, which states that God is "the Creator, [Redeemer], Preserver, and Ruler of the universe," expresses its belief about God the Father: "God as Father reigns with providential care over His universe, His creatures, and the flow of the stream of human history according to the purposes of His grace."[54] This doctrinal statement also affirms a basic belief in the special creation of human beings as divine image-bearers and their fall into sin.[55] The foundational documents of the United Methodist Church (with the Evangelical United Brethren Church) are similarly brief: The Articles of Religion acknowledge that God is "the maker and preserver of all things, both

---

54 The Baptist Faith and Message, II and IIA. The title "Redeemer," and the statement titled "God the Father," are not found in the 1925 version of the Baptist Faith and Message.
55 The Baptist Faith and Message, III.

visible and invisible."[56] The Confession of Faith states that God is "the Creator, Sovereign and Preserver of all things visible and invisible."[57] The Statement of Fundamental Truths of the General Council of the Assemblies of God affirms belief in God as "the Creator of heaven and earth."[58] It makes no affirmation about divine providence, and has only a brief statement about the fall into sin.[59] The Evangelical Free Church Statement of Faith affirms that God is the "Creator of all things" and that he "created Adam and Eve in His image."[60] In some statements of faith, the issue does not even appear. For example, the Evangelical Covenant Church does not address the doctrine of creation; nor does the United Church of Christ.

There are exceptions to this trend. For example, the Lutheran Church Missouri Synod has an explicit statement affirming the traditional doctrinal standard on creation and repudiating evolutionary theory:

> We teach that God has created heaven and earth, and that in the manner and in the space of time recorded in the Holy Scriptures, especially Gen. 1 and 2, namely, by His almighty creative word, and in six days. We reject every doctrine which denies or limits the work of creation as taught in Scripture. In our days it is denied or limited by those who assert, ostensibly in deference to science, that the world came into existence through a process of evolution; that is, that it has, in immense periods of time, developed more or less of itself. Since no man was present when it pleased God to create the world, we must look for a reliable account of creation to God's own record, found in God's own book, the Bible. We accept God's own record with full confidence and confess with Luther's *Catechism*, "I believe that God has made me and all creatures."[61]

56 The Articles of Religion of the Methodist Church, article 1.
57 Confession of Faith of the Evangelical United Brethren Church, article 1.
58 Statement of Fundamental Truths of the General Council of the Assemblies of God, 2.
59 Ibid., 4.
60 Evangelical Free Church Statement of Faith, 1, 3.
61 A Brief Statement of the Doctrinal Position of the Missouri Synod (1932), 5. The citation is from Martin Luther's Small Catechism, II. The Creed; The First Article, Of Creation; Answer.

This Lutheran statement continues with a denial of an evolutionary development of human beings—"We teach that the first man was not brutelike nor merely capable of intellectual development"—and an affirmation of God's creation of human beings in his image and of their tragic fall into sin.[62]

Another exception is the Presbyterian Church in America, which has the Westminster Confession of Faith for its doctrinal standards on creation, providence, Adam and Eve, the fall, and sin.[63]

With this amount of variation among churches and denominations, it is difficult to generalize about the compatibility or incompatibility of theistic evolution with doctrinal standards throughout Protestant churches, or even evangelical Protestant churches. This chapter's approach, however, which considers this matter from the historical position of the church, finds that *theistic evolution is incompatible with all the historical doctrinal standards that address these specific questions.*[64]

D. The Incompatibility of Theistic Evolution with the Church's Doctrinal Standards

The incompatibility of these doctrinal standards and theistic evolution can be demonstrated with regard to two versions of theistic evolution.

1. Theistic Evolution, Version 1

According to the first version, theistic evolution is the view that God created matter and after that did not guide or intervene to cause any empirically detectable change in the natural behavior of matter until all living things had evolved by purely natural processes. This version's incompatibility with the church's doctrinal standards can be demon-

---

62 A Brief Statement of the Doctrinal Position of the Missouri Synod (1932), 6, 7.

63 Westminster Confession of Faith, 4–6.

64 Theistic evolution also encounters problems with the doctrine of the inerrancy of Scripture, as emphasized in the Chicago Statement on Biblical Inerrancy: Article 12: "**We affirm** that Scripture in its entirety is inerrant, being free from all falsehood, fraud or deceit. **We deny** that Biblical infallibility and inerrancy are limited to spiritual, religious, or redemptive themes, exclusive of assertions in the fields of history and science. We further deny that scientific hypotheses about earth history may properly be used to overturn the teaching of Scripture on creation and the flood." The last two sentences oppose theistic evolution (but make no claim about the age of the earth).

strated in three points: (1) Theistic evolution's affirmation that God created matter is, in itself, neither wrong nor controversial, but it does not go far enough. Such a view falls short of affirming, as the church has historically believed, that God created not only inanimate matter but also all visible things, including the sun, moon, stars, land, seas, trees, fish, birds, animals, and human beings; and all invisible things, like the angelic realm. God's creation, therefore, was not a creation of generic material but of specific kinds and varieties of creatures.

(2) Theistic evolution's view that, after creating matter, God did not guide or intervene to cause any empirically detectable changes in the natural behavior of matter, is in clear conflict with the church's historical position. It must be noted that only some varieties of theistic evolution deny that the process was directed.[65] Other types of theistic evolution, like that of Francis Collins, do not specify the nature of the evolutionary process, whether it is undirected or directed.[66] In both cases, however, the idea of an undirected evolutionary process that produces no detectable change in what exists, encounters three problems with the church's doctrinal standards.[67]

---

65 Stephen Meyer underscores this in the opening essay ("Philosophical and Scientific Introduction") in *Theistic Evolution: A Scientific, Philosophical, and Theological Critique*, edited by J. P. Moreland, Stephen C. Meyer, Christopher Shaw, Ann K. Gauger, and Wayne Grudem (Wheaton, IL: Crossway, 2017). He writes, "Some proponents of theistic evolution openly affirm that the evolutionary process is an unguided, undirected process. Kenneth Miller, a leading theistic evolutionist and author of *Finding Darwin's God*, has repeatedly stated in editions of his popular textbook [*Biology*] that 'evolution works without either plan or purpose. . . . Evolution is random and undirected.'" The passage cited by Meyer is from Kenneth R. Miller and Joseph S. Levine, *Biology* (Upper Saddle River, NJ: Prentice Hall, 1991, 1993, 1995, 1998, 2000), 658. In *Finding Darwin's God*, Miller further describes the process of evolution in these terms: random, undirected, and blind. (Kenneth R. Miller, *Finding Darwin's God: A Scientist's Search for Common Ground between God and Evolution* [New York: HarperCollins, 1999], 51, 102, 137, 145, 244).

66 Again, as Meyer notes in his opening essay ("Philosophical and Scientific Introduction"), "Nevertheless, most theistic evolutionists, including geneticist Francis Collins, perhaps the world's best-known proponent of the position, have been reluctant to clarify what they think about this important issue. In his book *The Language of God*, Collins makes clear his support for universal common descent. He also seems to assume the adequacy of standard evolutionary mechanisms but does not clearly say whether he thinks those mechanisms are directed or undirected—only that they 'could be' directed." See Francis Collins, *The Language of God* (New York: Free Press, 2006), 205.

67 The lack of affirmation of a directed process would face similar objections from those who hold to the historical doctrinal standards of the church.

First, the early church clearly denounced the idea of an undirected process by which the universe and everything in it came into existence. The church has traditionally considered as absurd the notion that random collisions of existing elements fortuitously resulted in the development of what currently exists. Though the atomic theory against which the early church argued and the contemporary theory of theistic evolution are not the same theory, the basic tenet that some type of natural process acted on random variation to unexpectedly produce what exists today is at the heart of both theories. The church's denunciation of the basic tenet of the earlier theory would seem to carry over to the contemporary theory.

Second, the concept of the universe developing by means of an undirected process like natural selection acting on random mutations does not provide support for the deity of Jesus Christ, as proved by his creation of all things visible and invisible, whom the church has historically proclaimed to be both Savior and Creator. The church has repeatedly affirmed that Christ's work of creation furnishes proof of his divine nature.

Third, the concept of the universe developing by means of an undirected process that does not give evidence of divine activity contradicts the church's historical position, based on Scripture (e.g., Rom. 1:18–25), that God's creative handiwork reveals and prompts praise for his power, divinity, care, omniscience, sovereignty, wisdom, goodness, and kindness.

(3) Theistic evolution's view that, after creating matter, God did not guide or intervene in the development of that matter until all living things had evolved by purely natural processes, is at odds with the church's doctrinal standards, for several reasons. First, this view introduces an internal inconsistency in the church's historical position that God created not only the visible realm but the invisible realm as well. The church has always affirmed that God created angels, who were originally morally good. But this was a direct supernatural act of God. It could possibly be postulated that God used two very different processes in creating visible things (through an evolutionary process)

and in creating invisible things (through some type of supernatural process). But such a divergent approach does not accord well with the church's doctrinal standards, which at least imply a similarity of processes (neither of which was natural) by which God (supernaturally) created these two distinct realms of creatures.

Second, and more significantly, the view of the evolution of the world by purely natural processes stands in contrast with the church's doctrinal standard that God created Adam and Eve as the first human beings and the progenitors of the whole human race. Theistic evolution holds to some theory of pre-Adamite human beings who preceded Adam and Eve. The church has historically denounced this view.

One problem that any pre-Adamite view faces is its conflict with Scripture (Gen. 2:7, 18–25; 3:20; Hosea 6:7; Luke 3:23–38; Acts 17:26; Rom. 5:12–21; 1 Cor. 15:22, 45–48; 1 Tim. 2:13–14). Another problem is that the viewpoint diverges from the church's affirmation of God's creation of Adam and Eve in his image as complex (material and immaterial), originally sinless, moral beings.

Still another problem is that any pre-Adamite position entails natural death in the human realm. In this case, pre-Adamite humans would have died natural deaths, with legal death—the penalty for the violation of a divine command—being first introduced with Adam and Eve's sin. The church has historically denounced this view.

A final problem encountered by any pre-Adamite theory is explaining the relationship between the originating sin of Adam and Eve—their fall from original uprightness through disobedience to the divine command—and the original sin passed on to all their progeny.[68] Purely natural processes and the existence of thousands (and, through eventual multiplication, millions or billions) of human beings who are not descended from Adam and Eve do not result in

---

68 All these problems with the pre-Adamite theory present similar problems for the viewpoint espoused by Dennis R. Venema and Scot McKnight in *Adam and the Genome: Reading Scripture after Genetic Science* (Grand Rapids, MI: Brazos, 2017). As the church has historically refuted the pre-Adamite theory of human origins, it should be troubled by the stance promoted by that book. It goes against the doctrinal standards historically required for church leadership.

moral accountability, universal guilt before God, corruption of human nature passed down from generation to generation, liability to suffer divine punishment, enmity with God, enslavement to sin, depravity and inability, and so forth.[69]

2. Theistic Evolution, Version 2

According to the second version,[70] theistic evolution is the view that "God creates all living things through Christ, including human beings in his image, making use of intentionally designed, actively sustained natural processes that scientists today study as evolution."[71] Thus, God not only acted initially to create the world, but he continues an active involvement throughout the development of all that exists. He over-sees the evolutionary processes like natural selection, speciation, and random mutations to ensure that they engender both non-living and

---

69   Attention may be drawn to a controversial aspect of the doctrinal standards: the church has his-torically affirmed creation in six literal days in the not too distant past, while many church leaders today hold to a day-age theory, intermittent day theory, framework (literary) hypothesis theory, or gap theory. They deny, therefore, a recent creation in six literal days. Without entering into the debate between young earth creationists and old earth creationists (a debate on which this book takes no position), the following points underscore that this intramural contest is in a different category than the debate about theistic evolution:

(1) Both the young earth position and the old earth position affirm divine creation and deny theistic evolution as it is defined in this volume. Both are creationist positions, not evolutionist positions, and therefore accord well with the church's doctrinal affirmation of creation.

(2) The disagreement over the meaning of the Hebrew word *yom* (day) in Genesis 1 is a debate about the meaning of only one word in Scripture and does not involve extrabiblical considerations such as random mutations, natural selection, and the like, or a denial of major Christian doctrines such as the specific creation of "all things visible and invisible," the special creation of Adam and Eve as the first human beings, Adam and Eve as initially sinless, the entrance of human death into the world through Adam's sin, and the initial goodness of God's entire creation.

(3) Although some historical creeds affirmed that God created all things in six days, none of them specify that these were literal twenty-four-hour days.

70   Some of this material is adapted from Gregg Allison, "Can Christians Believe in Evolution?" desiringgod.org (February 9, 2019); used by kind permission.

71   Deborah Haarsma, "A Flawed Mirror: A Response to the Book 'Theistic Evolution,'" BioLogos blogpost April 18, 2018. https://biologos.org/blogs/deborah-haarsma-the-presidents-notebook /a-flawed-mirror-a-response-to-the-book-theistic-evolution. This definition represents Haarsma's draft of "a one-sentence definition of evolutionary creation for a Christian audience" that she, as president of BioLogos, culled from "several evolutionary creation leaders, inside and outside of BioLogos," as she prepared a response to *Theistic Evolution*. Therefore, the definition seems to represent broadly the second version of theistic evolution or, as BioLogos prefers, evolutionary creationism.

living beings in accordance with the divine design. As compared with the first version, this second version of theistic evolution maintains that the evolutionary process was divinely directed.

Even with this second version, however, theistic evolution is incompatible with the church's doctrinal standards. An important element in this second version is the axiom of common ancestry. To take the example of human beings and chimpanzees (often considered by evolutionists to be our closest relatives), common ancestry means that if we go back about 300,000 generations, we will find an "ancient population (which was neither human nor chimpanzee) [that] split into two groups, and these groups were reproductively isolated. . . . Eventually the characteristics of each group were different enough for scientists to recognize them as different species." Importantly for this version of theistic evolution, "a similar story could be told for the ancestral lineage of any two species that ever lived."[72] Clearly, this version of the origin and development of species in general[73] and of human beings in particular[74]—even when infused with an appeal to divine direction and purpose—conflicts with the biblical account. Moreover, the historical church would never have agreed with this position.

72 BioLogos, "What Is Evolution?" https://biologos.org/common-questions/scientific-evidence/what -is-evolution/.

73 Specifically, "[r]egarding creation other than humans, evolutionary creationists [this second version of theistic evolution] believe that God created fish, birds, and land animals as directly as he created the oceans, dry land, and stars: making use of natural mechanisms that he designed and actively sustains" (Haarsma, "A Flawed Mirror"). This is a denial of God's specific and immediate (not mediated by natural processes) creation of fish, birds, and land animals, as Genesis 1 recounts. At the same time, creationists of all stripes agree that microevolution has occurred.

74 Haarsma continues: "Regarding the biological origin of Adam and Eve, it is true that evolutionary creationists cannot affirm the traditional *de novo* view of human origins (in which God miraculously creates the first pair roughly 10,000 years ago, with this pair as the sole genetic progenitors of all humans today), because there is abundant evidence in God's creation that the early humans were a population of at least several thousand individuals roughly 200,000 years ago" (ibid.). This is a denial of God's specific and immediate (not mediated by natural processes) creation of Adam and Eve, as Genesis 1–2 recounts. On this troubling position, see the following chapters in this present book: Wayne Grudem, "Theistic Evolution Undermines Twelve Creation Events and Several Crucial Christian Doctrines," 177–236 (esp. 182–218); John D. Currid, "Theistic Evolution Is Incompatible with the Teachings of the Old Testament," 29–72; and Guy Prentiss Waters, "Theistic Evolution is Incompatible with the Teachings of the New Testament," 73–124.

E. What about Evangelical Leaders Who Affirm Theistic Evolution?

What, then, should we make of pastors and other Christian leaders who embrace(d) theistic evolution? The following citations from several leaders are representative: (1) John Stott sought to wed belief in a literal Adam and Eve with some form of theistic evolution:

> But my acceptance of Adam and Eve as historical is not incompatible with my belief that several forms of pre-Adamic "hominid" may have existed for thousands of years previously. These hominids began to advance culturally. They made their cave drawings and buried their dead. It is conceivable that God created Adam out of one of them. You may call them *Homo erectus*. I think you may even call some of them *Homo sapiens*, for these are arbitrary scientific names. But Adam was the first *Homo divinus*, if I may coin a phrase, the first man to whom may be given the biblical designation "made in the image of God."[75]

(2) Tim Keller thinks "God guided some kind of process of natural selection," yet he also "reject[s] the concept of evolution as an All-encompassing Theory."[76] (3) Keller relies to a great degree on Derek Kidner's *Genesis*, a commentary in the Tyndale Old Testament Commentaries series.[77]

(4) C. S. Lewis is claimed by evolutionists and creationists alike, depending on whether appeal is made to Lewis's embrace of evolution in the *Problem of Pain* (1940) or to the letter he wrote in 1951 to Bernard Acworth, author of *This Progress: The Tragedy of Evolution*:

> I have read nearly the whole of *Evolution* and am glad you sent it. I must confess it has shaken me: not in my belief in evolution, which was of the vaguest and most intermittent kind, but in my belief that

---

75 John Stott, *Understanding the Bible*, expanded ed. (Grand Rapids, MI: Zondervan, 1999), 55–56.

76 Tim Keller, *The Reason for God: Belief in an Age of Skepticism* (New York: Penguin, 2008), 94.

77 Derek Kidner, *Genesis*, Tyndale Old Testament Commentaries (Downers Grove, IL: InterVarsity Press, 1967), 26–31.

the question was wholly unimportant. I wish I was younger. What inclines me now to think that you may be right in regarding it as *the* central and radical lie in the whole web of falsehood that now governs our lives, is not so much your arguments against it as the fanatical and twisted attitudes of its defenders.[78]

(5) Princeton theologian B. B. Warfield (1851–1921) is often claimed as a supporter of evolution.[79] However, while Warfield allowed that it was possible that God used some kind of evolutionary process for parts of creation, he never explicitly affirmed this as his personal belief. In addition, he did not allow for the possibility of human sin or death before Adam and Eve, or the possibility that Adam and Eve were not created as sinless human beings.[80]

What is to be made of the views of these Christian pastors and leaders? None of them explicitly embraced theistic evolution as this book defines it: the view that God created matter and after that did not guide or intervene to cause any empirically detectable change in the natural behavior of matter until all living things had evolved by purely natural processes. Indeed, at least some of them gave evidence of confusion over the nature of theistic evolution and/or expressed hesitation about it. Additionally, none of them denied that Adam and Eve were created in the image of God, that Adam and Eve were originally sinless, that all human beings have descended from Adam and Eve,[81] and that human death began as a result of Adam's sin.

---

78 C. S. Lewis, *The Collected Letters of C. S. Lewis*, ed. Walter Hooper, 3 vols. (San Francisco: HarperSanFrancisco, 2007), 3:138. See the detailed discussion of Lewis by Lewis scholar John G. West in "Darwin in the Dock: C. S. Lewis on Evolution," chapter 26 in *Theistic Evolution*.

79 See B. B. Warfield, *Evolution, Scripture, and Science: Selected Writings*, ed. D. N. Livingstone and M. A. Noll (Grand Rapids, MI: Baker, 2000). For a detailed response, see Fred G. Zaspel, "B. B. Warfield on Creation and Evolution," *Themelios* 35, no. 2 (2010): 198–211.

80 See the detailed discussion of Warfield by Warfield expert Fred Zaspel in this volume's next chapter, "Additional Note: B. B. Warfield Did Not Endorse Theistic Evolution as It Is Understood Today."

81 An exception is Kidner, who allows for the possibility that, prior to Adam, there were many nearly human creatures, and that, after conferring his image on Adam, and after specially creating Eve (an action that "clinched the fact that there is no natural bridge from animal to man"), God may have "conferred His image on Adam's collaterals, to bring them into the same realm of being" (*Genesis*, 29).

Though in many respects the church looks up to pastors and leaders like these men, the overwhelming consensus of church history still argues against following their lead in embracing some form of theistic evolution.[82]

F. Conclusion

In summary, theistic evolution encounters numerous obstacles. The focus of this chapter has been on theistic evolution being incompatible with doctrinal standards required for church leadership, as those doctrinal standards have been developed throughout church history. Please note what this chapter does not do: it does not demonstrate or imply that Christian leaders who embrace theistic evolution are not or cannot be true disciples of Jesus Christ. But this chapter does show that Christian leaders who hold to theistic evolution stand outside the church's historical position on that issue.[83]

---

82 In this regard, see John Currid's comments on the controversy related to senior Old Testament scholar Bruce Waltke, as recounted in Currid's chapter 2 in this volume.

83 Many evangelical pastors and leaders would add that, by reason of holding similar responsibilities, leaders of parachurch organizations should also adhere to these doctrinal standards of the church and thus should not embrace theistic evolution.

5

Additional Note: B. B. Warfield Did Not Endorse Theistic Evolution as It Is Understood Today

Fred G. Zaspel

Summary

This chapter quotes extensively from published and unpublished writings of Princeton theologian B. B. Warfield on creation and evolution, demonstrating that Warfield did not endorse theistic evolution as it is understood and advocated today.

———

Despite the claims of some recent authors,[1] renowned Princeton theology professor Benjamin Breckinridge Warfield (1851–1921) was not a theistic evolutionist. In fact, those on both sides of the evolution

1 See especially David N. Livingstone, "B. B. Warfield, the Theory of Evolution, and Early Fundamentalism," *Evangelical Quarterly* 58, no. 1 (January 1986): 78; David N. Livingstone and Mark A. Noll, "B. B. Warfield (1851–1921): A Biblical Inerrantist as Evolutionist," *Journal of Presbyterian History* 80, no. 3 (Fall 2002): 153–71; see also B. B. Warfield, *Evolution, Scripture, and Science: Selected Writings* (hereafter *ESS*), ed. Mark A. Noll and David N. Livingstone (Grand Rapids, MI: Baker, 2000).

question who might like to claim him will find him somewhat of a disappointment, for different reasons. That is, he spoke with obvious openness to the possibility of evolution *if* it could be established with a reasonable degree of scientific certainty; however, throughout his career he remained skeptical on exactly this score, often even mocking the theory's speculative nature and lack of supporting evidence. Warfield maintained an obvious interest in the subject throughout his life, and through to the end his writings reflect both his openness and his critical suspicion regarding the theory. At the end of it all we must conclude that, although Warfield allowed for the possibility of evolution, he himself remained uncommitted to it, and he explicitly rejected most of the main components of theistic evolution as it is understood today.

A. Warfield on Evolution in Summary

Warfield makes it a point to affirm the complete truthfulness of both "volumes" of divine revelation—Scripture and the created order—and that there can be no conflict between the two. He is therefore very willing to allow the established facts of the one to check our interpretations of the other. He recognizes that biblical interpreters, no less than interpreters of physical science, can err, so he is willing to adjust even his own understanding of Scripture to the established facts of scientific findings *once and if* those facts are established. However, he does not view both volumes of revelation as equal in clarity, so he argues that due weight of consideration must be granted accordingly: interpretations of general revelation must give way to the clearer statements of special revelation. Remarks in his review of Luther Townsend's *Evolution or Creation* illustrate his thinking well:

> Rejecting not merely the naturalistic but also the timidly supernaturalistic answers, he insists that man came into the world just as the Bible says he did. Prof. Townsend has his feet planted here on the rock. When it is a question of scriptural declaration versus human conjecture dignified by any name, whether that of philosophy or that of science, the Christian man will know where his belief is due. . . .

[Professor Townsend's] trust in the affirmations of the Word of God as the end of all strife will commend itself to every Christian heart.[2]

Here Warfield is clear in his conviction that, where physical scientists' claims contradict the plain written Word, they must be rejected. Scripture alone is the final test of truth.

It must be emphasized that Warfield continually reflected a willingness to consider the evolutionists' scientific claims. Throughout his life he very clearly kept abreast of their writings and seems very much at home distinguishing the arguments of one scientist over against another, and of one evolutionary theory over another. And often he reflects striking openness to the idea. For example, in his lecture titled "Evolution or Development," prepared in 1888, he writes,

The upshot of the whole matter is that there is no *necessary* antagonism of Christianity to evolution, *provided that* we do not hold to too extreme a form of evolution. To adopt any form that does not permit God freely to work apart from law and that does not allow *miraculous* intervention (in the giving of the soul, in creating Eve, etc.) will entail a great reconstruction of Christian doctrine, and a very great lowering of the detailed authority of the Bible. But if we condition the theory by allowing the constant oversight of God in the whole process, and his occasional supernatural interference for the production of *new* beginnings by an actual output of creative force, producing something *new*, i.e., something not included even *in posse* [potentially] in preceding conditions, we may hold to the modified theory of evolution and be Christians in the ordinary orthodox sense.

2   (1897) *ESS* 177–78. See also (1895) *ESS* 153–54, where Warfield complains about the view that in "modern thinking . . . it is to science that we must go for the final test of truth." Also (1888) *ESS* 130, where Warfield insists that biblical pronouncement is "the test point" in the discussion and that an evolutionary theory that would "reverse" clear biblical teaching is unacceptable. See also (1896) *The Works of Benjamin B. Warfield*, vol. 9 (Grand Rapids, MI: Baker, 1991), 60–61, where Warfield argues pointedly for the superiority of written over natural revelation. (Note that I am including, in parentheses, the year for each Warfield citation.)

I say we may do this. Whether we ought to accept evolution, even in this modified sense, is another matter, and I leave it purposely an open question.[3]

This kind of openness on the question is common in Warfield. Throughout his many reviews of evolutionary literature, he routinely speaks of evolution as impossible apart from divine intrusion and purpose ("mediate creation"), and he can even assume evolution as a given[4]—until, that is, particular arguments are taken up for dispute. And in these same pieces he can often express his skepticism and doubt also.

It is also important to note that in addressing the question of evolution—as in the sample above—Warfield makes careful distinction between theism and Christianity. That is, he argues on the one hand that the upward progress of evolution is impossible apart from teleology (purpose)—a fact which he comments would necessarily define evolution as a theistic concept. But he further argues that to acknowledge evolution as theoretically possible within a theistic worldview is one thing; affirming that it is a specifically Christian option is quite another.[5] Again, by this he means to say that Scripture just may not allow what a broader theistic view perhaps could.

It must be noted additionally that, within his openness to the possibility of evolution thus considered, Warfield makes a pointed argument that evolution cannot by itself explain the world as it is. Here he makes careful distinction between creation, mediate creation, and evolution. Only creation can explain origins, he insists. And if God has providentially directed various developments of his created order (evolution), this process can never account for factors such as life, personality, consciousness, the human soul, Christ, and so on. Such realities as these require divine, creative "intrusions" (mediate creation). Providence is not creation:

---

3   *ESS*, 130–31, emphasis original.
4   E.g., (1899) *ESS* 189.
5   (1901) *ESS*, 202.

What he [the Christian] needs to insist on is that providence cannot do the work of creation and is not to be permitted to intrude itself into the sphere of creation, much less to crowd creation out of the recognition of man, merely because it puts itself forward under the new name of evolution.[6]

Warfield was very insistent on this point. He specifically denied that evolution could account for *everything* after Genesis 1:1. Whatever evolution there might have been, it cannot account for the arrival of anything specifically *new*. It cannot explain the original "stuff" of the created order, and it cannot account for other subsequent realities that depend for their existence on divinely creative acts. Thus, for example, Warfield could never accept abiogenesis (spontaneous generation of life), and he explicitly denied that evolution could account for life, the origin of the human soul, the human sense of morality, the continued existence of the soul ("immortality") in the afterlife, or the incarnate Christ.

Yet this careful distinction still leaves open the possibility of a theistic evolution carefully defined, and so it becomes necessary to address specific questions that are determinative of Warfield's understanding. The short answer here is that Warfield remained both open to some kind of evolution, within prescribed limits, and yet very skeptical of it.

In agreement with his theological mentor, Charles Hodge, Warfield condemns Darwinian evolution as atheistic, and he complains often of the naturalistic (and anti-supernaturalistic) bias that drives so much of the evolutionists' agenda—and that has rubbed off on the church.[7] He understands the distinction between Darwinian evolution and other theories (although at times, as was increasingly the case generally, Warfield can use the terms "Darwinism" and "evolution" interchangeably), but even so he judges the evolutionary notion itself as essentially atheistic[8] and comments that "the whole body of these evolutionary theories" is "highly speculative," even "hyperspeculative." "None" of

6 (1901) *ESS*, 210; cf. 100.

7 (1897) *ESS*, 177.

8 (1901) *ESS*, 196.

them, he insists, "have much obvious claim to be scientific. . . . The whole body of evolutionary constructions prevalent today impresses us simply as a vast mass of speculation which may or may not prove to have a kernel of truth in it."[9]

Warfield insists that any claim that evolution has been proven betrays an overly zealous enthusiasm that exceeds the evidence.[10] And despite his frequent open tone regarding evolution, when he addresses the proffered evidence for it he consistently speaks in a skeptical—and often even mocking—tone. Evolutionary theories, he insists, cry out with questions they cannot answer and rest on faulty logic even of the most elementary sort:[11]

> The lay reader [speaking inclusively of himself, it seems] is left with strong suspicion that, if their writers did not put evolution into their premises they would hardly find so much of it in their conclusions. . . . The time has already fully come when the adherents of evolution should do something to make it clear to the lay mind that a full ac-cumulation of facts to prove their case can never come—or else abate a little of the confidence of their primary assumption.[12]

Warfield finds no evidence for abiogenesis (that is, the spontaneous generation of life from nonliving matter), as I have already mentioned. He also criticizes evolution on grounds of the geological record, which, "when taken in its whole scope and in its mass of details is confessed as yet irreconcilable with the theory of development by descent." Likewise, he finds the appeal to embryology unable to account for the fact that supposed later stages of development retain a transcript of previous stages. So also the evolutionist faces difficulty, he says, with the "limits to the amount of variation to which any organism is liable."[13]

---

9   (1907) *ESS*, 244–45; cf. (1908) *ESS*, 255–56.
10 Cf. his 1888 review of James McCosh's *The Religious Aspect of Evolution* (Cornell University Library, 1890); *ESS*, 67.
11 (1891) *ESS*, 143; (1898) *ESS*, 184–87, etc.
12 (1898) *ESS*, 184, 187.
13 (1888) *ESS*, 122–24.

Similarly, Warfield makes much over the seemingly limitless and impossible demands the evolutionary theory makes on time. This, he notes, is becoming more a problem recognized within the evolutionary-scientific community itself. "The matter of time that was a menace to Darwinism at the beginning thus bids fair to become its Waterloo."[14] Warfield allows that the age of the earth—and the age of humanity, for that matter—are not questions of biblical or theological interest. Warfield is willing to allow an "immense" age of the earth, and he is open to a great age of humanity also, but he notes the general consensus of his day that the age of man is probably not more than twenty thousand years.[15] And he contends often that science has not demonstrated the time it demands for the theory of evolution.

Warfield speaks often along these lines in criticism of evolutionary theories, insisting throughout his career that evolution remains an unproven hypothesis. But is it not likely that it will be proven? "Is it not at least *probable*?" he asks rhetorically. Cannot prescient minds expect that proof will be forthcoming? He responds, "Many think so; many more would like to think so; but for myself, I am bound to confess that I have not such prescience. Evolution has not yet made the first step" toward explaining many things. "In an unprejudiced way, looking over the proofs evolution has offered, I am bound to say that none of them is at all, to my mind, stringent."[16]

Warfield insists that laymen have the right to affirm with confidence that the evolutionary hypothesis remains "far from justified by the reasoning with which it has been supported." If the facts are with the evolutionist, they "have themselves to thank for the impression of unreality and fancifulness which they make on the earnest inquirer."[17] In another place he cautions, "We would not willingly drag behind the evidence, indeed—nor would we willingly run ahead of it."[18] Again,

---

14 (1888) *ESS*, 124.
15 (1911) *ESS*, 272–79.
16 (1888) *ESS*, 121–22.
17 (1891) *ESS*, 143.
18 (1893) *ESS*, 153.

"Most men today know the evolutionary construction of the origin of man; there are many of us who would like to be better instructed as to its proofs."[19] Similarly, he writes in 1908,

> What most impresses the layman as he surveys the whole body of these evolutionary theories in the mass is their highly speculative character. If what is called science means careful observation and collection of facts and strict induction from them of the principles governing them, none of these theories have much obvious claim to be scientific. They are speculative hypotheses set forth as possible or conceivable explanations of the facts. . . . For ourselves we confess frankly that the whole body of evolutionary constructions prevalent today impresses us simply as a vast mass of speculation which may or may not prove to have a kernel of truth in it. . . . This looks amazingly like basing facts on theory rather than theory on facts.[20]

In a 1916 review, Warfield speaks optimistically of evolution as demonstrating teleology (design): "Imbedded in the very conception of evolution, therefore, is the conception of end." Here he seems to be more open to evolution. But later in this same review he writes more critically of the woeful lack of proof for it:

> The discrediting of [Darwin's] doctrine of natural selection as the sufficient cause of evolution leaves the idea of evolution without proof, so far as he is concerned—leaves it, in a word, just where it was before he took the matter up. And there, speaking broadly, it remains until the present day. . . . Evolution is, then, if a fact, not a triumph of the scientist but one of his toughest problems. He does not know how it has taken place; every guess he makes as to how it has taken place proves inadequate to account for it. His main theories have to be supported by subsidiary theories to make them work at all, and these subsidiary theories by yet more far-reaching subsidiary

19 (1896) *ESS*, 171.
20 (1908) *ESS*, 244–46.

theories of the second rank—until the whole chart is, like the Ptolemaic chart of the heavens, written over with cycle and epicycle and appears ready to break down by its own weight.[21]

So although Warfield can speak of evolution as theistically allowable, his skepticism remains, as do the biblical hurdles as he understands them. Moreover, it is surely significant that the skepticism expressed here was in 1916. This late in his career, only a few years before his death, Warfield remained skeptical of evolution.

Of the specifically biblical problems, he sees God's creation of Eve as the most obvious, the account of which in Genesis 2 would seem impossible to reconcile with any evolutionary theory. But there are further problems he sees also, such as the origin of the human soul, the human sense of morality, the continued existence of the soul ("immortality") and the afterlife, and the incarnate Christ, none of which can be accounted for on evolutionary grounds.

It is common to hear it said that Warfield understood the creation "days" of Genesis 1 in terms of ages, and this in order to allow time for evolutionary development. This rumor may have arisen from Warfield's openness to a very old earth, if such could be scientifically demonstrated, and his affirmation (with Henry Green) of gaps in the genealogies of Genesis 5 and 11. But it is in fact something Warfield nowhere affirms. Indeed, he explicitly rejects the view that the days represent geological ages, as well as the view that understands them as literal but representative days that stand at the end of a long process of development.[22] And more generally he comments in agreement with another author that "the necessity for indefinitely protracted time does not arise from the facts, but from the attempt to explain the facts without any adequate cause."[23] Warfield speaks similarly in 1908.[24] That is, Warfield was very skeptical even of the time required for evolution. And as will

21 (1916) *ESS*, 319–20.
22 (1892) *ESS*, 145–46.
23 (1903) *ESS*, 228–29.
24 *ESS*, 242–43.

be shown below, he tended to understand the age of humanity in terms of thousands, not millions, of years. At any rate, beyond this, Warfield nowhere specifies his own understanding of the days of Genesis.

B. Elements of Theistic Evolution That Warfield Would Not Accept as Consistent with the Christian Faith

Warfield argues that there are observable gaps in the genealogies of Genesis 5 and 11 and, thus, that Scripture does not speak to the age of earth or of man. He insists that this is not a theological question. Yet he seems to think—presumably on scientific grounds—that humanity cannot be more than ten thousand or perhaps twenty thousand years old.[25] This observation alone seems to rule out most any evolutionary theory of human origins.

More to the point, in his discussion of the evidence available to evolutionists, Warfield seems clearly to rule out the notion of a progressive rise of human forms, asserting that "the earliest human remains differ in type in no respect from the men of our day."[26] He scorns the evolutionary idea of "primitive man," and he expresses agreement with John Laidlaw that "to propound schemes of conciliation between the Mosaic account of creation and the Darwinian pedigree of the lower animals and man would be to repeat an old and, now, an unpardonable blunder."[27] Even so, he also writes that the creation of man by the direct act of God need not "exclude the recognition of the interaction of other forces in the process of his formation." Again, he speaks with allowance, but he goes to pains to emphasize that, in the creation of man, God made something specifically "new," and that the Genesis narrative itself makes this plain. "He was formed, indeed, from the dust of the ground, but he was not so left; rather, God also breathed into his nostrils a breath of life," making him something distinct from all other creation. Thus, he concludes, a "properly limited evolution" is not excluded by the Genesis text *if*—and as always he emphasizes

25 (1911) *Works of Benjamin B. Warfield*, vol. 9, 235–45; *ESS*, 272–79.
26 (1888) *ESS*, 124.
27 (1895) *ESS*, 165.

the "if"—an evolutionary process was, in fact, involved. That is to say, he allows for some kind evolution, carefully defined, but he does not commit to it.[28]

In Warfield's 1906 review of James Orr's *The Image of God in Man*, he notes Orr's argument that disparate development of mind and body is impossible, that it would be absurd to suggest an evolutionary development of the human body from a brutish source and a sudden creation of the soul by divine fiat. Warfield commends Orr's grasp of man as body and soul in unity and refers to this as "the hinge of the biblical anthropology." Warfield seems in obvious agreement, but in terms of the argument against evolution, he characterizes this as a "minor point"; that is, he does not think this argument will be effective given that it could be answered with a theory of evolution *per saltum*.[29]

Two factors in context militate against taking this as a statement of Warfield's own belief, however. First, earlier in the same review, Warfield praises Orr for his "courage to recognize and assert the irreconcilableness of the two views and the impossibility of a compromise between them" and that "the Christian view is the only tenable one in the forum of science itself." Second, Warfield commends Orr's thesis explicitly:

> That he accomplishes this task with distinguished success is the significance of the volume. . . . The book is a distinct contribution to the settlement of the questions with which it deals, and to their settlement in a sane and stable manner. It will come as a boon to many who are oppressed by the persistent pressure upon them of the modern point of view. It cannot help producing in the mind of its readers a notable clearing of the air.[30]

It may be helpful to recall here Warfield's 1897 affirmation, cited above, that "man came into the world just as the Bible says he did,"

---

28 (1903) *ESS*, 214–16.

29 *Per saltum* is a Latin phrase meaning "by leap or bound," by which Warfield seems to refer to some form of macroevolution.

30 *ESS*, 230–36.

and his understanding of the creation of Eve as the leading obstacle to believing in evolution.

We find this same tone in the extensive 1898 class notes of a student (N. W. Harkness) from Warfield's lectures on the origin of man. Here Warfield makes repeated references to Adam's creation from the dust by God, in his image, God having breathed into him the breath of life, in order to make him a living being. Never is the plain understanding of the Genesis narrative questioned; it is always taken at face value and treated as both theology and historical fact. Several times Warfield is quoted as speaking of evolution as "modern speculation" that "runs athwart" the biblical record. Warfield concedes—as throughout his writings—that evolution and creation are not necessarily mutually exclusive, so long as evolution is not understood in reference to origins.[31] "Man is not improved organic matter, but was created new out of nothing, the in-trusion of divine power for something entirely new," Harkness records his professor as saying. At this point evolution cannot be reconciled to Scripture. "To agree with us," Warfield argues, the evolutionist "must admit that the chain was broken at one or more points by intrusion of divine power." We must insist, he says, that man was created.

Warfield further instructed his students that Adam was "created perfect" and that this perfection must be understood in physical as well as moral terms. Adam, the first man, was created "mature and without defect." War-field also debunks the evolutionary idea of "primitive man" and insists that "there is no proof of progressive stages in man." Indeed, sin, having entered, debased and degenerated humanity. Adam was created in God's image, in righteousness and holiness—"an intellectual, moral, voluntary being" who is "like God" and "different from the beasts." Harkness reports that Warfield affirmed, in summary, "We hold that God made Adam well and good."[32]

31 Note that Warfield can speak of creation and evolution as mutually exclusive at times and as *not* mutually exclusive at other times, but the contradiction is only apparent. His point is that creation speaks of origins while evolution can only speak of modification. In this sense they are mutually exclusive: evolution cannot account for origins. But a modification (evolution) of previously cre-ated matter is possible, and in this sense the two are *not* mutually exclusive. This is the sense here.

32 Unpublished class notes of N. W. Harkness Jr., from Warfield's Princeton Seminary course on Systematic Theology (1898), 1–5 (Princeton Theological Seminary Archives). For more reflections

This material from the student's lecture notes is in keeping with what we find in Warfield's lecture itself, prepared originally in 1888, in which he explicitly affirms that Adam is the "first man," that Adam and Eve were created with "a fully developed moral sense" and in "moral perfection," that in Adam the human race stood on probation and fell into sin, and that an evolutionary model would seem to reverse the biblical order of original perfection followed by sinfulness.[33]

All of this from Warfield's lectures is in keeping with what we have of his published writings. Every reference in Warfield to Adam and Eve and to human origins asserts or presumes the historicity of that original pair as the first humans, from whom all the race has descended and by whom sin entered the race—a traditional reading of the Genesis narrative. And often the references, always unqualified, are so brief that the reader is left with the impression that this was for Warfield "assumed" ground, scarcely in need of defense or further explication.

Warfield touches on the question of the origin of human death only briefly, in his review of James Orr's *God's Image in Man*, and he expresses surprise at Orr's ambivalence on this question:

The problem of the reign of death in that creation which was cursed for man's sake and which is to be with man delivered from the bondage of corruption, presses on some with a somewhat greater weight than seems here to be recognized.[34]

Warfield does not here state this explicitly as his own belief (he says the problem "presses on some," which of course might include himself), and in fact he never failed to point out a better argument for either side in this discussion. But he clearly considers this a strong argument for Orr's position that he should have employed. And given his strong endorsement of Orr's defense of Adam's creation, along with

---

on the original perfection of man, see also Warfield's (1903) *The Power of God unto Salvation* (Grand Rapids, MI: Eerdmans, 1930), 1–9.

33 *ESS*, 128–30.

34 (1906) *ESS*, 236.

our previously mentioned considerations, it seems that this affirmation, stated in his conclusion, does reflect Warfield's own thinking. The implications of this are telling: Warfield does not allow any room for previous generations of humanity who lived and died prior to Adam.

It is also significant that Warfield here (in his 1906 Orr review) describes the fallenness and hostility of this present world as "the reign of death in that creation which was cursed for man's sake." That is, he seems to indicate that not just human death but also the general fallenness of the larger created order came about as a result of Adam's sin.[35] Warfield reflects this condition elsewhere. First, in 1902 Warfield reviews an essay that treats *4 Esdras*, where the author laments the suffering that is in the world and of Israel in particular. Warfield characterizes this problem as "the sin and misery of the whole world, plunged by the fall of Adam into every kind of evil."[36] And in his brief 1908 participation in "A Symposium on the Problem of Natural Evils," Warfield again traces all calamity to Adam's sin. Commenting on Luke 13:1ff., he says,

> On the other hand, your questioner in the Bible class argues apparently on the assumption that there is no necessary relation between sin and calamity. He seems to suppose that calamity can fall when there is no sin. In other words he has forgotten (as many forget nowadays) the Fall. Given the Fall, and there is a place for the use of calamity in the moral government of the world. God may then visit or withhold the suffering which is due to all, as best suits his ends. . . . If there had been no Fall, however, there would be no such use made of calamity.[37]

Warfield speaks only in passing to the question of God's direct intervention in the creation of animals "after their kind." He held that God created all this "lower creation," but he nowhere exactly specifies

---

35 (1906) *ESS*, 236.

36 *The Bible Student*, September 1902, 177.

37 *The Biblical World* 31, no. 2 (February 1908): 124. Cf. (1916) B. B. Warfield, *Faith and Life* (Carlisle, PA: Banner of Truth, 1974), 330–32.

it as *immediate* creation. He can allow only the possibility of "mediate creation," and he remarks that "let the sea/earth bring forth" can be so understood. But at the same time he argues vigorously that even a divinely guided developmental process (providence) cannot do the work of creation. He simply affirms God's creation of the animals "after their kinds."[38]

Moreover, given (1) Warfield's general assessment of the theory of evolution as speculative, (2) his expressed acceptance of the Genesis record elsewhere, (3) his criticism of abiogenesis and his insistence that life is a divinely creative act (something specifically "new" that evolution cannot accomplish), and (4) his observations that the fossil records provide no indication of transitional forms,[39] it is safe to assume that he held to God's direct intervention in the creation of animal "kinds."

Warfield's thinking on these defining issues is rather traditional. We may say in summary that Warfield held the following:

- the creation of Adam from the dust of the ground
- the creation of Eve from Adam
- that Adam and Eve were the original human pair
- that Adam and Eve were not highly developed animals
- that all humanity has descended from Adam and Eve
- that humanity was created in moral and physical perfection
- that sin entered humanity by Adam
- that humanity has not progressed from primitive man upward but has fallen because of sin
- that human death entered by Adam
- that the created order itself is in disarray because of Adam's sin
- that the arrival of the animal world, as it is, also required divine, creative intervention

In chapter 1 of this book, Wayne Grudem has enumerated twelve points at which theistic evolution as currently endorsed differs from

38 (1903) *ESS* 211–15. Cf. Harkness class notes.
39 (1908) *ESS* 253.

the biblical account.[40] We can review these twelve points and describe Warfield's understanding regarding each:

1. Adam and Eve were not the first human beings (and perhaps they never even existed).
Warfield would deny this. He affirmed that Adam and Eve were historical persons and were the original human pair.

2. Adam and Eve were born of human parents.
Warfield would deny this. He affirmed repeatedly that Adam and Eve were created by God as the first human pair.

3. God did not act directly or specially to create Adam out of dust from the ground.
Warfield would deny this. He affirmed Adam's creation by God from the ground as per the Genesis narrative.

4. God did not directly create Eve from a rib taken from Adam's side.
Warfield would deny this. He affirmed that Eve's creation from Adam was the leading obstacle to a Christian's embracing of evolution.

5. Adam and Eve were never sinless human beings.
Warfield would deny this. He affirmed the original perfection of Adam and Eve and their fall from that perfect state.

6. Adam and Eve did not commit the first human sins, for human beings were doing morally evil things long before Adam and Eve.
Warfield would deny this. He affirmed that sin entered humanity by Adam.

7. Human death did not begin as a result of Adam's sin, for human beings existed long before Adam and Eve and they were always subject to death.

40 See pages 25–26.

Warfield seemed to deny this. He consistently affirmed that death came to humanity and to the created order by Adam's sin.

8. Not all human beings have descended from Adam and Eve, for there were thousands of other human beings on Earth at the time that God chose two of them as Adam and Eve.
Warfield would deny this. He affirmed that Adam and Eve were the original humans and that all humanity descended from them and is united in them.

9. God did not directly act in the natural world to create different "kinds" of fish, birds, and land animals.
Warfield would deny this. Although he spoke to this issue only in passing, he spoke to it and the related discussion sufficiently to affirm God's intervention in the creation of animal "kinds."

10. God did not "rest" from his work of creation or stop any special creative activity after plants, animals, and human beings appeared on the earth.
Warfield would deny this. He affirmed God's rest on the seventh day:

> He who needed no rest, in the greatness of his condescension, rested from the work which he had creatively made, that by his example he might woo man to his needed rest. The Sabbath, then, is not an invention of man's, but a creation of God's. . . . God rested, not because he was weary, or needed an intermission in his labors; but because he had completed the task he had set for himself (we speak as a man) and had completed it well. "And God *finished* his work which he had made"; and God saw everything that he had made, and behold it was *very good*."[41]

41 (1915) "The Foundations of the Sabbath in the Word of God," *Selected Shorter Writings of Benjamin B. Warfield*, vol. 1, John E. Meeter, ed. (Philipsburg: Presbyterian & Reformed, 1980), 309, 318.

11. God never created an originally "very good" natural world in the sense of a safe environment that was free of thorns and thistles and similar harmful things.

Warfield would deny this. He affirmed the fallenness of the perfect created order in Adam.

12. After Adam and Eve sinned, God did not place any curse on the world that changed the workings of the natural world and made it more hostile to mankind.

Warfield would deny this. He affirmed the fallenness of the created order as a result of Adam's sin.

C. Warfield in Transition?

One question remains: Did Warfield change his position later in life? The notion that Warfield was a theistic evolutionist is common, fueled especially by various works by David Livingstone and Mark Noll, most notably their collection of Warfield's writings in *Evolution, Scripture, and Science: Selected Writings*.[42] Livingstone and Noll argue that Warfield's position on this question changed—that late in his career he came again to embrace an evolutionary theory of origins. I have addressed this point at greater length elsewhere,[43] but I can make a few summary remarks here.

First, all sides acknowledge that Warfield's lecture "Evolution or Development," prepared in 1888, reflects his clear skepticism regarding the theory. At least six observations are worthy of note here.

1. It would be possible to trace sentiments of Warfield's skepticism expressed here throughout his later writings also.
2. Warfield's later "positive" statements about evolution are substantively no more positive or open than some found in his 1888

---

42 This is the work cited in note 1 above and cited thereafter as *ESS*.

43 See my "B. B. Warfield on Creation and Evolution," *Themelios* 35, no. 2 (2010): 198–211. Also chapter 9 in my *The Theology of B. B. Warfield: A Systematic Summary* (Wheaton, IL: Crossway, 2010).

lecture. If we agree that in 1888 he was also skeptical of evolution, then his later allowances can scarcely indicate anything more. This observation is especially relevant given Warfield's continued expressions of skepticism. *Both* his openness to evolution and his skepticism regarding it continued to the last.

3. It appears that Warfield continued to use this 1888 lecture, with various emendations, at least through 1902 (when he began to share the teaching load with C. W. Hodge Jr., who eventually succeeded him, and whose lectures, interestingly, followed Warfield's closely).

4. Some of the emendations Warfield added to the lecture along the way seem in fact to reflect a strengthening of his convictions against evolution, not a weakening.

5. We have no later or replacement lecture from Warfield on this topic—this was the last he used, and he preserved it along with his other works to be examined by those coming after him.

6. For a theologian of the stature of Warfield to change course after passing the age of 50 on an issue so well studied and on which he had pronounced so often and so clearly, would be remarkable indeed. I don't see any evidence for it.

One major factor lending confusion to the question of Warfield's later commitments regarding evolution is a 1915 essay on Calvin's doctrine of creation in which Warfield argued that Calvin understood the work of the creation week (Genesis 1) in evolutionary terms. On the face of it, this may seem to reflect Warfield's own persuasion—why else would he make such an unprecedented claim regarding the Reformer?

But there is more to the story. In this essay, Warfield points out that Calvin held to a literal six-day creation week and a young earth of less than six thousand years, so we must at least say that, in his famous (notorious?) claim that Calvin's doctrine of creation was "an evolutionary one," Warfield makes no connection to any evolutionary theory current in his own day. There is not enough time allowed.

More substantively, what Warfield refers to as "evolution" in this essay is nothing more than "second causes" which God employed in forming the world. (Of course, Calvin would have had no idea of Darwin's theory of evolution, which was published nearly three hundred years after Calvin's death.) Warfield argues that, for Calvin, "creation" proper refers only to the original fiat of Genesis 1:1 (and to the origin of each human soul). God "created" the original world stuff (Gen. 1:1), and it is from this that the rest of the created order was brought forth and formed.[44] This is what Warfield refers to as Calvin's "evolutionary" view. And he acknowledges that Calvin makes no indication as to just how the rest of the created order thus "evolved." Clearly, Warfield uses the term "evolution" somewhat loosely here. He certainly does not refer to any particular *theory* of evolution. Indeed, he notes that Calvin held no such "theory" but simply believed that the Creator employed "second causes" in the development of the world in six days from the original world-stuff. Moreover, Warfield judges this "evolutionary" teaching of Calvin to be "inadequate." All considered, whatever Warfield's motivations were in describing Calvin's teaching as evolutionary, there just is not enough evidence to attribute any evolutionary theory to Warfield himself.

Indeed, one year later, as noted above, Warfield remains skeptical and insists that evolution necessarily entails teleology, purpose, mind, intelligence, and therefore a Designer. He argues that, given the current rejection of natural selection, evolution is left without explanation. Then he offers his latest (final) assessment of the various evolutionary theories:

> The discrediting of [Darwin's] doctrine of natural selection as the sufficient cause of evolution leaves the idea of evolution without proof. . . . And there, speaking broadly, it remains until the present day. . . . Evolution is, then, if a fact, not a triumph of the scientist but one of his toughest problems.[45]

Finally, we must note that in a 1916 piece written for the college newspaper, Warfield reminisces on his time as an undergraduate student

44 *Works of Benjamin B. Warfield*, vol. 5, 304–5.
45 (1916) *ESS*, 319–20. For the larger quote, see page 162 above.

in Princeton. Here Warfield affirms that he was a convinced (theistic) evolutionist in his teenage years when he entered the College of New Jersey (Princeton), but he also affirms that he had abandoned the theory by the time he was thirty years old (1881). That is, although theistic evolution was championed by his revered professor and college president James McCosh, Warfield says that he had outgrown it himself early on, and the clear implication is that as he was writing now at age 67, just four years before his death, his evolutionary beliefs remained a thing of the past.[46]

D. Conclusion

The claim that Warfield held to theistic evolution goes beyond the evidence. Throughout the years of his writing on the subject, Warfield spoke with marked openness and even allowance of evolution. Many of these statements were obviously made simply for the sake of argument, and many are not so obvious. But it must be recognized that all along, at the very same time and through to the end, Warfield spoke very critically of evolution, pointing out the obstacles to accepting it, characterizing it as mere speculation, and commending refutations of it (such as Orr's). He spoke with evidently genuine openness to the idea, and this is doubtless the source of the confusion on the question; in fact, it may be said that the confusion is Warfield's own fault. But his openness to evolution is only half the picture, for all along he also spoke critically of its purely "speculative" character. And in fact he said late in life that he had left it in his youth.

Moreover, he very clearly held that Adam and Eve (created from Adam) were historical persons, that they were created perfect, that the entire human race is descended from them, that theirs was the first human sin, and that the human race and all creation with it is fallen in Adam. This would seem to rule out theistic evolution as we understand it today, and in fact it must be admitted that it would be impossible to identify any theory of evolution that Warfield himself held. Again, the

---

46 "Personal Recollections of Princeton Undergraduate Life IV—The Coming of Dr. McCosh," *Princeton Alumni Weekly* 16, no. 28 (April 19, 1916): 652.

claim that Warfield held to theistic evolution goes beyond the evidence. Indeed, the claim seems to go *against* the evidence. Only a selective reading of Warfield can portray him as accepting of any evolutionary theory. Reading him "whole" and from beginning to end reveals a sustained skepticism.

We may say this in summary:

- Warfield seemed very open to evolution and spoke allowingly of it.
- Warfield at the same time was very critical of evolution, questioned its scientific grounding, mocked its speculative character and logical fallacies, and recognized the biblical obstacles to it. Indeed, his last assessment of evolutionary theories is sharply critical.
- It would be impossible to identify any specific evolutionary theory that Warfield allegedly held.
- Warfield did not hold to the essentials of any theistic evolutionary theory held today (as enumerated in Grudem's twelve points cited above).
- Warfield asserted in 1916 that he had left theistic evolution behind him years earlier.

There, it seems, we must leave it also.

6

Theistic Evolution Undermines Twelve Creation Events and Several Crucial Christian Doctrines

Wayne Grudem

Summary

This chapter provides an overview of the issues raised by theistic evolution in relation to the truthfulness of the Bible and several historical Christian doctrines. First, it enumerates twelve specific affirmations about the origin of human beings and other living creatures that are held by the most prominent advocates of theistic evolution today. It then seeks to show that these affirmations are in direct conflict with multiple passages of Scripture, including passages not only from the Old Testament but also from ten books in the New Testament. In addition, it shows how theistic evolution undermines eleven significant Christian doctrines. It concludes that belief in theistic evolution is inconsistent with belief in the truthfulness of the Bible.

A. Twelve Theistic Evolution Beliefs That Conflict with the Creation Account in Genesis 1–3

I ended chapter 1 with a list of twelve points at which theistic evolution (as currently promoted by its prominent supporters) differs from the biblical creation account if it is taken as a historical narrative. (It should be noted that the BioLogos objections to the 2017 book *Theistic Evolution: A Scientific, Philosophical, and Theological Critique*[1] did not disagree with any of these twelve points in the two chapters that I contributed to that book.)

According to theistic evolution:

1. Adam and Eve were not the first human beings (and perhaps they never even existed).
2. Adam and Eve were born of human parents.
3. God did not act directly or specially to create Adam out of dust[2] from the ground.
4. God did not directly create Eve from a rib[3] taken from Adam's side.
5. Adam and Eve were never sinless human beings.
6. Adam and Eve did not commit the first human sins, for human beings were doing morally evil things[4] long before Adam and Eve.
7. Human death did not begin as a result of Adam's sin, for human beings existed long before Adam and Eve and they were always subject to death.

---

1   *Theistic Evolution: A Scientific, Philosophical, and Theological Critique*, ed. J. P. Moreland *et al.* (Wheaton, IL: Crossway, 2017). See the discussion of the objections from BioLogos on pages 16–17 above. The responses to the book *Theistic Evolution* can be found at biologos.org.

2   As I noted in chapter 1, it is possible that "dust" in Genesis 2:7 refers to a collection of different kinds of nonliving materials from the earth. My argument in this chapter does not depend on that interpretative detail. See the further discussion of the Hebrew word for "dust" by John Currid on pages 61–62.

3   As I noted in chapter 1, it is possible that the "rib" was accompanied by other material substances taken from Adam's body, for Adam himself says, "This at last is bone of my bones *and flesh of my flesh*" (Gen. 2:23). My overall argument is not affected by that difference. See the further discussion of the Hebrew word for "rib" on pages 51–52 and 198–199.

4   As I noted in chapter 1, some advocates of theistic evolution may claim that human beings prior to Adam and Eve did not have a human moral conscience, but they would still admit that these human beings were doing selfish and violent things, and worshiping various deities, things that from a biblical moral standard would be considered morally evil.

8. Not all human beings have descended from Adam and Eve, for there were thousands of other human beings on Earth at the time that God chose two of them as Adam and Eve.

9. God did not directly act in the natural world to create different "kinds" of fish, birds, and land animals.

10. God did not "rest" from his work of creation or stop any special creative activity after plants, animals, and human beings appeared on the earth.

11. God never created an originally "very good" natural world in the sense of a safe environment that was free of thorns and thistles and similar harmful things.

12. After Adam and Eve sinned, God did not place any curse on the world that changed the workings of the natural world and made it more hostile to mankind.

B. Genesis 1–3 Is Both Similar to and Different from Other Historical Narratives in Scripture

Anyone who reads Genesis 1–3 immediately realizes that in some ways these chapters are different from other historical chapters in the Bible. The subject matter is different, for these chapters do not talk about kings and armies and battles but about the origins of the universe before any human beings existed. The method of collecting the information also had to be different, for there were no human observers when God created light and darkness, the sun, moon, and stars, and plants and animals. And the setting is different, because Genesis 2 portrays the garden of Eden, an idyllic place with no sin or shame, no suffering or death.

In addition, the style in Genesis 1 is distinctive, because it is written with an elegant six-day structure with majestic repetitive phrases such as "And God said. . . . And it was so," and, "God saw that it was good." C. John Collins appropriately refers to Genesis 1 as "exalted prose narrative."[5]

---

5 C. John Collins, "Response from the Old-Earth View," in *Four Views on the Historical Adam*, ed. Matthew Barrett and Ardel B. Caneday (Grand Rapids, MI: Zondervan, 2013), 74; also 248.

But these distinctives do not nullify the fundamentally historical na-ture of Genesis 1–3. As John Currid demonstrated in chapter 2, a careful reading of Genesis 1–3 in its historical context reveals the following:

(1) It cannot rightly be understood as *describing functions* rather than origins in similarity to other ancient Near Eastern texts, for both Egyptian and Mesopotamian creation texts give significant attention both to function and to the material origins of things.

(2) It cannot rightly be understood as *myth* in the sense of a legend-ary story without a basis in historical facts, because the Jewish people had a deep antagonism toward prevalent myths in other ancient Near Eastern religions, and there are numerous anti-mythic polemical ele-ments in Genesis 1–3.

(3) It cannot rightly be understood as *figurative and theological* (but not historical) literature, because the Hebrew text of Genesis 1–3 re-peatedly uses several grammatical and syntactical features that are char-acteristic of Hebrew historical narrative but rare in poetic or figurative writings, and because Genesis 1–3 stands at the beginning of the whole Bible, whose overall structure is historical and moves from the begin-ning of history (in Genesis) to its final consummation (in Revelation).

(4) It cannot rightly be understood as a *sequential scheme*, with Gen-esis 2 reporting events tens of thousands of years later than Genesis 1, because Genesis 2:7 and 2:21–22 report specific details about the creation of man and woman that was summarized briefly in Genesis 1, and the whole of Genesis 2 contains numerous markers of Hebrew historical narrative, not of figurative, allegorical, or poetic language. In addition, the Hebrew expression in Genesis 2:4 that is translated "these are the generations of" (the *toledoth* formula, also translated "this is the account of") indicates that a new topic is being discussed, and does not usually form a sequential "bridge" from what went before.

(5) It cannot rightly be understood as an example of *etiology*, that is, the construction of a story that explains how something came to be, even if the story does not record any true historical facts. Following this interpretative method, some have argued that Genesis 1–3 does

not reflect actual creation events but was a story written after the exile (that is, after 586 BC) as a sort of allegory (the character in the story who is called "Adam" symbolically representing Israel) to explain why the people of Israel have been carried off to Babylon as exiles. But this view depends much more on questionable assumptions than on convincing evidence. It must hold that the entire preexilic history of Israel, beginning with the calling of Abraham in Genesis 12 and continuing through Genesis, Exodus, Leviticus, Numbers, Deuteronomy, Joshua, Judges, Ruth, 1–2 Samuel, 1–2 Kings, and 1–2 Chronicles, all happened before Genesis 1–3 was written as an allegorical explanation for the exile.

In addition, interpreters who make this assumption cannot reach agreement on exactly when Genesis 1–3 was composed. This interpretation also assumes that the later Jewish author of Genesis 1–3 borrowed from pagan myths in the surrounding culture and then purged the myths of their objectionable content, itself an unlikely assumption. It is much better to read Genesis 1–3 as real history that *also* serves as a prototype for Israel: just as Adam disobeyed God and was exiled from the garden of Eden, so Israel disobeyed God and was exiled from its Promised Land.

Currid concludes, I think rightly, that none of these approaches finds enough factual support in the text to convince us that Genesis 1–3 should be read as anything other than historical narrative to report events that actually happened.

Then in chapter 3, Guy Waters showed how eight different New Testament passages regard Adam as a real historical person and assume that the events of Adam's life reported in Genesis 1–3 actually happened. In addition, Waters showed that there are thirteen distinct New Testament passages that treat the early chapters of Genesis (Genesis 1–11) as trustworthy historical narrative. Finally, Waters explained in detail why Romans 5:12–21 and 1 Corinthians 15:20–22, and 44–49 demonstrate that Paul's gospel about Jesus Christ depends heavily on the historicity of the narrative about Adam and Eve in Genesis 1–3 and on the reality of the physical descent of all human beings from Adam and Eve. In short, Waters says, "Absent either a historical Adam or the universal descent of humanity from Adam, Paul's gospel is incoherent" (page 104), and he adds, "Affirming the historicity of Jesus Christ requires affirming the historicity of Adam" (page 106).

In the remainder of this chapter I will investigate how Genesis 1–3 supports twelve specific details that are denied by theistic evolution, and then how each detail in Genesis 1–3 is viewed by the rest of the Bible. I will attempt to show that several passages in the rest of the Old Testament and multiple passages in the New Testament affirm or at least assume the historical validity of twelve significant details in Genesis 1–3 that are denied by theistic evolutionary theory.

Then in the closing section of this chapter, I will argue that the denial of these twelve details in Genesis 1–3 by theistic evolution supporters undermines the historical foundation on which several crucial New Testament doctrines are built. My conclusion is that theistic evolution is incompatible with the doctrinal teaching of the Bible as a whole. If we are to maintain faithfulness to the teachings of the Bible, Genesis 1–3 must be understood as historical narrative, reporting events that actually happened.

C. Analysis of Twelve Theistic Evolution Beliefs That Conflict with Teachings of the Bible

1. Adam and Eve Were Not the First Human Beings (and Perhaps They Never Even Existed)

As I indicated in chapter 1 (see pages 19–20), some Christians who support theistic evolution believe that the early chapters of Genesis are merely symbolic stories, and that *Adam and Eve never existed*. Others believe that *Adam and Eve were actual historical persons*, but that they were just one man and one woman out of many thousands of human beings on Earth, and God chose to relate to them personally and designate them as representatives of the entire human race. Both of these groups claim that Adam and Eve were not the first human beings on Earth.

A. THE EVIDENCE FROM GENESIS The claim that Adam and Eve were not the first human beings creates tension with specific statements in Genesis 1 and 2, chapters that present Adam as the first human being and Eve as a woman specially created to be his wife. The initial evidence is seen in Genesis 1:

> Then God said, "Let us make man in our image, after our likeness. And let them have dominion over the fish of the sea and over the birds of the heavens and over the livestock and over all the earth and over every creeping thing that creeps on the earth."
>
> So God created man in his own image,
> > *in the image of God he created him;*
> > *male and female he created them.*
>
> And God blessed them. And God said to them, "Be fruitful and multiply and fill the earth and subdue it, and have dominion over the fish of the sea and over the birds of the heavens and over every living thing that moves on the earth." (Gen. 1:26–28)

Is this passage intended to be understood as historical narrative? The larger literary context is important here. The passage occurs in the first chapter of the first book in the entire Bible, a chapter that tells how all things in the universe began. The subject matter is an explanation of how things originally came into being—which is a historical question. The chapter speaks sequentially of the original creation—*the beginnings*—of light, land and sea, plants, the heavenly bodies, fish and birds, animals, and finally human beings. Such a report of the beginning of each type of thing in the creation leads us to think that this is not just a story about choosing one man and one woman to represent thousands of human beings who were already living, but that it is a story of the *beginning* of the human race—the creation of the *first* man and first woman.

There is in fact nothing in this passage that would cause us to think that it is nonhistorical literature. Only a prior commitment to an evolutionary framework of interpretation would cause a reader to search for a way to understand this as figurative or poetic literature rather than historical narrative. But the science and philosophy chapters in the larger book from which these essays were taken[6] provide abundant evidence that such a prior commitment to evolution is unjustified, and therefore Genesis 1–3 should be approached with an open mind rather than with a prior commitment to consider only materialistic explanations for the origin of human beings and a prior commitment to consider only those explanations of Genesis that are consistent with evolutionary theory.

In addition, Genesis 1 does not stand alone in the biblical text. Genesis 2 is closely tied to Genesis 1 and provides a more detailed account of the initial creation of a man and a woman in God's image.[7] In Genesis 2 we read,

> the Lord God formed the man of dust from the ground and breathed into his nostrils the breath of life, and the man became a living creature. (Gen. 2:7)

This passage asks us to believe that there was no other human being on Earth at this time, for the narrative goes on to say that the man was alone when he was created: "Then the Lord God said, 'It is not good that the man should be *alone*; I will make him a helper fit for him'" (Gen. 2:18).[8] After that, God brought the animals to Adam, so that he could name them (vv. 19–20), but "for Adam there was not found a helper fit for him" (Gen. 2:20; here the first man is named as

---

6   See the seventeen scientific essays and nine essays on philosophy of science in *Theistic Evolution: A Scientific, Philosophical, and Theological Critique*, edited by J. P. Moreland, Stephen Meyer, Christopher Shaw, Ann K. Gauger, and Wayne Grudem (Wheaton, IL: Crossway, 2017).

7   See pages 65–67 for John Currid's detailed argument that Genesis 2 must be understood as a detailed recapitulation of Genesis 1, not as a contradictory account and not as an account of some later events.

8   Someone might object that the verse means only that Adam was alone *in the garden*, but that there were thousands of other human beings outside the garden (cf. John H. Walton, *The Lost World of Adam and Eve: Genesis 2–3 and the Human Origins Debate* [Downers Grove, IL: InterVarsity Press, 2015], 109). However, that is an unlikely proposal because then no special creation of Eve would have been necessary, for God could simply have taken a woman from outside the garden and brought her into the garden.

"Adam").[9] This again affirms that there was no other human being on Earth at that time.

Finally, God "caused a deep sleep to fall upon the man, and while he slept took one of his ribs and closed up its place with flesh. And the rib that the Lord God had taken from the man he made into a woman and brought her to the man" (Gen. 2:21–22). The narrative in this way presents Eve as the second human being on the earth, and the first woman.

We find these ideas reaffirmed in later Old Testament passages. Genesis 5 reinforces the idea that Adam was the first human being:

> This is the book of the generations of *Adam. When God created man, he made him in the likeness of God. Male and female he created them,* and he blessed them and named them Man [Hebrew *'ādām*] when they were created. When *Adam* had lived 130 years, he fathered a son in his own likeness, after his image, and named him Seth. The days of Adam after he fathered Seth were 800 years; and he had other sons and daughters. (Gen. 5:1–5)

This passage links the specific man "Adam" to the initial creation account in Genesis 1 with the words "When God created man" and with the clear echoes of Genesis 1 in "he made him in the likeness of God" and "Male and female he created them."[10] Therefore Adam is viewed as the specific man created by God in Genesis 1:27, the very first man, and a man who had a son named Seth. Then, almost as if he wants to reinforce to his readers that this is a report of specific historical events,

9 Walton, *Lost World of Adam and Eve*, 60–61, prefers to translate this verse, "But for the *man*" instead of "but for *Adam*," which would support his view of the man in Genesis 1–2 as an "archetype," but he admits that he has to repoint the Masoretic text (changing indefinite *le-* to definite *lā-*) in order to translate it this way. Most translations (including ESV, NASB, NIV, NET, KJV, NKJV) prefer "Adam" at this verse, following the Masoretic text. Walton also prefers to translate "the man" instead of "Adam" in Genesis 3:17 and 21, but the Masoretic text and most translations read "Adam" in those places as well.

10 C. John Collins provides a longer argument showing that "Genesis 1–11 Is a Unity on the Literary Level"; see C. John Collins, "A Historical Adam: Old-Earth Creation View," in Barrett and Caneday, *Four Views on the Historical Adam*, 155–57.

the writer immediately specifies a whole line of descendants leading from Seth directly to Noah and Noah's three sons (Gen. 5:6–32).[11] Adam and Eve are directly connected to historical persons in this subsequent historical narrative.

A later genealogy traces the beginning of the human race back to Adam: "Adam, Seth, Enosh" (1 Chron. 1:1). Following this verse, we find nine chapters of genealogies—names of specific people who descended from Adam, bringing us into the families of David and Solomon (1 Chronicles 3) and even into the exile (1 Chronicles 9). In this genealogy, Adam is again viewed as a historical person who stands at the beginning of the human race.

B. IS THIS POETIC, FIGURATIVE, OR ALLEGORICAL LITERATURE?

Francis Collins says Genesis 1–3 should be understood as "poetry and allegory."[12] But in chapter 2 above, John Currid showed that none of the five major attempts at interpreting Genesis 1–3 as nonhistorical literature have been persuasive. What is the evidence in the text that would cause us to understand it as nonhistorical?

Should we understand it as poetry? No Bible translation known to me presents the entirety of Genesis 1–3 as Hebrew poetry, which uses relatively short lines, one after another, and shows evident parallelism in succeeding sets of balanced lines.

Notice how translation committees present the Psalms, for example:

> The Lord is my shepherd; I shall not want.
>> He makes me lie down in green pastures.
> He leads me beside still waters.
>> He restores my soul. (Ps. 23:1–3)

---

11 Even if there are gaps in the genealogies, so that only certain individuals are mentioned, they are still intended to be accurate historical records that name actual people. Regarding Genesis 5:1–2, C. John Collins notes, "that Adam and Eve are presented as a particular pair, the first parents of all humanity, is pretty widespread in the exegetical literature" (C. John Collins, *Did Adam and Eve Really Exist?: Who They Were and Why You Should Care* (Wheaton, IL: Crossway, 2011), 57.

12 Francis Collins, *The Language of God* (New York: Free Press, 2006), 206; also 150, 151, 175, 207.

This is poetry. It contains successive short lines that reemphasize similar or related ideas, typical of Hebrew parallelism. But Genesis 1–3 is not written in this way, and Genesis 1–3 is not poetry.[13] It is written as a narrative of historical events. That is why the New Testament authors uniformly treat it as truthful history.

In chapter 2 of this book, John Currid points to several additional features in the Hebrew linguistic structure and in the interconnectedness of the narrative that demonstrate that these chapters must be taken as historical narrative, not as poetic, figurative, or allegorical literature. He concludes, "If we remove the profoundly historical nature of Genesis 1–3, we will remove the historical foundation on which all the remainder of the Bible rests."[14]

Nor is Genesis 1–3 an extended *metaphor*. We do find metaphorical language in Scripture, but we recognize it as metaphor because it cannot be literally true. When Jesus says, "I am the light of the world" (John 8:12), or "I am the true vine, and my Father is the vinedresser" (John 15:1), we know that he is not literally the sun or a grapevine, and so we understand it as a metaphor. But there are no such features in Genesis 1–3. For thousands of years, interpreters have readily understood the details in Genesis 1–3 to be actual historical events.

Nor is Genesis 1–3 an extended *allegory*. Essential to allegorical stories is that they have a continuous second level of meaning.[15] For example, in the book of Judges, Jotham told an allegorical story:

[Jotham] went and stood on top of Mount Gerizim and cried aloud and said to them, "Listen to me, you leaders of Shechem, that God

---

13 There are some poetic verses, such as Genesis 1:27; 2:23; and 3:14–19; but even these recount historical facts using a poetic form of expression, as here:

So God created man in his own image,
    in the image of God he created him;
    male and female he created them. (Gen. 1:27)

14 See page 54.

15 I am grateful to my friend Leland Ryken (professor of English emeritus at Wheaton College) for a telephone conversation in which he explained this characteristic of allegories.

may listen to you. *The trees once went out to anoint a king over them,* and they said to the olive tree, 'Reign over us.' But the olive tree said to them, 'Shall I leave my abundance, by which gods and men are honored, and go hold sway over the trees?' And the trees said to the fig tree, 'You come and reign over us.' But the fig tree said to them, 'Shall I leave my sweetness and my good fruit and go hold sway over the trees?'" (Judg. 9:7–11)

Readers realize at once that this is an allegory, both because trees don't actually talk to each other or go out "to anoint a king over them," and because readers recognize that the reactions of the different kinds of trees are specific details that carry a continuous second level of meaning (describing, in this case, various men who had refused to lead the people).

But Genesis 1–3 is not like this, and it is not an extended allegory. It is not possible to link together the details in a coherent second level of meaning, with each part corresponding to something else in the reader's experience, as in Jotham's allegory. To label a narrative passage in a historical book as an allegory when nothing in the context demands that it be taken as an allegory is not proper interpretation; it is "allegorizing." Genesis 1–3 should rather be understood as historical narrative.

Scot McKnight has recently proposed that Genesis 1–3 does not present a "historical Adam" but rather a "literary Adam," who is later viewed as a "genealogical Adam" in Jewish literature.[16] But in order to argue this, McKnight over-specifies what is meant by a "historical Adam" so that he makes it include not only what is explicitly recorded in Genesis 1–2 but also elements that would not be clearly taught until the New Testament (that Adam and Eve "passed on their sin natures . . . to all human beings"), some theological conclusions that are implied but not explicitly affirmed by the New Testament (e.g., "if one denies the historical Adam, one denies the gospel of salvation"), and one factor that would not be understood until modern genetics ("their DNA is our DNA").

16   Scot McKnight, in Dennis R. Venema and Scot McKnight, *Adam and the Genome: Reading Scripture after Genetic Science* (Grand Rapids, MI: Brazos, 2017), 107–8, 118, 145–46.

McKnight then denies that this kind of a "historical Adam" can be found in Genesis 1–2. He writes, "I have major doubts that when Genesis 1–2 was written, any of that or at least most of that was what was meant by 'Adam and Eve.'"[17] But to argue that Genesis 1–2 is not "historical" because it does not explicitly contain doctrinal material found in Romans 5 and 1 Corinthians 15 is surely not what "historical" means in ordinary English.

A better understanding is found in the statement of C. John Collins that I quoted earlier: "In ordinary English a story is 'historical' if the author wants his audience to believe the events really happened" (see page 13, note 4). In that sense of "historical," McKnight has not disproved that Genesis 1–2 presents Adam and Eve as historical persons.

McKnight also explores various discussions of Adam in extrabiblical Jewish literature, showing that different authors used the Genesis story of Adam and Eve as a platform for *expanding* on the Genesis narrative with various kinds of moral lessons, philosophical allegories, and creative elaborations on the Genesis story,[18] but his extensive survey turns up no Jewish authors who deny the historical reality of the events that are recorded in Genesis 1–2. Even McKnight admits that "Paul, *like the Jews of his day*, would have thought that the *literary* Adam and Eve were also the genealogical Adam and Eve, and that as such they were persons in the history of Israel."[19]

Therefore, while McKnight claims that we should not view Adam and Eve in Genesis as "*historical*" but rather as "*literary* Adam and Eve," his claim fails to be persuasive. The fact that Adam and Eve are viewed as actual historical persons elsewhere in the Old Testament, in later Jewish literature, and also in Paul's writings, argues for, not against, their historicity. In addition, McKnight fails to even discuss several other New Testament books that also affirm the historicity of Adam and Eve (see the evidence presented below).

---

17   Ibid., 108, cf. 158, 169.
18   Ibid., 147–69.
19   Ibid., 189, emphasis added for "*like the Jews of his day*."

C. THE LARGER STRUCTURE OF GENESIS After Genesis 1 gives an overview of the entire process of creation, Genesis 2 begins a long, continuous historical narrative that carries all the way through until the death of Joseph in Genesis 50:26, the end of the book.

The entire book of Genesis is connected together as a single historical document in two ways:

(1) The genealogies in later chapters (see Genesis 5, 10, 11) explicitly tie all of the later historical persons and events back to their direct descent from Adam and Eve in Genesis 1–3, showing that the entire story of Genesis from the beginning is intended to be understood as one historical narrative, reporting people who actually existed and events that actually happened. Abraham, Isaac, and Jacob are presented as real historical persons who descended from Adam and Eve, and therefore Adam and Eve are also viewed as real historical persons.

(2) The introductory phrase "These are the generations of . . ."[20] (or a similar expression) occurs eleven times in Genesis (see Gen. 2:4; 5:1; 6:9; 10:1; 11:10, 27; 25:12, 19; 36:1, 9; 37:2). This literary device begins with the first link in the chain at Genesis 2:4, "*These are the generations of* the heavens and the earth when they were created." This phrase is the introductory heading for Genesis 2:4 to 4:26, a section that includes the details of the creation of Adam and Eve, the fall, and the stories about Cain, Abel, and Seth. The second link in the chain is Genesis 5:1, "This is the book of the generations of Adam," and it introduces a long list of Adam's descendants including Enoch, Methuselah, and Noah.

The eleventh and final link in this literary chain is the story of Jacob and his twelve sons, beginning with the introduction in Genesis 37:2, "These are the generations of Jacob," and ending with the death of Joseph in Genesis 50:26, the end of the book.

This literary device links together the story of Adam and Eve with the stories about the lives of Abraham, Isaac, Jacob, and Jacob's twelve sons, stories that are unquestionably intended as factual historical narratives. Therefore, the entire book is intended to be understood as historical

---

20 Some translations render this as, "This is the account of . . ." (so NASB, NIV, NET, NLT).

narrative. This significant literary feature is analyzed in more detail by John Currid and Guy Waters in chapters 2 and 3 above.[21]

The interconnectedness of the whole of Genesis because of the unbroken links of genealogy from Genesis 1–3 all the way to the stories of the patriarchs in Genesis 12–50 must not be minimized. Gordon Wenham, professor emeritus of Old Testament at the University of Gloucestershire and author of a highly respected two-volume commentary on Genesis, writes,

> If the later figures in the genealogies are real people—and they certainly behave in very human fashion—then *the earlier characters, the ancestors of Abraham, must also be viewed as real persons.* . . . As an interim conclusion we may say that Gen 1–11 is a genealogy, which has been expanded with stories from ancient times to produce an account of the development of the human race from its origin to the time of Abraham. . . . The backbone of Gen 1–11 is an expanded linear genealogy: ten generations from Adam to Noah and ten generations from Noah to Abram.[22]

James Hoffmeier, professor of Old Testament and Near Eastern Archaeology at Trinity Evangelical Divinity School, similarly affirms that Genesis 1–11 must be understood as historical:

> Genealogical texts in the ancient Near East, by their very nature, are treated seriously by scholars and not cavalierly dismissed as made-up or fictitious, even if such lists are truncated or selective. . . . The "family history" structuring of the book [of Genesis] indicates that *the narratives should be understood as historical,*

---

21 See pages 53–54, 62–63, and 89. As Waters points out, it seems that Matthew is connecting his Gospel to the stories in Genesis when he begins the Gospel with, "*The book of the genealogy of* Jesus Christ, the son of David, the son of Abraham" (Matt. 1:1).

22 Gordon Wenham, "Genesis 1–11 as Protohistory," in *Genesis: History, Fiction, or Neither? Three Views on the Bible's Earliest Chapters*, ed. Charles Halton (Grand Rapids, MI: Zondervan, 2015), 85, 95, emphasis added. Wenham is the author of *Genesis 1–15* and *Genesis 16–50*, the two-volume Word Biblical Commentary on Genesis (Waco, TX: Word, 1987, 1994).

focusing on the origins of Israel back to Adam and Eve, the first human couple and parents of all humanity. . . . *The narratives are dealing with real events involving historical figures*—and this includes Genesis 1–11. . . . The author of the narrative goes to great lengths to place Eden within the known geography of the ancient near East, not some made-up mythological, Narnia-like wonderland.[23]

D. THE EVIDENCE FROM THE NEW TESTAMENT In the New Testament, Jesus reinforces the idea of Adam as the first human being, for he says,

[He] who created them from the beginning made them male and female, and said, "Therefore a man shall leave his father and his mother and hold fast to his wife, and the two shall become one flesh" (Matt. 19:4–5).[24]

Jesus must be referring to the narrative about Adam and Eve in Genesis 2, because "a man shall leave his father and his mother" is taken directly from Genesis 2:24. But Jesus also ties this Adam and Eve narrative *in Genesis 2* to the first creation of man on the earth *in Genesis 1*, for "from the beginning" echoes "In the beginning" in Genesis 1:1. Moreover, Jesus quotes Genesis 1:27 with the words "*made them male and female.*"[25] Jesus thus affirms the historicity of both Genesis 1 and Genesis 2, and thus affirms Adam and Eve as the first human beings on the earth, not (as theistic evolution would have it) as two among thousands of other human beings on the earth.

Luke's Gospel traces the genealogy of Jesus all the way back to Adam, at the beginning of the human race: "the son of Enos, the son of Seth,

---

23 James Hoffmeier, "Genesis 1–11 as History and Theology," in Charles Halton, ed., *Genesis: History, Fiction, or Neither?* (Grand Rapids, MI: Zondervan, 2015), 30, 32, emphasis added.

24 See page 90 for Guy Waters's discussion of the necessary historical nature of the basis of marriage as Jesus affirms it in this passage.

25 Jesus's words in Matthew 19:4, ἄρσεν καὶ θῆλυ ἐποίησεν αὐτούς, are an exact word-for-word citation of the Septuagint translation of Genesis 1:27.

the son of Adam, the son of God" (Luke 3:38).[26] Luke considers Adam the very first human being, the one directly created by God as specified in the narrative in Genesis 1–2.

When Paul is speaking to Greek philosophers on the Areopagus, he says,

> And he made from one man every nation of mankind to live on all the face of the earth. (Acts 17:26)

Paul says that "one man" was the first human being on the earth (for all were "made" from him), and in Paul's understanding, this one man is Adam (for Paul repeatedly calls Adam the "one man" in referring to the beginning of the human race in Romans 5:12, 14, 15, 16, 17, 19).[27]

In 1 Corinthians, Paul explicitly calls Adam the "first man":

> Thus it is written, "The first man Adam became a living being"; the last Adam became a life-giving spirit. (1 Cor. 15:45)

Therefore, the literary setting and content of the whole of Genesis 1–2 indicate that the author intends these chapters to be understood as a historical narrative of the beginnings of everything in creation, including the creation of Adam as the first human being. In addition, later Old Testament records, in Genesis 5 and 1 Chronicles 1, place Adam first in long lists of people descended from Adam, people whom they understand to be historical persons in subsequent generations. In the New Testament, Luke, Jesus, and Paul all affirm the historicity of the Genesis account of Adam as the first human being.

But advocates of theistic evolution all deny that Adam and Eve were the first human beings, and some deny that Adam and Eve even existed.[28]

---

26 See pages 76–78 for Guy Waters's discussion of this genealogy in Luke.

27 See the more detailed discussion of Acts 17:26 by Guy Waters on pages 79–80, demonstrating that the "one man" must be Adam.

28 Denis Lamoureux writes, in an article posted on the BioLogos website, "Did the apostle Paul believe that Adam was a real person? Yes, well of course he did. Paul was a first-century-AD Jew and like every Jewish person around him, he accepted the historicity of Adam. . . . It is understandable

2. Adam and Eve Were Born of Human Parents

This idea is the second point of tension between theistic evolution and Genesis 1–3. Our friends who hold to theistic evolution maintain that Adam and Eve (if they even existed) were ordinary human beings with human parents, but this presents a conflict with the text of Genesis, which affirms that God directly *"formed the man of dust from the ground* and breathed into his nostrils the breath of life, and the man became a living creature"* (Gen. 2:7). If this is understood as historical narrative, Adam had no human parents but was formed directly from the earth.[29]

Eve is also portrayed as having no human parents, for we read that she was created from a rib taken from Adam's body: "and the rib that the LORD God had taken from the man he made into a woman and brought her to the man" (Gen. 2:22).

Luke's Gospel similarly portrays Adam as having no human parent, for his genealogy leads backward from Jesus ultimately to "Seth, the son of Adam, the son of God" (Luke 3:38).

Paul also affirms that Adam had no human parent, for he calls him "the first man Adam" (1 Cor. 15:45; also verse 47). But if Adam had had a human father, he would not be the first man.

This is another point of tension with theistic evolution, which requires that Adam and Eve were born of human parents, and that they were only two out of many thousands of human beings on Earth at that time.

---

why most Christians believe that Adam was a real historical person. This is exactly what Scripture states in both the Old and New Testaments" (Denis Lamoureux, "Was Adam a Real Person? Part 3," *BioLogos*, September 17, 2010, http://biologos.org/blogs/archive/was-adam-a-real-person -part-3).

But in spite of the fact that he thinks the Bible says this, Lamoureux himself does not believe that Adam ever existed: "My central conclusion in this book is clear: Adam never existed, and this fact has no impact whatsoever on the foundational beliefs of Christianity" (Denis Lamoureux, "Was Adam a Real Person, Part 2," *BioLogos*, September 11, 2010, http://biologos.org/blogs /archive/was-adam-a-real-person-part-2, citing Lamoureux's summary statement from his 2008 book, *Evolutionary Creation* [Eugene, OR: Wipf & Stock]).

29 For a discussion of John Walton's alternative interpretations of this verse and the verse about Eve's creation from Adam's rib, see the following two sections of this chapter.

3. God Did Not Act Directly or Specially to Create Adam out of Dust from the Ground

This point is the counterpart to the previous point about Adam and Eve having human parents. Theistic evolution requires that "Adam" (if there was an Adam) descended from a long line of previously existing human beings, but the account in Genesis 2 claims that God made the first man from the dust:

> then the LORD God *formed the man of dust from the ground* and breathed into his nostrils the breath of life, and the man became a living creature. (Gen. 2:7)

As John Currid demonstrates in chapter 2, the expression "formed the man of dust from the ground" specifies the material from which God made the man, because "verbs of forming often require two accusatives, an object accusative (the thing made) followed by a material accusative (the material from which the thing is made)."[30] The material is "dust," that is, "the dry, fine crumbs of the earth"[31]—specifying that God directly created man from the ground, not from a line of previously existing human beings and nearly human animals.

However, in defending the possibility of theistic evolution, John Walton argues that "the LORD God formed the man of dust from the ground" simply means that Adam was mortal, subject to death. He argues that the verb for "formed" need not refer to forming a material object.[32] He also argues that "formed . . . of dust" simply means that human beings are subject to death because "dust refers

---

30 See page 61. Vern Poythress rightly notes that "dust from the ground" simply "hints at the common material stuff making up his body" (Poythress, *Did Adam Exist? Christian Answers to Hard Questions* [Phillipsburg, NJ: P&R, 2014], 16).

31 See chapter 2, note 88 and text.

32 As evidence, he points to other verses where the Hebrew verb for "formed" (Hebrew *yātsar*) "is used in a variety of nonmaterial ways," such as forming days and forming events to happen (Walton, *Lost World of Adam and Eve*, 71). But this is simply an exegetical mistake on Walton's part, because he fails to give sufficient attention to this specific context: when the verb is used *in contexts that specify the material that is used and the object that is formed* (as in Gen. 2:7), and when those are both physical items, then it evidently is speaking about a material creation.

to mortality."[33] He quotes Psalm 103:14: "For he knows how we are formed, he remembers that we are dust" (NIV), where the Hebrew words for "formed" and "dust" are the same or similar to the words in Gen. 2:7, and the Psalm is speaking about our mortality.

But Walton does not give sufficient attention to the decisive differences in the contexts of Genesis 2 and Psalm 103. Psalm 103 is poetic literature that speaks elegantly about the fleeting nature of human life (the next verse says, "As for man, his days are like grass"). When David says, "He remembers that we are dust," it is an evident allusion to God's punishment in Genesis 3:19: "You are dust, and to dust you shall return."

The context of Genesis 2:7 is different. As we have seen, it is a detailed explanation of how God created human beings. Walton makes a verse about the creation of man into a verse predicting man's death!

Here is what Genesis 2:7 says:

> then the LORD God formed the man *of dust from the ground* and breathed into his nostrils the breath of life, and the man became a living creature. (Gen 2:7)

But according to Walton's interpretation, "formed from dust" simply means that man is mortal. If we insert that idea back into the verse, this is what Genesis 2:7 would mean:

> then the LORD God formed the man *so that he would die* and breathed into his nostrils the breath of life, and the man became a living creature.

C. John Collins says, "Walton's treatment of the verb in Genesis 2:7 ('form') lacks appropriate lexical rigor. No doubt other things can be formed (as in Zech. 12:1); but the specific syntactical structure in Genesis 2:7 employs what some call a double accusative, which is common for verbs that denote making or preparing: the first accusative ('the man') is the object of the verb, the thing made; the second accusative ('dust from the ground') is the stuff out of which the thing is made" (Collins, "Response from the Old-Earth View," in Barrett and Caneday, *Four Views on the Historical Adam*, 129).

33 Walton, *Lost World of Adam and Eve*, 73.

On this reading, the text tells us that man would die before man even began to live (by receiving the breath of life). The very passage that proclaims to us that God amazingly made *nonliving* "dust" into a *living* human being now becomes a passage that tells us that God made a man who would die. But death is continually seen as a flaw, an enemy (1 Cor. 15:26), a tragedy that according to Genesis 3 came only as a judgment for Adam's sin, not at the very beginning of creation.

Therefore Walton's proposed interpretation is unpersuasive, both because of the specific linguistic construction in Genesis 2:7 and because of the Bible's consistent claim that death was not part of the way God originally created man but was a horrible punishment that came later because of sin.

The next chapter of Genesis also affirms Adam's creation directly from the earth:

> By the sweat of your face
> > you shall eat bread,
> till you return to the ground,
> > *for out of it you were taken;*
> *for you are dust,*
> > *and to dust you shall return.* (Gen. 3:19)

Then the narrative continues, "therefore the LORD God sent him out from the garden of Eden to work *the ground from which he was taken*" (Gen. 3:23).

In the New Testament, Paul reaffirms Adam's creation from the dust of the earth as reported in Genesis 2 when he says, "the first man was from the earth, *a man of dust*" (1 Cor. 15:47).

4. God Did Not Directly Create Eve from a Rib Taken from Adam's Side

Theistic evolution requires that "Eve" (if there was an Eve) had human parents, but the narrative in Genesis 2 gives a different explanation of how God created Eve:

The man gave names to all livestock and to the birds of the heavens and to every beast of the field. But for Adam there was not found a helper fit for him. So the LORD God caused a deep sleep to fall upon the man, and while he slept *took one of his ribs* and closed up its place with flesh. *And the rib that the Lord God had taken from the man he made into a woman* and brought her to the man. Then the man said,

> "This at last is bone of my bones
>   and flesh of my flesh;
> she shall be called Woman,
>   because she was taken out of Man."

Therefore a man shall leave his father and his mother and hold fast to his wife, and they shall become one flesh. And the man and his wife were both naked and were not ashamed. (Gen. 2:20–25)

The text does not present the creation of Eve from Adam's rib[34] as a minor detail, for it is immediately presented as an explanation for the institution of marriage in the human race and for sexual union within marriage as a reuniting of two halves that were originally one ("for a man shall . . . hold fast to his wife, and they shall become one flesh"; v. 24).

God's forming of Eve from Adam's body also demonstrates that Eve is not an inferior creature but one who is of the same substance as Adam, and therefore someone who is fully human, of equal value to Adam in God's sight. In addition, it provides the historical basis for affirming that all human beings, including Eve, have descended from

---

34 Christopher Shaw, one of the science editors of *Theistic Evolution*, the larger volume from which this present book is taken (see note 5, above), pointed out to me the interesting fact that a rib is one of the few bones in the human body that can be removed without significant loss of function. In addition, he called my attention to a 2011 letter to the editor published in *American Journal of Hematology*, which noted that "The rib, in particular, represents an anatomic type of long bone with a wide, spongious component rich in hematopoietic bone marrow, containing multipotent, pluripotent, and unipotent stem cells" (Francesco Callea and Michelle Callea, "Adam's Rib and the Origin of Stem Cells," *American Journal of Hematology* 86, no. 6 (2011): 529; http://online library.wiley.com/doi/10.1002/ajh.22005/full).

Adam, something that is more explicitly affirmed in the New Testament (see Acts 17:26; 1 Cor. 15:22).

John Walton argues that God did not create Eve from Adam's rib, but that Adam had a "visionary experience" where he saw "himself being cut in half[35] and the woman being built from the other half." This was "something he saw in a vision."[36] But once again Walton has offered an implausible interpretation that does not fit with the actual wording of the text. Elsewhere in Genesis, when someone sees a vision or has a dream, the text makes this clear:

The word of the LORD came to Abram *in a vision*. (Gen. 15:1)

But God came to Abimelech *in a dream* by night. (Gen. 20:3)

And [Jacob] *dreamed*, and behold, there was a ladder set up on the earth, and the top of it reached to heaven. (Gen. 28:12)

Now Joseph had a *dream*, and when he told it to his brothers they hated him even more. (Genesis 37:5; also "He said to them, '*Hear this dream* that I have dreamed'"; Gen. 37:6)

Then [Joseph] dreamed another dream and told it to his brothers and said, "Behold, *I have dreamed another dream*. Behold, the sun, the moon, and eleven stars were bowing down to me." (Gen. 37:9)

---

35 Walton argues for the translation, "he took one of Adam's sides" instead of "one of his ribs," and thus the text means that God "cut Adam in half" (Walton, *Lost World of Adam and Eve*, 78–79). The Hebrew word *tsēlā'* can mean either "rib" or "side," depending on the context, but "closed up its place with flesh" suggests removal of a smaller part of Adam, not his entire side, and this idea is more suitable in a context in which Adam immediately afterward is able to function normally (not as a half-person) as he welcomes God's gift of Eve. The same Hebrew word *tsēlā'* is used elsewhere to refer to the wooden bars that support the fabric of the tabernacle (Ex. 26:26; 36:31) or the boards of wood that Solomon used to line the inside of the temple (1 Kings 6:15). This same word is used to mean "rib" in rabbinic literature: see Marcus Jastrow, *A Dictionary of the Targumim, the Talmud Babli and Yerushalmi, and the Midrashic Literature* (New York: Judaica Press, 1971), 1285. In the phrase "took one of his ribs," the translation "ribs" is found in the ESV, RSV, NRSV, NASB, NIV, NLT, CSB, NKJV, and KJV (I found no translation with "sides").

36 Walton, *Lost World of Adam and Eve*, 80.

Pharaoh *dreamed* that he was standing by the Nile. (Gen. 41:1)

There are no such contextual indicators of a dream or vision in Genesis 2. It is presented as straightforward narrative in which God causes a deep sleep to fall on Adam (presumably to anesthetize him), then removes one of his ribs, then closes up the place where the rib was removed, and then creates Eve and brings her to Adam, and Adam welcomes her. The passage does not say that Adam had a dream or saw a vision.

Jesus also affirms the historicity of Genesis 2 when he says,

Have you not read that he who created them from the beginning made them male and female, and said, "*Therefore* a man shall leave his father and his mother and hold fast to his wife, and the two shall become one flesh"? (Matt. 19:4–5)

His words "Have you not read" indicate that he is relying on the narrative in Genesis 1–2, and his report in Matthew 19:5 of what God "said" is a direct quotation from Genesis 2:24. It is significant that Jesus includes the word "Therefore" in his quotation, for this word in the text of Genesis 2:24 links it explicitly to the story of how God created Eve from a rib from Adam's side in the immediately preceding verses (vv. 21–23).

The reasoning is, "Eve was taken out of Adam's side, and *therefore* a man shall hold fast to his wife, and the two shall become one flesh, and what was separated will be reunited." This "therefore" statement cannot work unless the reader believes that Eve was created from the rib taken from Adam's side, as reported in Genesis 2:21–23. Jesus is relying on and affirming the historical accuracy of the record in Genesis—that Eve was created from a rib from Adam's side.

Paul affirms the historicity of Eve's creation from Adam's body when he says, "For man was not made from woman, *but woman from man*" (1 Cor. 11:8).[37] Paul is not saying that Adam dreamed this, but that it actually happened.

---

37 See the further discussion of this passage by Guy Waters on pages 80–81.

Paul also affirms the accuracy of the history of Eve's creation in Genesis 2 in another epistle when he writes, "For Adam was formed first, then Eve" (1 Tim. 2:13). He could not have known this from Genesis 1, where no details are given about the sequence of the creation of man and woman; he could only have known it from Genesis 2.[38] Once again he is affirming the historicity of the creation of Eve from Adam's side.

Therefore both Paul and Jesus understand Genesis 2 as a historical narrative, and they claim that the specific details of Genesis 2 are factually true—they actually happened. But theistic evolution must say that Eve was not created from Adam's rib—or from any part of Adam's body at all. Are we willing to say that both Paul and Jesus were wrong?

5. Adam and Eve Were Never Sinless Human Beings

Our friends who hold to theistic evolution maintain that Adam and Eve were ordinary human beings, doing sinful deeds for their entire lives just as all other human beings do. By contrast, the entire story of the creation of Adam and Eve as recorded in Genesis 1–2 indicates only blessing and favor from God, and gives no hint of the existence of any human sin or God's judgment on sin.

God created them, and "God blessed them" (Gen. 1:28), and then,

God saw everything that he had made, and behold, *it was very good*. (Gen. 1:31)

"Very good" in the eyes of a holy God implies there was no sin present in the world.[39]

---

38 Paul's statement that "Adam was formed first" uses the Greek verb *plassō*, "to form, mold," which is the same verb used in the Septuagint of Genesis 2:7, "the LORD God formed the man of dust from the ground."

39 John Walton argues that "good" (Hebrew *tôb*) in Genesis 1:31 does not imply freedom from sin or suffering, because "in reality the word never carries this sense of unadulterated, pristine perfection" (*Lost World of Adam and Eve*, 53). But his argument is unpersuasive because (1) this is a unique, pre-fall context, unlike the post-fall contexts in which the word later occurs; (2) this verse gives an evaluation of what is "very good" in the eyes of an infinitely holy God, not in the eyes of sinful human beings; (3) Walton inexplicably considers only the word *tôb*, "good," not

Where there is no sin or guilt, there also is no shame, and so the picture of a sinless world is confirmed by this statement that closes the narrative in Genesis 2: "And the man and his wife were both naked and were not ashamed" (Gen. 2:25).

But then sin, and the guilt and shame that accompany sin, begin with Adam and Eve eating the forbidden fruit in Genesis 3, and it is only then that "the man and his wife hid themselves from the presence of the Lord God among the trees of the garden" (Gen. 3:8).

This perspective on a sinless creation followed by the fall is also seen in Ecclesiastes: "See, this alone I found, that *God made man upright*, but they have sought out many schemes" (Eccles. 7:29).

In the New Testament, the first entrance of sin into the world through the disobedience of Adam is affirmed when Paul says, "sin came into the world through one man" (Rom. 5:12).[40]

If sin "came into the world through one man," and specifically through that "one man's trespass" (Rom. 5:15), then Paul is affirming that there was no sin in the world before Adam's sin. This means that God created Adam and Eve as sinless human beings, as the narrative in Genesis 1–2 indicates.

But theistic evolution argues that Adam and Eve (if they existed at all) were never sinless human beings. Therefore theistic evolution once again implies that Paul himself was wrong.

6. Adam and Eve Did Not Commit the First Human Sins, for Human Beings Were Doing Morally Evil Things Long before Adam and Eve

This is the counterpart to the previous point about God not creating Adam and Eve as sinless people. According to theistic evolution, human beings have always committed morally evil deeds, and therefore human beings were sinning for thousands of years before Adam and Eve.[41]

---

the emphatic expression *tôb me'od*, "very good" which occurs in this verse. It is unthinkable that God would look at a world filled with moral evil and declare it to be "very good."

40 See the extensive discussion of this passage by Guy Waters on pages 104–107 of this volume, especially its implications for the origin of human sin.

41 John Walton says, "Anthropological evidence for violence in the earliest populations deemed human would indicate that there was never a time when sinful (= at least personal evil) behavior was not present" (*Lost World of Adam and Eve*, 154).

But this claim is again in tension with the biblical witness, for just as the Genesis narrative shows that God created Adam and Eve as sinless human beings (see previous section), it also shows that Adam and Eve committed the *first* human sins in a world that was perfect and free from human sin. God had commanded Adam not to eat of the fruit of the tree of the knowledge of good and evil (Gen. 2:17), but the serpent tempted Eve (Gen. 3:1–6), and she ate of the fruit, and then Adam also ate:

> So when the woman saw that the tree was good for food, and that it was a delight to the eyes, and that the tree was to be desired to make one wise, she took of its fruit and ate, and she also gave some to her husband who was with her, and he ate. (Gen. 3:6)

After that, sin quickly proliferates as the narrative unfolds. God drives Adam and Eve out of the garden (Gen. 3:16–24), and then Cain murders Abel (Gen. 4:8), Lamech murders a man in vengeance (Gen. 4:23), and eventually, "the LORD saw that the wickedness of man was great in the earth, and that every intention of the thoughts of his heart was only evil continually" (Gen. 6:5). All this is pictured in Genesis as something that began with the initial sin of Adam and Eve.

A reference to the sin of Adam is also the most likely interpretation of a passage in Hosea:

> But *like Adam* they transgressed the covenant (Hos. 6:7).[42]

---

42 Denis Alexander says, "Most scholars maintain that the 'Adam' referred to in Hosea 6:7 refers to a place not a person" (Denis Alexander, *Creation or Evolution: Do We Have to Choose?*, 2nd ed., rev. and updated (Oxford: Monarch, 2014), 475n164). He gives no basis for this assertion. The translation "like Adam" (referring to Adam as a person) is found in ESV, NASB, NLT, and CSB, while the translation "at Adam" is found in NIV, NET, RSV, and NRSV.

The *ESV Study Bible* note says, "to whom or to what does 'Adam' refer? Many commentators suggest a geographical locality. The difficulty is that there is no record of covenant breaking at a place called Adam. . . . And it requires a questionable taking of the preposition 'like' (Heb. *ke-*) to mean 'at' or 'in'. . . . It is best to understand 'Adam' as the name of the first man" (*ESV Study Bible* [Wheaton, IL: Crossway, 2008], 1631).

Paul reaffirms that sin began with Adam and Eve[43] in an extensive discussion in Romans 5:

> Therefore, just as *sin came into the world through one man.* . . .
>
> For if many died through *one man's trespass*, much more have the grace of God and the free gift by the grace of that one man Jesus Christ abounded for many. And the free gift is not like the result of that *one man's sin.* For the judgment following *one trespass* brought condemnation, but the free gift following many trespasses brought justification. For if, because of *one man's trespass*, death reigned through that one man, much more will those who receive the abundance of grace and the free gift of righteousness reign in life through the one man Jesus Christ.
>
> Therefore, as *one trespass led to condemnation for all men*, so one act of righteousness leads to justification and life for all men. For as *by the one man's disobedience the many were made sinners*, so by the one man's obedience the many will be made righteous (Rom. 5:12, 15–19).[44]

Paul also affirms the historicity of the account of the sin of Adam and Eve with reference to a specific detail in Genesis 2: "But I am afraid that as *the serpent deceived Eve by his cunning*, your thoughts will be led astray from a sincere and pure devotion to Christ" (2 Cor. 11:3).[45]

Paul returns to this theme in a later epistle: "and Adam was not deceived, but the woman was deceived and became a transgressor" (1 Tim. 2:14).[46]

Therefore the theistic evolution claim that thousands of human beings were committing sinful acts long before the time of Adam and Eve would require us again to say that Paul was wrong in what he wrote.

---

43 Although Eve sinned first in the narrative in Genesis 3, Paul focuses on the sin of Adam, apparently because Adam alone had a representative role with respect to the entire human race, a role in which Eve did not share. Similarly, Paul elsewhere says, "For as in Adam all die, so also in Christ shall all be made alive" (1 Cor. 15:22).

44 See pages 113–118 for Guy Waters's answer to Walton's claim that Romans 5 simply means that people were not accountable for their sin before Adam.

45 Guy Waters discusses this passage more fully on pages 81–83.

46 See the discussion of this passage by Guy Waters, pages 83–86.

7. Human Death Did Not Begin as a Result of Adam's Sin, for Human Beings Existed Long before Adam and Eve and They Were Always Subject to Death

All living things known to evolutionary science, including human beings, eventually die, and therefore theistic evolution requires that human beings have always been subject to death, and that human beings were dying long before Adam and Eve existed.

But according to the biblical narrative, when God first created Adam and Eve, they were not subject to death (as I argued in section 3 above, in response to John Walton's view of "formed the man of dust from the ground"). The absence of death when Adam and Eve were created is implied by the summary statement at the end of the sixth day of creation, "and God saw everything that he had made, and behold, *it was very good*" (Gen. 1:31). In light of later biblical teachings that death is the "last enemy to be destroyed" (1 Cor. 15:26), and the prediction that in the age to come, "death shall be no more" (Rev. 21:4), the initial "very good" creation should be understood to imply that Adam and Eve were not subject to death when they were first created.

In addition, in the next chapter, God said to Adam, "But of the tree of the knowledge of good and evil you shall not eat, for in the day that you eat of it *you shall surely die*" (Gen. 2:17). This implies that death would be the *penalty for disobedience*, not something to which they were initially subject. (Nothing is implied in Genesis 2 about animal death, for God's statement directed to Adam implies only human death: "*you shall surely die.*") After Adam sinned, God pronounced the promised judgment, which would be carried out over time through a life filled with painful toil, culminating in death:

> By the sweat of your face
>   you shall eat bread,
> *till you return to the ground,*
>   for out of it you were taken;

for you are dust,

and to dust you shall return." (Gen. 3:19)

In the New Testament, Paul states explicitly that human death came into the world through Adam's sin, for he says,

Therefore, just as sin came into the world through one man, *and death through sin*, and so death spread to all men because all sinned— (Rom. 5:12)[47]

Once again, the emphasis is on human death, for Paul's statement, "and so death spread to all *men*" uses a plural form of the Greek term *anthrōpos*, a term that refers only to human beings, not to animals. (The entire Bible says nothing one way or another about the death of animals before the fall.)

In 1 Corinthians, Paul affirms again that death came through Adam's sin:

For as *by a man came death*, by a man has come also the resurrection of the dead. For as *in Adam all die*, so also in Christ shall all be made alive (1 Cor. 15:21–22).[48]

But theistic evolution requires us to deny that human death began as a result of Adam's sin,[49] and this once again requires us to say that the Genesis account is not a trustworthy historical narrative, and that Paul was wrong.

8. Not All Human Beings Have Descended from Adam and Eve, for There Were Thousands of Other Human Beings on Earth at the Time That God Chose Two of Them as Adam and Eve

The "Adam and Eve" advocated by theistic evolution were just two individuals among many thousands on the earth at that time, and therefore not all human beings have descended from Adam and Eve.

---

47 See Guy Waters's discussion of this passage and its implications for human death, pages 104–107.

48 See Guy Waters's discussion of this passage and its implications for human death, pages 108–113.

49 See, e.g., Walton, *Lost World of Adam and Eve*, 144; also 72–77 and 159.

But Genesis portrays Adam and Eve as the first human beings (see section 1 above), and that is why God then says to them, "Be fruitful and multiply and fill the earth and subdue it" (Gen. 1:28). The earth had no human beings, so Adam and Eve were to begin to fill it.

Later in Genesis, "The man called his wife's name Eve, because *she was the mother of all living*" (Gen. 3:20). The sentence cannot mean "all living things," because plants and animals existed before Adam or Eve (Gen. 1:11–25), and so the intended sense must be "all living human beings." All human beings have descended from Adam as the male progenitor, and from Eve, his wife, as the female progenitor.

By contrast, several theistic evolution authors claim that there must have been many other human beings on the earth at the time of Adam and Eve. The evidence they give is that Cain's wife (Gen. 4:17) had to come from somewhere, and Cain expected that there were other people who would want to kill him (Gen. 4:14). Genesis even says that Cain built a "city," which had to be a place populated by numerous people (Gen. 4:17).

But are we to think that the author of Genesis (whom I believe to be Moses) was unaware of this difficulty? The text of Genesis itself provides an obvious solution to this problem, because it says that Adam lived 930 years, "*and he had other sons and daughters*" (Gen. 5:4–5). How many? The text does not say, but Adam and Eve, created as full-grown adults, could have begun to have children in their very first year. Adam was 130 years old when Seth was born (Gen. 5:3), but he and Eve could well have had many dozens of children both prior to that time and after that time—the text does not tell us.

Yes, this requires that Cain and Seth and others would have married their sisters in the first generation, but that was necessary in order to have the entire human race descend from Adam and Eve, and the prohibitions against incest were not given by God until much later (see Lev. 18:6–18; 20:11–20; Deut. 22:30).

In the New Testament, Paul said that God "made *from one man* every nation of mankind to live on all the face of the earth" (Acts 17:26). This implies that all human beings descended from Adam.

Such a descent of the entire human race from Adam is important (a) because it shows the actual physical unity of the human race, thus precluding any ideas of racial superiority or inferiority. It is also important (b) because it explains how *the guilt of Adam's sin* could be justly imputed to all his descendants, and it also provides the mechanism by which *a sinful nature* (or disposition toward sin) has been transmitted from generation to generation throughout the entire human race. Finally, it is important (c) because it provides a category of people who are "in Adam" in such a way that Adam's sentence of death also applied to all who descended from Adam: "For as *in Adam all die*, so also in Christ shall all be made alive" (1 Cor. 15:22).

But theistic evolution denies that all human beings have descended from Adam, and so the actual physical unity of the entire human race is denied, and Adam's role as representative head of the entire human race is nullified, because it is inextricably tied to the physical descent of every human being from Adam. As Guy Waters argues in a detailed analysis of 1 Corinthians 15 in chapter 3, "Were there a human being not descended from Adam, he would not be eligible for redemption. Only those who have borne Adam's image may bear Christ's image."[50]

9. God Did Not Directly Act in the Natural World to Create Different "Kinds" of Fish, Birds, and Land Animals

Theistic evolution claims that God created matter and after that did not guide or intervene to cause any empirically detectable change in the natural behavior of matter until all living things had evolved by purely natural processes.

But this proposal is in tension with the picture presented in Genesis, where God carries out *distinct and separate actions* to directly create different specific parts of creation, and then, in further distinct actions, creates specific kinds (or types) of animals.

---

50 See pages 98–124. Waters maintains that theistic evolution supporters fail to adequately explain, in a way consistent with New Testament teaching, just how Adam could represent the entire human race if not all human beings have descended from him.

For example,

And God said, "Let the earth sprout vegetation." . . . And it was so.
(Gen. 1:11)

That was on day 3. Then in a separate act on day 5,

And God said, "Let the waters swarm with swarms of living creatures,
and let birds fly above the earth across the expanse of the heavens."
(Gen. 1:20)

Then on day 6 there is more creative activity:

And God *made the beasts of the earth* according to their kinds and
the livestock according to their kinds, and *everything that creeps on
the ground* according to its kind. And God saw that it was good.
(Gen. 1:25)

The Hebrew text includes the direct object marker [*'eth*] three times
in this verse, showing that there are three distinct direct objects of
the verb "made" (Hebrew *ʿāsāh*): the verse says that God specifically
made (1) the beasts of the earth, and also (2) the livestock, and also
(3) everything that creeps on the ground. In addition, within each of
these groups he made creatures "according to their kinds," indicating
a number of different specific types of animals within each group
(though Scripture gives us no indication of the size of each category
that is called a "kind"). This verse pictures a direct, active involvement
of God in making different kinds of animals, which is far different
from the "hands-off" allowing of matter to evolve following its own
properties that we find in theistic evolution.

Later, in a separate action on this same day, God said, "Let us *make*
[once again, another distinct action designated by Hebrew *ʿāsāh*] man in
our image. . . . So God created man in his own image, in the image of
God he created him; male and female he created them" (Gen. 1:26–27).

Finally, at the end of the sixth day, "God saw everything *that he had made*, and behold, it was very good" (Gen. 1:31). The scope of "everything that he had made" (once again, Hebrew *'āsāh*) must include both the separate kinds of animals (from day 6) and also man himself (from day 6), which have just been specified as things that God "made."

The picture given in Genesis, therefore, is that God *directly made* various kinds of animals and also made human beings in distinct, separate acts. But theistic evolution says that God did not "make" these things in any sense that the Hebrew reader of these verses would understand from the verb "made" (Hebrew *'āsāh*), but only in the sense that inanimate matter that God had created billions of years earlier at the beginning of the universe evolved by virtue of its own properties, with no additional creative action from God, into all these animals and human beings.[51]

The Psalms also speak about God's *specific acts* of creating individual parts of nature. David says to God that "the moon and the stars" are things that "you have set in place" (Ps. 8:3). Then he says to God that many different kinds of animals fall in the category of "the works of your hands":

what is man that you are mindful of him. . . .

You have given him dominion over *the works of your hands*;
    you have put all things under his feet,
all *sheep* and *oxen*,
    and also the *beasts* of the field
the *birds* of the heavens, and the *fish* of the sea,
    whatever passes along the paths of the seas. . . .

---

51 Theistic evolution advocates frequently affirm that they believe in God's ongoing providential involvement in all of creation, but by this they do not mean that God intervened in, or in any way directed, the actions of the material universe, but rather that God sustained the materials of the universe so that they continually acted according to the physical properties with which they were initially created. Denis Alexander speaks about "the precious materials God has so carefully brought into being in the dying moments of exploding stars" and says it is wrong to deny that they have the "potentiality to bring about life" (*Creation or Evolution*, 436). But if matter merely acting according to its own created properties can create life, then there would have been no need for God to repeatedly *act* in the natural world, in a way different from ordinary providence, to create different kinds of living things, as Genesis 1 portrays him doing.

O Lord, our Lord,
how majestic is your name in all the earth! (Ps. 8:4–9)

These creatures are nowhere said to be the product of "materials that assembled themselves" (the theistic evolution view); they are specifically the *works of God's hands.*

A similar understanding is found in Psalm 104, which views various creatures as specific indications of God's wisdom:

O Lord, how manifold are your works!
In wisdom have you made them all;
the earth is full of *your creatures.*
Here is the sea, great and wide,
which teems with creatures innumerable,
living things both small and great. (Ps. 104:24–25)

In the New Testament, Paul speaks of "the God who made the world *and everything in it*" (Acts 17:24). In this statement, "everything in it" must refer to something different from "the world" itself, and therefore it is best understood to include all the varieties of plants and animals that exist on the earth. Paul does not say that God made the raw materials of the universe and then these materials made themselves into living creatures, but that God himself made "everything" that exists in the world (see also John 1:3: "all things were made through him"—showing that the Son of God, the eternal second person of the Trinity, was the active personal agent in bringing all things into existence, a view far different from the idea that matter itself brought all things into existence).

In a similar way, Paul says that God's "invisible attributes, namely, his eternal power and divine nature" have been "clearly perceived, ever since the creation of the world, *in the things that have been made*" (Rom. 1:20). Created things, especially plants and animals and human beings in their complexity, bear witness to God's power and divine nature— a fact that has been evident to all generations of human beings, who instinctively realize, "Only God could create something as amazing as this flower or this hummingbird." But on a theistic evolution account, complex living things only bear witness to the *amazing properties of matter* that God made billions of years earlier, and bear no direct witness to God's wisdom or power in their specific creation.

When Paul writes, "by him *all things* were created, in heaven *and on earth*, visible and invisible" (Col. 1:16), he surely intends to include all living creatures. He says *Christ* specifically created them, not inanimate matter. Similarly, when Paul says that "everything created by God is good" (1 Tim. 4:4), he is speaking specifically about "foods that God created to be received with thanksgiving" (1 Tim. 4:3), foods which are made from living plants and animals. These things have not evolved by random mutation, for Paul says they have been "created by God."

The book of Revelation includes two additional references affirming that God himself, not inanimate matter, created all things that exist in the world, including specifically all the creatures of the sea:

Worthy are you, our Lord and God,
 to receive glory and honor and power,
for you created *all things*,
 and by your will they existed and were created. (Rev. 4:11)

. . . him who lives forever and ever, *who created* heaven and what is in it, *the earth and what is in it, and the sea and what is in it.* (Rev. 10:6)

None of the original readers of Genesis or of these New Testament writings would have understood these verses to mean that God originally created nonliving matter and that *this matter then created all living things* over the course of billions of years, without any additional intervention from God. Nor could this have been the intended meaning of any of the authors of these New Testament books. Rather, the intent of the human authors (and of the divine author), as rightly understood by the original readers, would be to affirm that God directly acted in the natural world to create all the different kinds of plants and animals that exist on the earth today.

But theistic evolution requires us to believe that these passages from Genesis, Psalms, Acts, Romans, Colossians, 1 Timothy, and Revelation are all mistaken in the way they tell us of God's direct and specific creation of all things in heaven and on Earth.

10. God Did Not "Rest" from His Work of Creation or Stop Any Special Creative Activity after Plants, Animals, and Human Beings Appeared on the Earth

Theistic evolution holds that, after the initial creation of matter, God did not intervene in the world to create any living things. Karl Giberson and Francis Collins say, "The model for divinely guided evolution that we are proposing here thus requires no 'intrusions from outside' for its account of God's creative process, except for the origins of the natural laws guiding the process."[52]

But this also means that, according to theistic evolution, there was no special activity of God from which he could have "rested" after the six days of creation recorded in Genesis 1. The biblical record, however, is incompatible with this theistic evolution viewpoint, for after narrating the events of God's six days of creative work, it says,

> Thus the heavens and the earth were finished, and all the host of them. And on the seventh day *God finished his work* that he had done, and *he rested on the seventh day from all his work that he had done.* So God blessed the seventh day and made it holy, because on it God *rested from all his work* that he had done in creation. (Gen. 2:1–3)

Oxford mathematics professor John Lennox explains why these verses cannot be reconciled with theistic evolution:

> According to Genesis, then, creation involved not just one, but a sequence of several discrete creation acts, after which God rested. This surely implies that those acts involved processes that are not going

---

52 Karl Giberson and Francis Collins, *The Language of Science and Faith* (Downers Grove, IL: Inter-Varsity Press, 2011), 115.

on at the moment. . . . In both Old and New Testaments, the Bible clearly distinguishes between God's initial acts of creation on the one hand and his subsequent upholding of the universe on the other. This distinction is also apparent in Genesis 1: it records a sequence of creation acts followed by God's resting. I also think, by contrast with my theistic evolutionary friends, that science supports this distinction.[53]

Two additional passages in Scripture also view this Genesis account of God's resting as an actual historical event—something that really happened. First, in the Ten Commandments, God himself says,

> For in six days the LORD made heaven and earth, the sea, and all that is in them, *and rested on the seventh day.* Therefore the LORD blessed the Sabbath day and made it holy. (Ex. 20:11)

Then the author of Hebrews also affirms that God rested from his work of creation:

> For he has somewhere spoken of the seventh day in this way: "And *God rested* on the seventh day from all his works." . . . for whoever has entered God's rest has also rested from his works as God did from his. (Heb. 4:4, 10)

Yet according to a theistic evolution viewpoint, there was no special kind of work that God did during these six days of creation, because the *providential* work of God in sustaining the materials of the universe while evolution was happening was no different from the ongoing *providential* work of God in sustaining the materials of the universe even today. *There was no particular creative work of God from which he could "rest."* This is another event in the history of the universe which the Bible claims to have happened but which theistic evolution says didn't happen.

---

53 John Lennox, *Seven Days That Divide the World: The Beginning according to Genesis and Science* (Grand Rapids, MI: Zondervan, 2011), 161, 170–71.

11. God Never Created an Originally "Very Good" Natural World in the Sense of a Safe Environment That Was Free of Thorns and Thistles and Similar Harmful Things

Theistic evolution requires that all plants and animals living today resulted from an unbroken line of evolutionary change, and therefore there never was a different kind of natural order from what we know today.

By contrast, for many centuries interpreters have understood Genesis 1–2 to speak of an idyllic garden of Eden, an earth in which there were no "thorns and thistles" (Gen. 3:18), no curse on the ground because of sin (Gen. 3:17), and, by implication, no weeds hindering beneficial crops, and no natural disasters such as hurricanes, tornadoes, earthquakes, floods, or droughts. It was also thought to be an earth where no animals were hostile to human beings, because of the prophetic predictions of God's future restoration of an earth where, "The nursing child shall play over the hole of the cobra, and the weaned child shall put his hand on the adder's den," and, "They shall not hurt or destroy in all my holy mountain" (Isa. 11:8–9).

This was understood (I think rightly) to be the kind of earth implied by the summary statement at the end of the sixth day of creation, "and God saw everything that he had made, and behold, *it was very good*" (Gen. 1:31). Indeed, the kind of earth we have today, with frequent earthquakes, hurricanes, floods, droughts, poisonous snakes and venomous scorpions, malaria-spreading mosquitoes, and man-eating sharks and lions, can hardly be thought to be the best kind of creation that God could make, a creation that would cause God to say, "and behold, *it was very good*."

This idea of an originally idyllic creation is reaffirmed by the passage where God pronounces judgment on Adam after he sinned, telling him that now the ground would be "cursed" and would bring forth "thorns and thistles." (See the further discussion of this idea in the next section.)

But theistic evolution cannot affirm such an originally idyllic creation, because it holds that all living things *as they exist today*, including all the things that are hostile to human beings, are the results of a fully natural evolutionary process. Therefore, the earth has always been the way it is today. Therefore, the picture of an idyllic creation given in Genesis is not a historically reliable narrative.

12. After Adam and Eve Sinned, God Did Not Place Any Curse on the World That Changed the Workings of the Natural World and Made It More Hostile to Mankind

This belief of theistic evolution advocates is the counterpart of the previous point. They do not believe in an original idyllic creation, and so they also do not believe that God placed a curse on the ground as judgment for Adam's sin, or that God altered the operation of nature in any way to make the world more hostile to human beings.

But the biblical text, if understood as a historical record of actual events, shows that God did indeed alter the workings of the natural world when he spoke to Adam in words of judgment:

And to Adam he said,

> "Because you have listened to the voice of your wife
>   and have eaten of the tree
> of which I commanded you,
>   'You shall not eat of it,'
> *cursed is the ground because of you*;
>   in pain you shall eat of it all the days of your life;
> *thorns and thistles* it shall bring forth for you;
>   and you shall eat the plants of the field.
> By the sweat of your face
>   you shall eat bread,
> till you return to the ground,
>   for out of it you were taken;
> for you are dust,
>   and to dust you shall return." (Gen. 3:17–19)

Adam's life would eventually end in death ("to dust you shall return"), but even while he continued alive, his life would consist of painful toil to provide enough food from the ground that had now become hostile ("cursed is the ground. . . . By the sweat of your face you shall eat bread").

God's statement that the ground would now produce "thorns and thistles" is best understood as a synecdoche, a common feature in biblical speech by which two or three concrete examples represent an entire category of things. Taken in this way, God's words of judgment mean that the earth would not only produce thorns and thistles but would also harbor insects that would destroy crops (such as locusts, Deut. 28:38; Amos 7:1), diseases that would consume them (see Deut. 28:22), foraging animals that would eat crops before they could be harvested, and floods and droughts, tornadoes and hurricanes that would make farming difficult and life precarious (see Eccles. 11:4).

Paul affirms in the New Testament that the present operation of the natural world is not the way God originally created it to work, but is a result of God's judgment. He pictures nature as longing to be freed from its bondage in much the same way as we long to be freed from our dying physical bodies and obtain new resurrection bodies:

> For I consider that the sufferings of this present time are not worth comparing with the glory that is to be revealed to us. For *the creation waits with eager longing* for the revealing of the sons of God. For *the creation was subjected to futility*, not willingly, but because of him who subjected it, in hope that *the creation itself will be set free from its bondage to corruption* and obtain the freedom of the glory of the children of God. For we know that *the whole creation has been groaning together* in the pains of childbirth until now. And not only the creation, but we ourselves, who have the firstfruits of the Spirit, groan inwardly *as we wait eagerly for* adoption as sons, *the redemption of our bodies*. For in this hope we were saved. (Rom. 8:18–24)[54]

---

54 See the further discussion of this passage by Guy Waters, pages 92–93.

Paul does not say that the creation will suddenly be raised to a brand-new, wonderful state of operation that it had never known before. Instead, he says that the creation will be "*set free* from its bondage," the bondage to which it was previously "subjected." Surely he is here referring to God's curse on the ground and his alteration of the functioning of nature because of sin in Genesis 3. But theistic evolution requires us to affirm that Paul was also wrong at this point.

D. Significant Christian Doctrines That Are Undermined or Denied by Theistic Evolution

Why is this entire issue of theistic evolution important? Ideas often have consequences in our lives, and theistic evolution, as an overarching explanation for the origin of all living things, leads to several destructive consequences for a number of Christian doctrines. Theistic evolution is not at all a harmless "alternative opinion" about creation, but will lead to progressive erosion and often even a denial of at least the following eleven Christian doctrines:

1. The Truthfulness of the Bible

As I have argued in the pages above, proponents of theistic evolution must deny that Genesis 1–3 should be understood as historical narrative in the sense of literature that intends to report events that actually happened. But, in contrast to theistic evolution, these chapters are understood as truthful historical narrative by later chapters in Genesis, as well as by later Old Testament passages in Exodus, 1 Chronicles, Psalms, and Hosea.

In addition, theistic evolution requires us to believe that both Jesus and the New Testament authors were wrong in their affirmations of the historical reliability of many details in Genesis 1–3. More specifically, theistic evolution requires us to believe that passages in Matthew, Luke, Acts, Romans, 1 Corinthians, 2 Corinthians, Colossians, 1 Timothy, Hebrews, and Revelation were all in error in what they affirmed about Genesis 1–3. This is much deeper than a challenge to the historicity of one verse or another. This is a challenge to the truthfulness of the three foundational chapters of the entire Bible, and to the truthfulness of ten of the twenty-seven books of the New Testament.[55]

Even if there were no other harmful consequences from this theory, this alone would be sufficient to conclude that theistic evolution is not a viewpoint that Christians should accept. In addition, when significant historical records in Scripture are explained away as not being truthful records of actual events, then eventually other passages of Scripture— usually those unpopular in modern culture at the moment—will eventually also be explained away as untrustworthy, for they will be seen simply as the result of God accommodating his words to the beliefs of the ancient world in order to communicate his larger saving message to his people.[56] By this process, many of the second- and third-generation followers of those who hold to theistic evolution today will abandon belief in the Bible altogether, and will abandon the Christian faith.

Several years ago the respected evangelical leader Francis Schaeffer used the example of a watershed in the Swiss Alps to illustrate what happens when some Christians begin to abandon the complete truthfulness of the Bible in places where it speaks to matters of history and science. When spring comes, two bits of snow that are only an inch apart in the high mountains of Switzerland will melt on two sides of a ridge in the rock, and the drop of water from one side of the watershed will eventually flow into the Rhine River and then into the cold waters of the North Sea, while the drop of water on the other side of

---

55 The "Chicago Statement on Biblical Hermeneutics," adopted at the Summit II conference sponsored by the International Council on Biblical Inerrancy, which was held November 10–13, 1982, appropriately included the following statement: "WE DENY that generic categories which negate historicity may rightly be imposed on biblical narratives which present themselves as factual" (Article XIII), quoted from *Hermeneutics, Inerrancy, and the Bible: Papers from ICBI Summit II,* ed. Earl Radmacher and Robert Preus (Grand Rapids, MI: Zondervan, 1984), 884.

56 Theistic evolution literature frequently appeals to the idea that God "accommodated" his words to the scientific knowledge of the day in order to communicate well. See Denis Lamoureux, "No Historical Adam: Evolutionary Creation View," in Barrett and Caneday, *Four Views on the Historical Adam,* 54, 57; Alexander, *Creation or Evolution,* 55–56. Whether or not this idea is consistent with belief in the complete truthfulness of the Bible depends on what is meant by "accommodation." If it means that God, through human authors, used language and concepts that would be *understood* by the original readers, this does not negate the truthfulness of what is said in Scripture. But if it means that God in Scripture *affirmed ancient ideas that were in fact false* (such as that the sky is a solid dome), then this concept is not consistent with the truthfulness of the entire Bible.

the watershed will eventually flow into the Rhône River and finally into the Mediterranean Sea. In the same way, Christians who seem so close together on many issues, if they differ on the watershed issue of biblical inerrancy, will in the next generation or two train up disciples who will be a thousand miles apart from each other on many of the most central matters taught in the Bible.[57]

I disagree, therefore, with the emphasis of Denis Alexander, who says, "Least of all should supporting one model [about creation] over another become a bone of contention among Christians, as if it were some central point of doctrine on a par with the death and resurrection of Jesus for our sin. . . . this is a secondary issue, which is not essential for salvation."[58]

But if the real issue here is the truthfulness of the Bible, then it is a central point of doctrine and it is not at all a secondary issue. I would not say that this issue is "essential for salvation," for people can be saved by simple faith in Jesus even while refusing to believe a number of important Christian doctrines.[59] But that does not mean this is a secondary issue—not at all. Once the truthfulness of Scripture is lost, the entire Christian faith begins to unravel.

It is important to recognize what is actually happening here. Proponents of theistic evolution are claiming, in essence, that there are whole areas of human knowledge about which they will not allow the Bible to speak with authority. They will allow the Bible to speak to us about salvation, but not about the origin of all living things on the earth, the origin of human beings, the origin of moral evil in the human race, the origin of human death, the origin of natural evil in the world, the

---

57 See Francis Schaeffer, *The Great Evangelical Disaster* (Westchester, IL: Crossway, 1984), 43–51.

58 Alexander, *Creation or Evolution*, 287. Later he adds, "Launching attacks on evolution is divisive and splits the Christian community" (462).

59 Denis Lamoureux, e.g., says, "I simply want evangelicals to be aware that there are born-again Christians who love the Lord Jesus and who do not believe there ever was a first man named 'Adam'" (Lamoureux, "No Historical Adam," 38). I have no reason to doubt Lamoureux's statement, but that does not make this a secondary issue. The question is not whether many people who hold to theistic evolution are themselves born-again Christians, but rather whether this belief undermines confidence in the truthfulness of the Bible and brings significant harmful consequences to the church.

perfection of the natural world as God originally created it, and even the nature of Christ's own personal involvement as the Creator of "all things . . . in heaven and on earth, visible and invisible" (Col. 1:16). These are massive areas of human knowledge, affecting our outlook on our entire lives. Yet theistic evolution has decreed that the Bible cannot authoritatively speak to us about these areas of human knowledge. Those topics are the exclusive domain of modern naturalistic science, off-limits for God to speak to us about.

But do Christians today really want to accept a theory that decrees that God is not allowed to speak to us about these vast areas of human knowledge? The appropriate response to such a claim would seem to be God's challenge to Job:

> "Where were you when I laid the foundation of the earth?
>   Tell me, if you have understanding.
> Who determined its measurements—surely you know! . . .
> On what were its bases sunk,
>   or who laid its cornerstone,
> when the morning stars sang together
>   and all the sons of God shouted for joy?
>
> "Or who shut in the sea with doors
>   when it burst out from the womb,
> when I made clouds its garment
>   and thick darkness its swaddling band. . . .
>
> "Have you commanded the morning since your days began,
>   and caused the dawn to know its place? . . .
>
> "Do you give the horse his might?
>   Do you clothe his neck with a mane? . . .
>
> "Is it by your understanding that the hawk soars
>   and spreads his wings toward the south?

Is it at your command that the eagle mounts up
and makes his nest on high?" . . .

And the LORD said to Job:

"Shall a faultfinder contend with the Almighty?
He who argues with God, let him answer it." (Job 38:4–9,
12; 39:19, 26–27; 40:1–2)

Theistic evolution supporters often claim that "the Bible doesn't teach science." Karl Giberson and Francis Collins write, "The Bible is not even trying to teach science. Nowhere in the entire Bible do we read anything that even hints that the writer is trying to teach science."[60] And John Walton writes, "There is not a single incidence of new information being offered by God to the Israelites about the regular operation of the world (what we would call natural science)."[61] These statements are offered as justification for the idea that the Bible cannot speak authoritatively to questions about the origin of life on Earth.

But the question is not whether the Bible "teaches science" (whatever that might mean). The question is *whether the Bible is truthful in all that it affirms*, on whatever topic it wishes to speak about.[62]

60 Giberson and Collins, *Language of Science and Faith*, 108.
61 Walton, *Lost World of Adam and Eve*, 21; see also 188. To ask whether the Bible reveals new information about the operation of the natural world is to ask the wrong question. The question is *whether the Bible is truthful in all that it affirms about the natural world*. The astounding fact is that there is no statement in the Bible about the natural world that is scientifically false (when interpreted according to sound principles of grammatical-historical exegesis). Even though the Bible was written by multiple authors in diverse ancient cultures over a period of 1,500 years (approximately 1400 BC–AD 90), nothing that it affirms as true has ever been shown to be false by modern standards of archaeology, history, and scientific inquiry—as is evident from multiple evangelical books that thoughtfully defend the inerrancy of the Bible. In its astounding freedom from falsehood, the Bible stands in stark contrast to all other ancient literature.
62 Some of our friends who support theistic evolution object that they do not want to affirm a "God-of-the-gaps" argument, a kind of argument that calls upon belief in God's activity as an explanation for events that scientists currently cannot explain. Francis Collins says, "Faith that places God in the gaps of current understanding about the natural world may be headed for crisis if advances in science subsequently fill those gaps" (Collins, *Language of God*, 93; see also 95, 193–95). But my argument throughout this chapter has not claimed that we need God as an explanation for events that science cannot currently explain. My argument instead has been that we should believe the

If the Bible tells us that God said, "Let the earth bring forth living creatures according to their kinds" (Gen. 1:24), is that statement historically true, or not? Did God speak these words and thereby cause living creatures to appear on the earth, or not? If the Bible tells us that "the rib that the LORD God had taken from the man he made into a woman and brought her to the man" (Gen. 2:22), is that a truthful report of a historical event, or not? And so it goes with every detail that Genesis 1–3 tells us about the earliest history of the earth and the human race. The most important issue at stake here is the truthfulness of the Bible as the Word of God.

In some theistic evolution literature, the authors double down on their denial of the historical truthfulness of the creation accounts and argue that the Bible affirms other scientifically false ideas as well—thus adding more examples to shore up their denial of the truthfulness of Scripture. Denis Lamoureux tells us that the Bible affirms a three-tiered universe with a solid sky overhead that holds back large reservoirs of water,[63] and that Jesus affirmed a scientific falsehood when he said that the mustard seed was "the smallest of all seeds on earth" (Mark 4:31).[64] John Walton says that the ancient writers "believed that the heart was the center of intellect and emotion, and the text affirms that belief."[65] Karl Giberson and Francis Collins say that the opening chapters of Genesis have "*two* stories of creation, not one," and "only an unreasonable interpretation that mutilates the text can resolve the differences."[66] Apparently the purpose for bringing up these additional affirmations of falsehood in other statements of Scripture is to demonstrate that the Bible cannot speak accurately to scientific issues, because it makes so many mistakes. But these challenges have been known for centuries,

---

Bible on whatever topic it speaks about, including the origin of living things, the origin of human beings, and the earliest history of the earth and human beings on the earth.

63 Lamoureux, "No Historical Adam," 49, 51, 61.

64 Ibid., 60.

65 Walton, *Lost World of Adam and Eve*, 201. He fails to consider the obvious possibility that the biblical authors were using "heart" in a metaphorical way to refer to the center of our deepest emotions and convictions, rather than referring to a literal physical heart.

66 Giberson and Collins, *Language of Science and Faith*, 101; see also 208.

and the standard evangelical commentaries contain reasonable, textually sensitive explanations that do not require us to conclude that the Bible anywhere affirms false statements about the natural world.[67]

John Walton claims that belief in theistic evolution does not entail a denial of biblical inerrancy, because no theological point is lost. He says, "Historical Adam is only tied to inerrancy to the extent that it can be demonstrated not just that the biblical authors considered him historical but that the biblical teaching incorporated that understanding into its authoritative message. . . . I do affirm the historicity of Adam. But I do not consider interpreters who are trying to be faithful to Scripture to be denying inerrancy if they arrive at a different conclusion."[68]

But Walton clearly misunderstands the doctrine of inerrancy. The inerrancy of Scripture does not apply merely to those details that the biblical writers "incorporated" into some "authoritative message" that is somehow less than what the Bible actually affirms as truthful. Rather, inerrancy applies to *everything* that the biblical text affirms to be true, for its "authoritative message," understood rightly, includes everything that it affirms: "*All Scripture* [not just some parts of it] is breathed out by God and profitable for teaching, for reproof, for correction, and for training in righteousness" (2 Tim. 3:16).

In a brief definition that is consistent with what many evangelicals have affirmed for generations, "The inerrancy of Scripture means that Scripture in the original manuscripts does not affirm anything that is contrary to fact."[69] The widely used Chicago Statement on Biblical Inerrancy (1978) gives a fuller explanation:

---

67 I will not discuss these passages in detail at this point, but interested readers could consult a standard reference work such as the *ESV Study Bible* (Wheaton, IL: Crossway, 2008), or the *NIV Zondervan Study Bible*, ed. D. A. Carson (Grand Rapids, MI: Zondervan, 2015), as well as any of a number of widely used commentaries.

68 Walton, *Lost World of Adam and Eve*, 201–2. Walton elsewhere says that someone who denied that Adam and Eve were the first human beings and the ancestors of all humanity, and also denied that there was material discontinuity between Adam and other species, still "could not be accused of rejecting the Bible or the faith" (John H. Walton, "A Historical Adam: Archetypal Creation View," in Barrett and Caneday, *Four Views on the Historical Adam*, 113.

69 Wayne Grudem, *Systematic Theology* (Leicester, UK, and Grand Rapids, MI: Zondervan, 1994), 91. Although these are my words, such an understanding of inerrancy did not originate with me

We affirm that inspiration, though not conferring omniscience, guaranteed true and trustworthy utterance on all matters of which the Bible authors were moved to speak and write. We deny that the finitude or fallenness of these writers, by necessity or otherwise, introduced distortion or falsehood into God's Word. (Article IX).

We affirm that Scripture . . . is true and reliable in all matters it addresses. (Article XI).

We affirm that Scripture in its entirety is inerrant, being free from all falsehood, fraud, or deceit. We deny that biblical infallibility and inerrancy are limited to spiritual, religious, or redemptive themes, exclusive of assertions in the fields of history and science. We further deny that scientific hypotheses about earth history may properly be used to overturn the teaching of Scripture on creation and the flood. (Article XII).[70]

These explicit explanations of inerrancy clearly differ from the much weaker understanding of biblical inerrancy advocated by John Walton.

While I consider the denial of the complete truthfulness of the Bible to be the most significant harmful consequence of theistic evolution, I must also mention several other harmful doctrinal consequences in the following points.

2. Direct Creation by God's Powerful Words

According to theistic evolution, there was no special action of God or intervention by God in the created order after the initial creation of matter. But the biblical picture is far different. It shows God speaking living

---

but is consistent with what evangelical Christians have believed for centuries about the truthfulness of the Bible.

70 "The Chicago Statement of Biblical Inerrancy," available at *Alliance of Confessing Evangelicals*, http://www.alliancenet.org/the-chicago-statement-on-biblical-inerrancy. The Evangelical Theological Society bylaws refer members to the Chicago Statement on Biblical Inerrancy to understand "the intent and meaning of the reference to biblical inerrancy in the ETS Doctrinal Basis" ("Bylaws," The Evangelical Theological Society, see item 12, available at http://www.etsjets.org/about/bylaws).

things into existence by his powerful creative words, and the picture it gives is that those powerful words of God bring immediate response:

> And God said, "Let the earth sprout vegetation, plants yielding seed, and fruit trees bearing fruit in which is their seed, each according to its kind, on the earth." And it was so. (Gen. 1:11)

> And God said, "Let the earth bring forth living creatures according to their kinds—livestock and creeping things and beasts of the earth according to their kinds." And it was so. (Gen. 1:24)

Several other passages of Scripture also emphasize that God's powerful words brought into existence various aspects of creation:

> By the word of the LORD the heavens were made,
>   and by the breath of his mouth all their host. . . .

> For he spoke, and it came to be;
>   he commanded, and it stood firm (Psalm 33:6, 9; see also
>   Psalm 148:5–6; Rom. 4:17; Heb. 11:3; 2 Pet. 3:5).

By contrast, the picture given by theistic evolution denies that there were any such powerful words of God, or any other direct intervention of God into the creation, that caused plants and animals to exist. Instead of appearing immediately in obedience to God's powerful creative words, these things evolved over billions of years, and new forms of life are the result of random mutations, not God's commands. The driving force that brings about mutations in living things is randomness, not God's command.[71] The Bible's emphasis on the wonder of God's direct activity in creation, and the power of God's creative words, is lost.

---

71 Theistic evolution supporters insist that the process is "not a random process." Giberson and Collins say, "We emphasize that there is nothing random about an organism that is better adapted to its environment having greater reproductive success. This is an orderly and predictable trajectory in the direction of better adaptation" (*Language of Science and Faith*, 38).

3. Overwhelming Evidence in Nature for God's Existence

The Bible claims that nature gives abundant evidence of God's existence.[72] Paul writes,

> For what can be known about God is plain to them, because God has shown it to them. For *his invisible attributes*, namely, his eternal power and divine nature, *have been clearly perceived*, ever since the creation of the world, *in the things that have been made*. So they are without excuse. (Rom. 1:19–20)

Paul's phrase "the things that have been made" certainly includes plants, animals, and human beings, all of which give clear evidence of God's power and other attributes (such as wisdom, knowledge, creativity, love, goodness, and faithfulness). This evidence is so strong that God's attributes are "clearly perceived" in the natural world. Therefore people who rebel against God are "*without excuse.*" *The evidence from creation for God's existence is so overwhelming that God holds people morally accountable for denying it.*

This means that when people ponder the astounding complexity of the human eye, or a bird's wing, or a single living cell, the evidence for God's existence is so strong that people have no good excuse for unbelief. Only an infinitely wise and powerful God could create things as wonderful as these. An old hymn put it this way:

This is my Father's world, the birds their carols raise,
The morning light, the lily white, declare their Maker's praise.

But that is not the point I'm making here. No one is claiming that it is a "random" process by which those creatures that survive are those that are best able to survive. The claim of randomness has to do not with which animals survive but with the driving force behind the beneficial mutations that (according to evolution) cause the development of a new type of animal. The fact remains that, according to evolutionary theory, these mutations are random. Giberson and Collins themselves say later in this same book, "*The process of evolution is driven in large part by random mutations,* so it certainly seems possible that earth could have been home to an entirely different assortment of creatures" (198, emphasis added).

72 I wish to thank Casey Luskin of the Discovery Institute for his suggestions that led to a significant strengthening of this section.

This is my Father's world: He shines in all that's fair;
In the rustling grass I hear Him pass;
He speaks to me everywhere.[73]

But theistic evolution *takes away that evidence for God completely.* While the Bible says that "the things that have been made" give clear evidence of God's "eternal power and divine nature" (Rom. 1:20), theistic evolution says that the living creatures give no such evidence, for the existence of all living things can be explained solely from the properties of matter itself.[74]

The contrast is clear. While the Bible says that everything in nature bears witness to God, theistic evolution says that no living creature in nature bears witness to God. When an unbeliever is confronted with the wondrous complexity of living things, theistic evolution allows him just to think that random mutations produce surprising results, and therefore he has no need for any thought of God. Evolutionary science has given him (so he thinks) a complete explanation for why life exists. Theistic evolution completely nullifies the evidence for God's existence in living things, and therefore significantly hinders evangelism.[75]

Now, sometimes scientists who support theistic evolution suggest that *maybe* God was working behind the scenes in an invisible way. Giberson and Collins say,

Another way to think about God's relationship to evolution is to view God guiding the evolutionary process, working within the random-

---

73 "This Is My Father's World," by Maltbie D. Babcock, 1901.

74 Some supporters of theistic evolution will say that the fine-tuning of the universe to make it suitable to support human life is evidence of God's existence, and we agree, but that kind of evidence from modern physics and chemistry, evidence which was unknown to ancient readers, would not have been Paul's intention in speaking of "the things that have been made" in Romans 1:20. He surely would have thought of all living creatures as included in "the things that have been made," an evident allusion to Genesis 1:31, "And God saw everything that he had made [LXX *poieō*, a verb cognate to poiēma in Rom. 1:20], and behold, it was very good."

75 Notice Paul's appeal to people's ordinary experience of "rains from heaven and fruitful seasons" in the natural world as a testimony to "a living God, who made the heaven and the earth and the sea and all that is in them" (Acts 14:15–17). Psalm 104:24 proclaims that the "creatures" who fill the earth are evidence for God's wisdom: "In wisdom you have made them all."

ness. . . . Mutations appear to be genuinely random occurrences that can be initiated by quantum mechanical events. . . . There is no reason why God could not work within such processes, shaping evolutionary history. What appear to be genuinely random events might actually be the subtle influence of God working within the system of natural law.[76]

But according to this viewpoint, there is still no visible or detectable evidence of God's working in the natural world. It is a proposal that says, essentially, "*Maybe* God was working secretly in a way that we cannot detect." In other words, even though science has shown us that *nothing* in nature bears witness to God's power and wisdom, *maybe* God was working in it anyway, but it must have been only in a way that cannot be detected.

This is the complete opposite of the perspective of Scripture, in which everything in nature gives undeniable, overwhelming testimony to God's existence. "For his invisible attributes, namely, his eternal power and divine nature, have been *clearly perceived*, ever since the creation of the world, *in the things that have been made*. So they are *without excuse*" (Rom. 1:20). But according to theistic evolution, unbelievers have a gigantic excuse, for they could say that all living things can be explained as a result of the properties of matter without any special creative action by God.

4. Evidence in Nature for Moral Accountability to God

In a society where a traditional belief in God as the Creator of all living things is prominent, the wonder of creation leads people to think of their moral accountability to God. When people (even many unbelievers) observe the wonder of tiny seeds growing into large trees or a mother robin caring for her chicks, they often have an instinctive sense of moral accountability to their Creator: "Only an infinitely powerful and wise God could have made such amazing creatures, and that means that I will one day be accountable for my actions to this very God."

---

76 Giberson and Collins, *Language of Science and Faith*, 199–200, emphasis original.

The apostle Paul himself reasoned in a similar manner, beginning with God's actions in creation and then going on to speak about moral accountability to this same God, when he spoke to pagan Greek philosophers in Athens: "*The God who made the world and everything in it,* . . . made from one man every nation of mankind. . . . now he commands all people everywhere to *repent*, because he has fixed a day on which *he will judge the world* in righteousness by a man whom he has appointed" (Acts 17:24, 26, 30, 31). This is similar to Paul's words in Romans 1:20, mentioned in the previous section, where Paul says that people are "without excuse"—and therefore are accountable to God—because of the evidence in nature for God's existence.

But theistic evolution severs the cord of connection between observing the creatures and fearing accountability to the Creator, because theistic evolution allows an unbeliever to think, not, "There must be an all-powerful God who made such amazing creatures," but rather, "*Matter* is so wonderful that it produced these amazing living creatures *all by itself.* Wow!" The next thought will often be, "I don't see any evidence for a Creator who will hold me accountable for my actions. Wow!" And in this way, within the theistic evolution system, the complexity of living things no longer leaves unbelievers "without excuse" (Rom. 1:20).

5. The Wisdom of God

Theistic evolution undermines the glory given to God for his unfathomable wisdom in the creation of all living things, because in theistic evolution no divine intelligence or wisdom beyond the properties present in inanimate matter is required for matter to evolve into all forms of life.

In addition, in theistic evolution God does not wisely create various kinds of animals on his first attempt, but clumsily, by his providence, brings about millions of failed mutations in each creature before he finds a beneficial change.

According to a traditional Christian view of creation, when we contemplate the beauty and complexity of a sunflower or hummingbird or rainbow trout, we are struck with a sense of awe at the wisdom and skill of the Creator. "God is an amazingly wise Creator!" But when we look at the same creatures through the eyes of theistic evolution, we first have to think, "*Matter* is really an amazing thing!" Then, perhaps later, a Christian believer might think, "God built remarkable properties into the matter that makes up the universe." But the connection between the original creation of matter and the existence of living creatures is so distant that it will lead to scant praise for God's wisdom.

That is so different from the perspective of the Bible, which repeatedly praises God for his great wisdom that is evident in the amazing creatures he has made:

> Is it by your understanding that the hawk soars
> and spreads his wings toward the south? (Job 39:26)

> Behold, Behemoth,
> which I made as I made you;
> he eats grass like an ox. (Job 40:15)

Denis Alexander does not think that theistic evolution robs glory from God by attributing such amazing potentialities to the materials of creation. He says, regarding the objection that life could not emerge out of chemicals by "blind, materialistic, naturalistic forces,"

> But wait a minute: these are God's chemicals, God's materials, that are being talked about here. . . . Is this God's world or isn't it? Imagine going into an artist's studio, seeing the tubes of paint arranged in neat rows on one side and then telling the artist, 'You've chosen the wrong type of paints, they're really hopeless!' I think we would all agree that would be insulting. But to confidently proclaim that the precious materials God has so carefully brought into being in the dying moments of exploding stars do not have the potentiality to bring about life seems to me equally insulting.[77]

---

77 Alexander, *Creation or Evolution*, 436.

John Lennox quotes this paragraph from Alexander and then effectively replies as follows:

> This argument is fatally flawed, since the analogy does not correspond to the application. No one is suggesting that the Creator's materials are "the wrong type" or "hopeless." What is being suggested is that the Creator's good materials cannot bring life into existence without the additional direct intelligent input of the Creator. This is no more an insult to the Creator than it would be an insult to the artist to suggest that his paints are incapable of producing a masterpiece without his direct input. It is rather the (ludicrous) suggestion that the paints could do it on their own without him that would be an insult to the painter![78]

Lennox is correct in his criticism. If inanimate matter, by itself, without any additional input from God, is responsible for all living things, then we ought to praise this remarkable matter that could accomplish such wonders without God's direction. Theistic evolution robs God of the glory he deserves for the infinite wisdom he exhibited in the creation of all living things. If God's providential control of nature is limited to maintaining the properties of matter, then created things do not give evidence of anything greater than matter. The properties of matter only give evidence of the properties of matter.

How different from theistic evolution is the perspective of Scripture, which sees evidence of God's wisdom in every created thing. Psalm 104 views all the creatures of the earth and the sea as evidence of God's wisdom in creation:

> O LORD, how manifold are your works!
> *In wisdom have you made them all;*
> the earth is full of your creatures.

---

78 Lennox, *Seven Days*, 176.

Here is the sea, great and wide,
    which teems with creatures innumerable,
    living things both small and great. (Ps. 104:24–25)

6. The Goodness of God

Theistic evolution also undermines belief in the goodness of God, because according to this view God is responsible for (somehow) creating a world filled with deadly diseases, dangerous animals, and natural disasters that have brought suffering and destruction to human beings for the entire duration of the human race on the earth. (By contrast, on a traditional view of Genesis 1–3, the blame for evil in the world belongs to Adam and Eve, and not to God.)

7. The Moral Justice of God

According to theistic evolution, the earliest human beings who were somehow "created" by God's use of evolution were sinful human beings, committing morally evil deeds from their earliest existence on Earth. But if that is the case, it is hard to escape the conclusion that God himself is responsible for human sin, for he never created sinless human beings who were able to obey him and not to sin.

8. Human Equality

According to theistic evolution, some human beings have evolved primarily from one group of early humans, while others have evolved primarily from another group of early humans. But that means there is no foundational physical unity to the human race, and it opens the possibility that some human beings (or even some racial groups) are superior to others—perhaps they are the recipients of more beneficial random mutations—and other human beings are therefore inferior.

The biblical picture of the unity of all human beings is a far different picture, because it teaches that we have all descended from the same man, Adam. The conviction that God "made *from one man* every nation of mankind to live on all the face of the earth" (Acts 17:26) leads to an affirmation of human equality.

9. The Atonement

Paul links the historicity of the sin of one man, Adam, and the unity of the human race as represented by Adam, to the effectiveness of the atonement worked by Christ for those whom he represented. Paul writes,

> Sin came into the world through one man, and death through sin, and so death spread to all men because all sinned. . . . For as by the one man's disobedience the many were made sinners, so by the one man's obedience the many will be made righteous. (Rom. 5:12, 19)

However, as Guy Waters explains more fully in chapter 3,[79] if we deny that sin came into the world through Adam, and if we deny that all human beings have descended from Adam, then Paul's argument about the unity of the human race as represented by Adam does not work. And then the parallel with the unity of the redeemed who are represented by Christ does not work. In this way, theistic evolution significantly undermines the doctrine of the atonement.

In this regard, it is not surprising that Scot McKnight, in denying a historical Adam, also denies the historical Christian doctrine of "original sin" (or "inherited sin"); that is, the idea that Adam in the garden of Eden represented the entire human race, with the result that, (1) when Adam sinned, God counted the entire human race as guilty (Rom. 5:12–19), and also that (2) all human beings are born with a sinful nature, a disposition to sin against God (Pss. 51:5; 58:3; Eph. 2:3). But McKnight does not think we have all descended from Adam and Eve.[80] Therefore he denies the doctrine of original sin and says instead that "each human being stands condemned before God as a sinner because each human being sins as did Adam (and Eve)."[81] He wants to keep Christ as our representative in his obedience,[82] but he

---

79 See pages 98–124.
80 Scot McKnight, in Venema and McKnight, *Adam and the Genome*, 93, 100, 145–46.
81 Ibid., 187.
82 Ibid., 186.

denies a similar representation by Adam in Adam's disobedience ("by one man's disobedience many were made sinners"; Rom. 5:19), and so undercuts Paul's argument about the atonement.

10. The Resurrection

Paul also links the unity of the human race in Adam, and the reality of death coming to the entire human race through the sin of Adam, to the efficacy of the resurrection of Christ to bring new life to all who are represented by him:

> For as by a man came death, by a man has come also the resurrection of the dead. For as in Adam all die, so also in Christ shall all be made alive. (1 Cor. 15:21–22)

However, if we deny that death came into the world through Adam, and if we deny the unity of the human race as descending from Adam, then once again the parallel between Adam and Christ does not work. In this way, theistic evolution undermines the effectiveness of the resurrection to give new life to all who are saved by Christ. Guy Waters also explains this parallel more fully in chapter 3.[83]

11. The Value of Improving upon Nature

According to a traditional Christian understanding of creation, the natural world is not the best it could be, because it is still under the curse that God placed on it as a result of the sin of Adam in Genesis 3:17–19. But God's plan in the history of redemption is that nature will one day "be set free from its bondage to corruption and obtain the freedom of the glory of the children of God" (Rom. 8:21).

Therefore, Christians have historically thought it is pleasing to God to work to overcome the "thorns and thistles" and other hostile forces in creation, because this is his ultimate goal for the end of history, and the ongoing advance of the kingdom of God properly manifests that

---

83 See pages 98–124.

final redemptive result *in partial form* even in this current age. As a result, Christians have worked "as for the Lord" (Col. 3:23) to develop improved, disease-resistant crops, hybrid plants that produce more food in the same acreage, healthier chickens and cattle and pigs, and more pleasant products such as seedless oranges and watermelons.

But according to theistic evolution, there never was a "better" form of the natural world. In fact, nature as it exists today is apparently the best natural world that God could have brought about through the millions of years of theistic evolution. In this view, the natural world is not currently under a curse from God as a result of human sin. Yet this conviction tends to undermine the value of seeking to improve on nature, and tends to discourage people from thinking that any part of the natural world might itself be evil, that is, something we should seek to change. Perhaps nature is already the best it can be?

E. Conclusion

Theistic evolution, as defined by its most respected defenders today, implies a denial of twelve specific events that are recorded in Genesis 1–3. The placement of these chapters at the beginning of Genesis, the absence of literary markers in these passages signaling to readers that they should be understood in a figurative way, and the matter-of-fact way in which subsequent chapters in Genesis assume that Genesis 1–3 is reliable historical narrative, provide convincing evidence that Genesis 1–3 is intended to be taken as a historical record of events that actually happened. In addition, all of these twelve events are affirmed or implied in various places in four other books in the Old Testament and ten books in the New Testament.

Because theistic evolution denies the historicity of these twelve events, it also denies or undermines eleven significant Christian doctrines. In sum, belief in theistic evolution is incompatible with the truthfulness of the Bible and with several crucial doctrines of the Christian faith.

General Index

Abel, 54, 88, 90–91, 91n57, 93–95, 97, 190, 203
abiogenesis, 159, 160, 169
Abraham, 20, 50, 54, 76, 77, 88, 89, 94, 181, 190–91
accidental vs. purposeful causes of creation, 130–31
Achan, 70
Acworth, Bernard, 152
Adam
  as first man, 77
  as first "significant" human (Walton), 78
  as having no human parents, 194
  parallel with Christ requires that he be real person, 75, 101
  as prototype of Israel, 71
  "sides" of, 199n35
  as "type" of Christ, 105–6, 105n83, 116, 121
Adam and Eve
  as "a couple of Neolithic farmers," 23, 110–11
  historicity of, 74–75, 78, 82, 86, 88, 95n63, 98–99, 101, 103, 104–8, 113, 116, 119, 121, 167, 181–82, 189, 192–93, 193n28, 200–201, 204, 224, 234
  See also theistic evolution; beliefs of that conflict with Genesis 1–3
age of the earth
  "old earth" position, 150n69, 163
  "young earth" position, 129–33, 129nn11–14, 150n69, 173
Ai, 65

Alexander, Denis, 23–24, 23n30, 50–51, 129n14, 203n42, 210n51, 220, 231;
  on Genesis 1–3 as figurative and theological literature, 48, 50
  on Paul's understanding of Adam, 108–13, 111n113
Alt, Albrecht, 64n93, 69
Amphilochius, 132n20
anthrōpos, 206
anti-mythic polemic in Genesis, 43–48
Aquinas. See Thomas Aquinas
Areopagus, 79, 193
Articles of Religion of the Methodist Church, 144–45
atomic theory of evolution, 130–31, 131n18, 148
Augsburg Confession of Faith, 135
Augustine, 110n104, 129–30, 129n14
Averbeck, R. E., 34n16, 41

Balaam, 87n47, 88, 98
Baptist Faith and Message, 144
Bauckham, Richard, 86n40, 87n43, 98n68
Bauer, D. R., 76n4
Belgic Confession of Faith, 135–36, 140, 142
Berkhof, Louis, 16n11
BioLogos, 15, 15n8, 16–21, 32, 32n8, 33, 67, 71–72, 150n71, 178, 178n1, 193–94, 193n28
Blenkinsopp, Joseph, 44, 66–67, 70
Bock, Darrell, 77n6
Bruce, F. F., 79n14, 94n62

Cain, 54, 87n47, 88, 91, 93–95, 97–98, 190, 203, 207

Caird, G. B., 78n13

Caleb, 60

Calvin, John, 173–74

Cassuto, Umberto, 56n73, 61n85

Chicago Statement on Biblical Hermeneutics, 219n55

Chicago Statement on Biblical Inerrancy, 146n64, 224–25, 225n70

Childs, Brevard, 70–71

Clement of Rome, 133

Collins, C. John, 13n4, 53, 58, 94n62, 95n63, 179, 179n5, 185n10, 186n11, 189, 195–96n32

Collins, Francis, 14, 15, 16–17, 16n11, 20, 21n26, 22, 22n27, 49, 147, 147n66, 186, 213, 222, 222n62, 223

Confession of Faith of the Evangelical United Brethren Church, 144–45

creation
   of Adam from dust. *See* dust.
   days of, 13, 13n3, 42, 63, 129, 129n11, 131, 133, 136, 145, 150, 150n69, 163–64, 173–74, 179–80, 195n32, 205, 213–14
   of different "kinds," 127–30, 128n9, 147, 169, 188, 208–13, 223, 226, 230
   doctrinal standards on, contemporary, 144–46
   doctrinal standards on, early church, 126–34
   of Eve, from Adam's rib. *See* rib
   ex nihilo, 127–28, 131, 134, 143
   first creation of life, 21n26
   by God's spoken word, 93, 145, 223, 225–26
   historicity of, 13n4, 44, 53–55, 58–60, 83n25, 84, 88–89, 91, 99, 99n70, 101–2, 106, 121, 187, 218, 219n55, 223. *See also* Adam and Eve, historicity of
   originally "very good," 19, 136, 171–72, 201–2, 201n39, 205, 210, 215–16, 228n74, 236
   as purposeful, 42, 142–44
   as special, supernatural act of God, 21n26, 39, 46, 77, 80, 81, 85, 96,
      106, 144, 150n69, 153n81, 184n8, 195–97, 225, 229

Darwin, Charles, 162, 164, 174

days. See creation, days of

dust, 30–31, 49–52, 56–58, 61–62, 72, 84, 101–3, 114, 136, 138, 164, 166, 169–70, 178, 178n2, 184, 194–97, 195nn30, 31, 201n38, 205–6, 216

Eden, garden of, 59, 61, 66, 67, 71, 137, 139, 140, 143, 179, 181, 192, 197, 215, 234

Edwards, James, 76n4

Egyptian creation texts, 35–39

Ellingworth, Paul, 94n62, 95n64

Elohim, 59

Emmrich, Martin, 66

Enns, Peter, 20, 20n19, 32, 43, 67, 77–78, 108, 118–22

Enoch, 76, 86–88, 93, 94, 190

Enuma Elish, 39–40, 47

eternality of matter (Plato), 127, 130n15

etiology as methodology, 63–71
   assumption that Genesis 2–3 was written after Israel's exile, 68–69
   use of to deny events of creation account, 65–67
   use of to deny historicity of some Old Testament events, 64–65

Evangelical Free Church Statement of Faith, 145

evangelical leaders wrongfully claimed as advocates of theistic evolution, 152–54

Eve. See Adam and Eve

"evolutionary creation," 16, 16n11, 21, 32–33, 71–72, 71n116, 150n71

"exalted prose narrative," Genesis 1 as, 53, 58

fall, the, 83–85, 83n25, 85n36, 90, 93, 102n76, 114n129, 116, 129n12, 135, 139–41, 145, 146, 168, 190, 202, 206

false teachers, 81–82, 86, 96, 97–98, 99n70

flood, the, 46, 54, 91, 92, 96, 96n65, 99n70, 137, 146n64, 225
France, R. T., 89, 91n56
Frankfort, Henri, 35
Futato, Mark, 60n83

Gaffin, Richard, Jr., 101, 103, 111, 122
Garland, David, 80n19
Genesis, book of
    chapters 1 and 2, relationship between, 55–63
    chapters 1–3, as both similar to and different from other historical parts of Scripture, 179–82
    chapters 1–3, as figurative or allegorical literature, not factual history, 19–20, 48–55
    chapters 1–3, as history, not poetic, figurative, or allegorical literature, 186–89
    chapters 1–3, as myth, 43–48
    context of chapters 1–3, 54–55
    functions and origins in chapters 1–3, 41–43
    genealogies in, 190
    genre of chapters 1–3, 52–54
    indicators of historical narrative in chapter 2, 58–60
    "J" (Jehovist) source, 68
    larger structure of, 190–92
Gibeath-haaraloth, 69, 69n112
Giberson, Karl, 14, 15, 17n13, 20n19, 21n26, 22n27, 24, 213, 222, 223, 226–27n71
God-of-the gaps fallacy, 222n62
Goppelt, L., 105n83
Gunkel, Hermann, 43

Haarsma, Deborah, 16–17, 150–51, 150n71, 151nn73–74
Harris, Murray, 82
Hasel, G. F., 45n44, 47
Harkness, N. W., class notes of on Warfield lectures, 166
Hebrews 11 as affirming creation, 94n62
Heidel, Alexander, 39, 47
Heidelberg Catechism, 135
Hodge, Charles, 159

Hoffmeier, James, 191
Hollaz, David Friedrich, 141

inerrancy of Scripture, 146n64, 219n55, 220, 222n61, 224, 224n69, 225, 225n70
Irenaeus, 128, 129, 130n15

Jastrow, Marcus, 199n35
Jesus Christ
    affirming historicity of requires affirming historicity of Adam, 75, 104–8
    assumes ramifications of Adam's sin for entire human race, 90
    as creator, 126n2, 132, 148, 212, 221
    descent of from Adam qualifies him as Redeemer, 77
    flood typological of his death for his people, 96
    as "last" or "second" Adam and "man of heaven," 101–3
    regarded Genesis as historical, 73, 92, 200, 218
    reinforces idea of Adam as first human being, 192
    teaching on marriage relies on Genesis 2:24, 192, 200
Joshua, 60, 65, 69, 70
Jotham, 187
Jude, 86–88, 87n43, 97–99, 126

Keller, Tim, 33, 152
Kidner, Derek, 152–53, 153n81
Kline, Meredith, 60
Knight, George, 83n25

Lactantius, 128n6
Laidlaw, John, 164
Lamoureux, Denis, 19, 19n17, 22, 90, 193–94, 193n28, 219n56, 220n59, 223
Lennox, John, 13n3, 213, 232
Le Peyrère, Isaac, 137–39
Lewis, C. S., on evolution, 152
Livingstone, David, 172
Longman, Tremper, 32–33, 32n9, 33n10
Luskin, Casey, 227n72

Luther, Martin, 134n25, 145
Lutheran Church Missouri Synod, 145–46

marriage, instituted at creation, 90
McCosh, James, 175
McKnight, Scot, 34n15, 49, 67n103, 71n116, 112–13, 149n68, 188–89, 234
Mesopotamian Creation Text, 39–41
Methodius, 129
Midrash Rabbah, 69n112
Miller, Kenneth, 147n65
Minucius Felix, 131n18
Moo, Douglas, 83n26, 84n27, 85n35, 86nn37–38, 93n59
Morenz, Siegfried, 36
Moses, 90, 94, 95, 106, 116, 128, 207
"from Adam to Moses," 106, 116
Mounce, William, 83n24, 84n27

nature
overwhelming evidence in for account-ability to God, 229–30
overwhelming evidence in for God's existence, 227–29
value of improving upon, 235–36
Nicene Creed, 27, 126, 126n2, 132
Nilsson, M. P., 64
Noah, 62, 63, 76–77, 79, 80, 91–92, 94–96, 186, 190–91
Noll, Mark, 33n13, 153n79, 172
Nolland, John, 89n51, 91n56
Noth, M., 64n93

O'Brien, Peter T., 94n62
Origen, 129–30, 129–30nn12, 14
Orr, James, 165–68

Pelagianism, 71n116, 111, 113
Peterson, David, 79
Poythress, Vern, 12n2, 195n30
pre-Adamite, 116–17, 117n145, 137–39, 139n43, 149, 149n68, 152
Promised Land/Land of Promise, 66, 68, 69, 71, 181
"propensity to sin" (Alexander), 109–11, 111n113

providence of God, 18–19, 133–35, 135n32, 141–46, 158–59, 169, 210n51, 230

Quenstedt, John, 138–39

Reeves, Michael, 86n39
rib, 25n37, 52, 56–58, 72, 84, 170, 178n3, 185, 194, 197–201, 198n34, 199n35, 223
Ryken, Leland, 187n15

Sarna, Nahum, 56
Satan, 81–82, 82n23, 97–98, 140
Schaeffer, Francis, metaphor of watershed in Swiss Alps, 219–20
Schreiner, Thomas, 83n26, 84n28, 85n33, 87n44, 96n65, 104n78, 105n81
Scripture
inerrancy of. *See* inerrancy of Scripture
organic character of, 74n2
truthfulness of, 218–25
Second Helvetic Confession, 135
Seth, 54, 76, 77, 185–86, 190, 192, 194, 207
Shaw, Christopher, 198n34
Smith, Frank, 31
Sodom and Gomorrah, 64
Solomon, 66, 186, 199
special revelation, 74, 156
Statement of Fundamental Truths of the General Council of the Assemblies of God, 145
Stott, John, 152
Stump, Jim, 18
Swiss Alps, metaphor of watershed in, 219–20

Tatian, 127
Tertullian, 128
theistic evolution, definition of, 15–18
theistic evolution, Christian doctrines undermined by
atonement, 234–35
direct creation by God's word, 225–26
existence of God, 227–29
goodness of God, 233

human equality, 233
moral accountability to God, 229–30
moral justice of God, 233
resurrection, 235
truthfulness of the Bible, 218–25
value of improving upon nature,
235–36
wisdom of God, 230–33
theistic evolution, beliefs of that conflict
with Genesis 1–3
Adam and Eve did not commit the first
human sins, 202–4
Adam and Eve were born of human
parents, 194–95, 197
Adam and Eve were never sinless,
201–3. *Compare* 33n13, 149,
150n69, 153, 233
Adam and Eve were not the first
human beings, 182–93. *Compare* 57,
78, 119n153, 137
after Adam and Eve sinned, God did
not curse the world, 216–18
God did not create Adam out of dust
from the ground, 195–97
God did not create different "kinds" of
creatures, 208–13
God did not create Eve from Adam's
rib, 197–201. *See also* rib
God did not create an originally "very
good" world, 215–16. *Compare* 236
God did not "rest" from his work of
creation, 213–14
human death is not a result of Adam's
sin, 205–6. *Compare* 12, 25, 33n13,
150n69, 153, 167–68, 220
not all human beings descended from
Adam and Eve, 206–8. *Compare*
22–23, 22n27, 25, 31, 81, 86, 98,
103, 111, 113, 149, 153, 171, 175,
186, 190, 193, 195, 198–99, 233–34
theophany, 50
Theophilus, 127
"This Is My Father's World" (Babcock),
228n73
Thomas Aquinas, 134–35, 134n26,
141–42

toledoth formula, 62–63, 180
Towner, Philip, 85n36
Turretin, Francis, 138–39

universalism, 100n72, 107n88

Van Kuiken, E. Jerome, 80n18
Venema, Dennis, 149n68
Versteeg, J. P., 77n5, 88, 105–6
Von Rad, Gerhard, 64
Vos, Geerhardus, 74n2

Waltke, Bruce, 32, 32n8
Walton, John, 20, 24n33, 32, 34–35,
34nn14–16, 39–42, 49, 49n56, 51–
52, 56–58, 62–63, 78–80, 84, 87,
108, 113–18, 114n133, 117n145,
121, 141, 180, 184n8, 185n9,
194n29, 195–97, 195–96n32, 199,
199n35, 201n39, 202n41, 204n44,
205, 222, 222n61, 223–25, 223n65,
224–25, 224n68
Warfield, B. B., 33n13, 153, 155–76
Wenham, Gordon, 191
West, John, 153
Westminster Confession of Faith, 54,
136, 140, 142, 146
Westminster Larger Catechism, question,
72
Wheaton College Statement of Faith,
139n43
Whybray, R. N., 68
Williams, R. J., 52n65
Wilson, John, 35
women, false claim of their inherent gull-
ibility, 85, 85nn33, 34, 36
Woodrow, James, 30–32, 72
Wright, N. T., 24, 33

Yahweh, 50, 59, 61
Yarbrough, Robert, 77n6

Zechariah, son of Barachiah, 90–91,
91n56

Scripture Index

Genesis

1	13, 13n3, 34, 41, 42, 43, 53, 55, 56, 57, 58, 59, 60, 63, 70, 128, 129, 129n12, 129n14, 137, 145, 150n69, 151n73, 163, 173, 179, 180, 184, 184n7, 185, 190, 192, 201, 210n51, 213, 214
1–2	19, 20, 58, 61, 72, 74, 77, 80, 81, 83, 151n74, 182, 185n9, 188, 189, 193, 200, 201, 202, 215
1–3	12, 13, 14, 19, 20, 25, 27, 29–30, 33, 34, 34n14, 34n15, 39, 41, 43, 44, 45, 48, 49, 50, 52, 53, 54, 55, 67n103, 73, 85, 98, 99, 106, 178, 179, 180, 181, 182, 184, 186, 187, 188, 190, 191, 194, 218, 223, 233, 236
1–5	88
1–11	44, 73, 75, 88, 99, 181, 191
1:1	41, 42, 59, 127, 129n12, 159, 174, 192
1:1–2	13n3
1:1–2:3	55, 58, 59
1:2	42
1:2–31	129n12

1:3	42, 52
1:3–5	13n3
1:3–31	127
1:4	52
1:9	42
1:11	42, 209, 226
1:11–12	60, 61, 128n9
1:11–25	207
1:14	42
1:15	42
1:16	47
1:20	209
1:20–21	128n9
1:24	42, 128n9, 223, 226
1:25	209
1:26	42, 43
1:26–27	61, 136, 209
1:26–28	183
1:26–31	82
1:27	46, 185, 187n13, 192, 192n25
1:28	42, 201, 207
1:28–29	79, 79n17
1:31	19, 201, 201n39, 205, 210, 215, 228n74
2	20, 35, 48, 49n56, 51, 56, 57, 58, 59, 60, 63, 84n27, 137, 145, 163, 179, 180, 184, 184n7, 190, 192, 196, 197, 200, 201, 204, 205
2–3	57, 59n81, 66, 67, 68, 69, 70, 71, 83, 84
2:1–2	19
2:1–3	213

2:2, 3, 7, 8, 9, 15,
   16, 19, 21, 22 52
2:4 ....53, 58, 59, 62, 63,
          63n91, 89, 180, 190
2:4ff. 59, 60
2:4–24 59
2:4b–25 89
2:4–3:24 55
2:5 ....55, 60, 61
2:7 ....25n36, 31, 49, 52,
          56, 61, 102, 104, 136,
          138, 178n2, 180,
          184, 194, 194n29,
          195, 195n32, 196,
          196n32, 197, 201n38
2:7, 18–25 149
2:7, 22 84
2:8 61
2:17 ....203, 205
2:18 ....81, 138, 184, 184n8
2:18–25 138
2:19–20 184
2:20 ....184, 185n9
2:20–25 198
2:21–22 ....52, 56, 180, 185
2:21–23 ....80, 200
2:22 ....194, 194n29, 223
2:23 ....25n37, 80n19,
          178n3, 187n13
2:23, 18–20 ....80n19
2:24 ....90, 192, 198, 200
2:25 202
3 ....49n56, 82, 197,
          204n43, 218
3:1 ....82n22
3:1–6 ....82, 203
3:6 203
3:7 82
3:8 ....50, 202
3:13 ....82n22, 84
3:14–19 ....187n13
3:15 93
3:16–24 203
3:17 215
3:17–19 ....216, 235
3:17, 21 ....185n9
3:18 215
3:19 ....196, 197, 206
3:20 ....138, 149, 207
3:23 197
4 ....54, 91, 94, 95, 97
4–11 ....73, 75, 76
4:8 203

4:10 95
4:14 207
4:17 207
4:23 203
4:26 190
5 ....54, 94, 163, 164,
          190, 193
5:1 ....53, 62, 63, 89, 190
5:1–2 ....186n11
5:1–5 185
5:3 207
5:4–5 207
5:6–32 186
6 94
6–9 ....54, 92, 95, 96, 97
6:5 ....47, 203
6:9 ....53, 62, 190
6:10 63
10 ....54, 190
10:1 ....53, 62, 63, 190
10:32 79
11 ....54, 163, 164, 190
11:10, 27 ....53, 62, 63, 190
12 ....20, 181
12–50 ....54, 191
12ff 88
13–14 64
15:1 199
18–19 64
18:1–2 50
18:13, 17 50
18:22 50
19 64
19:1 50
19:24–25 64
19:26 64
20:3 199
25:12 63
25:12, 19 ....53, 62, 190
25:19 63
28:12 199
36:1, 9 ....53, 62, 63, 190
37:2 ....53, 62, 63, 190
37:5 199
37:6 199
37:9 199
41:1 200
50:26 190

Exodus
9:30 ....59n81
19ff. 106

20:8–11 55
20:11 214
26:26 . . . . 199n35
36:31 . . . . 199n35

Leviticus
18:6–18 207
20:11–20 207

Numbers
3:1 63
16 98
22–24 98

Deuteronomy
4:15 50
4:32 . . . . 80n18
22:30 207
28:22 217
28:38 217

Joshua
4:9 70
5:3 69
5:9 70
7:26 70
8:28–29 65
8:28, 29 70
9:27 70
14:6–14 60
14:13–15 60
15:13–17 60

Judges
9:7–11 188

Ruth
4:18 63

1 Kings
6:15 . . . . 199n35
11:1–8 66

1 Chronicles
1 193
1:1 186
1:29 63
3 186
9 186

2 Chronicles
24:20–22 91
24:21 91

Job
38:4–9, 12 222
39:19, 26–27 222
39:26 231
40:1–2 222
40:15 231

Psalms
8:3 210
8:4–9 211
23:1–3 186
33:6, 9 226
51:5 234
58:3 234
103 196
103:14 196
103:15 196
104 55
104:24 . . . . 228n75
104:24–25 . . . . 211, 233
139:8 42
139:13 17
148:5–6 226

Ecclesiastes
1:9 29
7:29 . . . . 107, 202
11:4 217

Isaiah
11:8–9 215

Hosea
6:7 . . . . 149, 203, 203n42

Amos
7:1 217

Zechariah
12:1 . . . . 196n32

Matthew
1:1 . . . . 88, 89n51
1:1–17 89
10:29–30 . . . . 133n24
19:4 . . . . 192n25
19:4–5 . . . . 192, 200
19:4–6 90
19:5 200
19:8 90
23:35 . . . . 90, 91
24:37–38 91
28:20 . . . . 89, 89n51

Mark
4:31...................223

Luke
3:23...................76
3:23–38...............76, 138, 149
3:23c–38a.............77
3:38...................74, 76, 78, 193, 194
11:51.................90
13:1ff.................168
17:26–27.............91

John
1:3...................211
8:12..................187
15:1..................187

Acts
14:15–17.............228n75
17:24.................211
17:24, 26, 30, 31......230
17:26.................74, 79, 80, 80n18,
                     138, 149, 193,
                     193n27, 199, 207,
                     233
17:31.................80

Romans
1:18–25...............148
1:18–32...............117
1:19–20...............227
1:20..................211, 228, 228n74,
                     229, 230
4:17..................226
5....................109, 113, 116, 118,
                     119, 189, 204,
                     204n44
5:6–11................107
5:12..................80, 107, 138, 202,
                     206
5:12–19...............234
5:12, 14, 15, 16, 17, 19..193
5:12, 15, 16, 17, 19.....104
5:12, 15–19...........204
5:12, 19..............234
5:12–21...............73, 75, 79, 80, 104,
                     107, 108, 114, 117,
                     119, 149, 181
5:13..................106, 115, 116,
                     117n145
5:13–14...............106, 116, 117
5:14..................74, 104, 105, 106,
                     121

5:15..................104, 106, 202
5:15, 17, 19..........104
5:15, 17, 21..........104
5:16..................106n87
5:16, 18..............105
5:16–19...............107
5:17..................105, 107
5:17–18, 21...........105
5:17, 21..............105
5:18..................107, 107n88
5:18–19...............105, 112
5:19..................107, 107n88, 235
5:20..................105
5:21..................105, 107
8:18–23...............92
8:18–24...............217
8:21..................235

1 Corinthians
11:8..................74, 80, 200
11:8–9................80
11:8, 12..............80n19
11:9..................81
11:10.................81
11:11–12..............85n34
15....................104, 109, 109n99,
                     113, 116, 118, 119,
                     189, 208
15:1..................100
15:1–11...............99
15:2..................100
15:3–4................101, 121
15:12–34..............100
15:20–22..............100
15:20–22, 44–49.......73, 75, 79, 81, 99,
                     107, 108, 116, 181
15:21.................100, 101
15:21–22..............100, 101, 102, 206,
                     235
15:22.................100, 199, 204n43,
                     208
15:22, 45.............74, 114,
15:22, 45–48..........138, 149
15:26.................197, 205
15:35–58..............100
15:44–49..............101, 102
15:44b–49.............101
15:45.................71, 102, 104, 111,
                     193
15:45a................102
15:45, 47.............194

15:47 .... 102, 197
15:47, 45 121
15:47–48 .... 116n144
15:47, 48, 49 104
15:48 .... 102, 109
15:48, 49 103
15:48–49 109
15:49 .... 103, 111
15:54–57 110

2 Corinthians
11 82
11:2–3 82
11:3 .... 82, 204
11:13 81
11:14, 15 81
11:15 82

Ephesians
1:11 142
2:3 234

Colossians
1:16 .... 212, 221
1:17 17
3:23 236

1 Timothy
2 .... 85n36
2:1–15 83
2:11–14 83
2:11–15 .... 83n25
2:12 .... 83, 83n24, 85, 86
2:13 .... 83, 83n24, 84,
                       84n27, 85, 201
2:13–14 .... 74, 85, 149
2:14 .... 83, 83n25, 84, 85,
                       204
3:2 126
4:3 212
4:4 212
5:17 126

2 Timothy
3:16 224

Titus
1:9 126

Hebrews
1:1–2 74

1:3 17
4:4, 10 214
10:39 94
11 .... 94n62
11:1–3 94
11:1–7 93
11:1–40 94
11:2 .... 94n62
11:3 226
11:4 94
11:5 94
11:7 94
11:8–19 94
11:15–16 71
11:20 94
11:21 94
11:22 94
11:23–29 94
11:32–38 94
11:39–12:1 94
12:24 95

James
3:9 .... 102n76

1 Peter
3:20 95
3:21 96

2 Peter
2:1–3 96
2:5 96
2:9 96
3:1–7 .... 99n70
3:5 226
3:8 129

1 John
3:9, 13 97
3:12 97
3:12, 15 97
3:15 97

Jude
3 126
3–16 86
4 98
5 88
5–11 87
7 88
11 .... 88, 97

14..................74, 78, 86
14–15.................86, 87

Revelation
4:11...................212
10:6...................212
21:4...................205
22:13 42

APOCRYPHAL AND OTHER
EXTRABIBLICAL SOURCES
1 Enoch
1:9....................86–87, 87n44

4 Esdras...............*168*

1 Maccabees
2:51–60...............94n62

4 Maccabees
16:20ff................94n62
18:11ff................94n62

Sirach
44:1–50:21 ....94n62

Also Available from Wayne Grudem

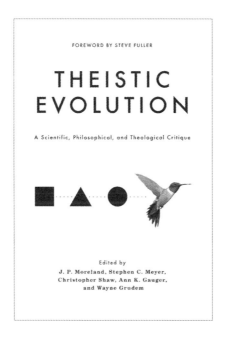

This volume of more than two dozen essays written by highly credentialed scientists, philosophers, and theologians from Europe and North America provides the most comprehensive critique of theistic evolution yet produced, opening the door to scientific and theological alternatives.

"Theistic evolutionists, and those swayed by their arguments, owe it to themselves to read and digest this compendium of essays. This book is timely and necessary—quite literally a godsend."

JAMES N. ANDERSON
Professor of Theology and Philosophy,
Reformed Theological Seminary, Charlotte

For more information, visit **crossway.org**.